THE FIRESIDE TREASURY OF NEW HUMOR

EDITED BY

AL SARRANTONIO

A FIRESIDE BOOK · PUBLISHED BY SIMON & SCHUSTER INC.
NEW YORK · LONDON · TORONTO · SYDNEY · TOKYO

FIRESIDE

SIMON & SCHUSTER BUILDING
ROCKEFELLER CENTER
1230 AVENUE OF THE AMERICAS
NEW YORK, NEW YORK 10020

DESIGNED BY KATHY KIKKERT
MANUFACTURED IN THE UNITED STATES OF AMERICA

1   3   5   7   9   10   8   6   4   2   PBK.
LIBRARY OF CONGRESS CATALOGING IN PUBLICATION DATA

THE FIRESIDE TREASURY OF NEW HUMOR / EDITED BY AL SARRANTONIO.
P.   CM.
"A FIRESIDE BOOK."
1. AMERICAN WIT AND HUMOR.   2. ENGLISH WIT AND HUMOR.
I. SARRANTONIO, AL.
PN6162.F484   1989

814'.008—DC19   89-1599
                                                      CIP

ISBN 0-671-67303-3 PBK.

The author is grateful for permission to reprint the following:

"A Reading List for Young Writers" from *Dating Your Mom* by Ian Frazier. Copyright © 1975, 1976, 1977, 1978, 1980, 1981, 1982, 1983, 1984, 1985, 1986 by Ian Frazier. Originally published in *The New Yorker*. Reprinted by permission of Farrar, Straus and Giroux, Inc. "Am I White?" by Martin Mull and Allen Rucker reprinted by permission of the Putnam Publishing Group from *The History of White People in America* by Martin Mull. Copyright © 1985 by MCA Publishing Rights, a division of MCA Inc.

(continued at back of book)

ACKNOWLEDGMENTS

My thanks to Jim Menick, Liz Cunningham, and my wife, Beth Martin, for their excellent suggestions; and to Joe Lansdale, Pat LoBrutto, and three Laura's—Laura Yorke of Simon & Schuster, Lora Porter and Laura Rogers of the Putnam Valley, New York, Library—for their valued help.

FOR
TIM MCGINNIS,
WHO ALSO KNEW HOW TO LAUGH.

CONTENTS

INTRODUCTION

Any chucklehead (including me, of course—but I'm not just *any* chucklehead) who turns to the copyright page of this book will see that none of the stuff printed (or, to be more exact, *re*printed) herein is brand-spanking new.

So why the word "new" in *The Fireside Treasury of New Humor*?

There are two reasons. The first has to do with Mr. Webster, who, in his *NEW* WORLD DICTIONARY, lists eleven entries under the word "new." The seventh reads: "modern; recent . . . recently current."

That's the usage that pertains to this book.

And let's face it—*The Fireside Treasury of Recently Current Humor* stinks as a title.

The second reason is that, keeping in mind our usage of the word "new" as "modern; recent . . . recently current," I put this book together to try to prove a thesis.

Any chucklehead who turns back to the copyright page might notice that nothing in this volume is more than about fifteen years old. That's not a very long period of time. As I write this, Ronald Reagan has been in the White House for half that period; the hounding of Richard Nixon from office (brilliantly, and hilariously, chronicled by Hunter S. Thompson in one of this book's oldest pieces) roughly marks the beginning of what I believe to be a *new* Golden Age of humor writing.

What makes a Golden Age? Well, the humorists nurtured by *The New Yorker* magazine in the first two decades of its existence, including Algonquin Round Tablers Robert Benchley and Dorothy Parker, as well as James Thurber, E. B. White, and, ultimately, S. J. Perelman—*they* made a Golden Age. They were a group of writers, working in a defined period of time, doing one thing extremely well.

That's just what we have between these covers: a *new* group of writers, doing the same thing at about the same time—and just as well as their forebears.

That, to me, makes a Golden Age.

I had only one standard of judgment when I edited this book, the same one I employed in compiling my previous volume, the *Fireside Treasury of Great Humor*. In that book, I was free to choose pieces from any era, and had no trouble gathering top-notch material from authors as diverse (in time and style) as Mark Twain, Stephen Leacock, and Dorothy Parker. The one test each piece had to pass was that it had to make me laugh—*out loud*.

I used the same test this time, but, frankly, I was a little nervous that, having stuck my neck out making a claim for a Golden Age of humor, I wouldn't be able to fill the volume with quality material. Which would leave me, as far as my thesis goes, an editor who cried wolf (or, specifically, Golden Age).

But, lo and behold (*whew!*), my fears proved groundless, I laughed loud and often, and had no trouble assembling a book with *more* material than the first one.

One note: happily, I was able to include a larger number of women contributors this time. The first book was *very* thin on women, because there just haven't been that many working in the field. But the last few years, especially, have seen a relative upsurge in the number of excellent female humorists (a parallel phenomenon seems to be occurring in stand-up comedy), and I'm happy to be able to chronicle this rise in talent, which will no doubt continue.

I've made my case for a Golden Age, so I think I'll get out. The proof—forty very talented and funny authors, who, if they make you laugh out loud, only pass the test, and prove my thesis—follows.

—*AL SARRANTONIO*

IAN FRAZIER

A READING LIST FOR YOUNG WRITERS

Ian Frazier is one of the latest of a long and illustrious line of humorists cultivated by The New Yorker *magazine. His output has not been great (his only book to date,* Dating Your Mom, *measures only 123 pages—plus a few blank pages for "Notes" at the end) but his impact has, as the following piece illustrates.*

When aspiring young authors come to me and ask what books I think it essential for a modern writer to have read, I am hard pressed for an answer. I dislike talking about writing, because I believe that the job of a writer is to write rather than talk, and that real writing is something so deep within one that any discussion profanes it. In addition, I have a profound distrust of lists—the ten-best this, the twenty-worst that. Such lists strike me as a characteristically American oversimplification of life's diversity. Like most writers of any experience, I fear making lists simply because I fear leaving something out. Young writers, however, can be very insistent (I have found), and, as no less an authority than Flaubert once said, "what a scholar one might be if one knew well merely some half a dozen books." So I have decided to tackle this difficult task despite my misgivings. The following six works are ones that I believe every writer—in fact, every educated person—should know as well as he knows his own name and telephone number:

Remembrance of Things Past. Marcel Proust's lyric, luminous evocation of lost time is arguably the greatest novel of the twentieth century. Moving from private to public scope, from the narrator's boyhood in the small provincial town of Combray, through the glittering salons of the Faubourg-Saint-Germain in Paris, to the sun-blinded hotels and beaches of Hawaii's Diamond Head, this monumental work has as its intent the precise description of Time itself. Time is as much a character in the book as the narrator, Marcel, or his ex-wife, Valerie. When Marcel meets Valerie on a flight to Honolulu, she is much changed since he saw her last; now she is an international diamond smuggler, and the mob has put a hundred-thousand-dollar price on her head. Again, Time is the genie who reveals to Marcel unguessed secrets about a woman with whom he was once deeply in love. Many writers have imitated Proust's generous, untrammeled, multihued prose; none has ever equaled it.

Madame Bovary. In Emma Bovary, Flaubert created a character who will live as long as there are books and readers. Flaubert, we are told, wrote slowly and carefully; I try to take the same care when I read him. In the marvelous scene when Emma first discovers that the petit-bourgeois pharmacist, Homais, is operating a baby-stealing ring, the intricate chiastic imagery switches from the look of horror on Emma's face to the happy, gurgling laughter of the innocent babies in their makeshift cribs in the garage behind the drugstore. Flaubert's genius for the accumulation of observed detail in delineating character showed the way for many later writers—particularly James Joyce.

War and Peace. Tolstoy's epic novel of Russia during the Napoleonic era is, in essence, a parable about the power of the media. Pierre Bezuhov is the ambitious young reporter who will go to any length to get a story—including murder. What he doesn't know is that Natasha Rostov, Moscow's feared "Dragon Lady," wants Pierre iced, and the hit man is Prince Andrei, Pierre's old college roommate! No writer who ever lived possessed a surer sense of plot than Tolstoy.

Buddenbrooks. Meet Antonie. She's beautiful. She's talented. She's sexy. She's the daughter of rich German businessman Jean Buddenbrook. And she's a walking time bomb. Somebody wants her dead, and she has been infected with a deadly virus that takes twenty-four hours to work. Half the city of Frankfurt goes underground looking for the antidote, and the police, in desperation, join forces with the mob. Author Thomas Mann interweaves these many strands so effortlessly that it is easy to see why he, along with Proust and Joyce, was considered one of the three main architects of twentieth-century literature.

Bleak House. This is the one with the car chase, right? And the exploding helicopter at the end? Excellent! A neglected book but one of Dickens's best.

Ulysses. Stephen Dedalus, star of James Joyce's *Ulysses,* teams up with twelve beautiful lady truckers to find the madman responsible for a series of brutal murders. When Stephen himself becomes a suspect, he turns to his old buddy from 'Nam, Jim Rockford. Jim comes up with a great plan, which is to pretend that Stephen is dead and to plant a fake obituary in his brother-in-law's newspaper. Then Jim, Angel, Molly Bloom, Buck Mulligan, Rocky, Stephen, and the twelve beautiful lady truckers fly over to Dublin, Stephen's hometown. It is St. Patrick's Day, and in the mass of people the killer escapes. Then the action moves to New Orleans, where Mardi Gras is in full swing. Then it's down to Rio, for Carnaval. All this time, Joyce keeps the reader informed as to what is going on inside each character's head.

My list is, of course, only a beginning. View it as the foundation of a literary mind; do not mistake it for the edifice itself. If you approach these books with passion, with an eye to their symmetries and harmonies and violent dissonances, you will not necessarily learn how to write. But you will certainly come nearer an understanding of what it is, gloriously, to read.

MARTIN MULL AND ALLEN RUCKER

AM I WHITE?

In The History of White People in America, *Martin Mull (recognizable for his many film and television appearances— most notably as the cheesy talk-show host on "Fernwood Tonight") and Allen Rucker have created a goofy ethnic document quite unlike any other. The appendix to the book lists selected readings, among them "Harriet, Where Are My Pajamas!!!," a psychosexual study of Ozzie Nelson.*

The search for personal identity is as old as man, and maybe older. Most of us begin this search when we are eighteen, eighteen and a half, or nineteen, sitting around in a college dorm or army barracks, chatting with friends. But many of us, in the hubbub of daily life, never get around to such introspection, and when we die no one knows where to bury us or what to say at the funeral. If that's a potential problem for you, read on.

The following questionnaire was developed after years of intense research at the Institute for White Studies (IFWS), Zanesville, Ohio, under a grant from the J. C. Penney Company, Expand-A-Belt Division. It is intended for the private use of our readers and cannot be used or reproduced on job or home loan applications, résumés, civil service entrance exams, or census reports without the express written consent of the Institute. Furthermore, no question or answer should be construed to reflect directly on the effectiveness or durability of the Expand-A-Belt line of fine fashions.

This test should be administered only under optimum conditions. These include:

1. A quiet room, preferably a licensed Christian Science Reading Room. Or a study room at your local library if you don't believe that bunk about not going to a doctor when you're sick, as if a shot of penicillin spells the difference between Heaven and the Hot Place.
2. A No. 2 lead pencil, well sharpened. Mongol makes a good one. (Please initial all erasures.)
3. If you need a radio to help you think, keep it tuned to mild, middle-of-the-road music, no lyrics.
4. Upon completion, write at the bottom of your exam: "I have neither given nor received help on this paper." Sign your name, date it, and send, along with $106 (cash or money order—no checks, please), to:

Tell Me If I'm White or Not
THE INSTITUTE FOR WHITE STUDIES
Miracle Whip Square
Zanesville, Ohio 60605

You may now begin. You have fifteen minutes. Keep your own time.

1. Do you wear Expand-A-Belt trousers?
   - ☐ Always.
   - ☐ Only at home.
   - ☐ Wish I could.
   - ☐ Not available in my area.

2. Can you slam-dunk a basketball?
   - ☐ Yes.
   - ☐ No.
   - ☐ Could touch the rim in high school.

3. How many ways does Wonder bread help build strong bodies?
   - ☐ Eight.

☐ More than eight.
☐ At least eight.

4. How many neckties do you own? (Men only)
  ☐ One.
  ☐ One hundred.
  ☐ Several hundred.

5. When a sultry, raven-haired Latin temptress in a low-cut sequined gown slinks up to you at the bar and asks for a light, you . . . (Men only)
  ☐ Tell her she shouldn't smoke.
  ☐ Shake hands and give her your business card.
  ☐ Shout "Hoy-oh!" loudly, like Ed McMahon on "The Tonight Show."

6. A great hamburger does not contain which of the following:
  ☐ Lipton's onion soup mix.
  ☐ Mayonnaise, and tons of it.
  ☐ Artificial grill marks.
  ☐ Jewish pickles.

7. The first thing you notice about another's home is:
  ☐ How it smells.
  ☐ Its resale value.

8. You are traveling to Europe on an expensive cruise ship. At seven in the morning there is a knock on your stateroom door and a man with a thick accent you can't pinpoint announces what sounds like breakfast. You . . .
  ☐ Make an attempt to learn his language.
  ☐ Insist that he learn yours.
  ☐ Tip him lavishly and bow, praying to God that it's the custom and he's really a waiter and not a terrorist.

9. A game of Scrabble becomes unbearable when:
  ☐ Your opponent won't stop talking about the storm-window business.
  ☐ Everybody leaves the room when it's your turn.

☐ There's no more Cheetos.

☐ Your Italian neighbor gets a triple on the word "goombahz" (with a "z").

10. The beauty of Expand-A-Belt trousers is:

☐ You don't need a belt.

☐ They stay up anyway.

☐ They are a perfect gift idea.

☐ They go great with the Expand-A-Jacket.

11. Your teenage daughter announces that she is a born-again Christian. There's a long silence, and then you:

☐ Jokingly ask what it cost, because the first time she was born set you back $600 and change.

☐ Tell her she's adopted.

☐ Go over your will with an eraser.

☐ Act like you didn't understand and say "Gesundheit."

12. How often do you check your breath?

☐ Upon reading this.

☐ When others wince.

☐ Once a year.

Take a breather. If these questions are tough for you, you probably aren't White and can go home now. Good night. If you're still not sure, keep working.

13. The world's most nearly perfect food is:

☐ Processed cheese.

☐ Stinky French cheese.

☐ Stinky German cheese.

☐ Donuts.

14. It's two days before Christmas. Your mail carrier, a non-White, announces that he's been fired from the post office, effective today, and that his wife is expecting triplets. He's provided excellent mail service for fourteen years, so you:

☐ Give him a lecture on birth control.

☐ Complain about all the junk mail you get.

☐ Tell him to wait while you go in the house and send your wife out with a check for one dollar.

15. A condominium is:
☐ Less than a home.
☐ A perfect home for your mother-in-law.
☐ Something that leaves a ring in your son's wallet.

16. You are waiting in your boss's car as he ducks into a 7-Eleven store for some Tums. The glove compartment inexplicably opens and out pops a large white bed sheet with two eyeholes and a hood. You:
☐ Ask if he's been sleeping in his car.
☐ Put it on as a joke and go into the 7-Eleven after him, yelling, "Woogie, woogie, woogie!"
☐ Write a TV movie about your discovery.

17. You just bought a new car and that evening, you must hand it over to a Third World parking valet at your favorite restaurant. You:
☐ Ride with him as he parks it.
☐ Drive home and walk back to the restaurant.
☐ Empty the glove compartment into the trunk and give him only the ignition key.
☐ Eat at Denny's.

18. Upon hearing the oft-used phrase "Man's Best Friend," you immediately think of:
☐ Brut.
☐ A five iron.
☐ Bob Guccione.
☐ Expand-A-Belt trousers.

You're through. Push your paper away and take another breather. Better yet, stand up and stretch. It can't hurt. If it does hurt, sit down. No reason to kill yourself. It's just a harmless questionnaire, not an insurance physical.

If you are like any of the hundreds of people who have completed this exam, you are excited and confused. How did I do? Where do I stand? What's my score? Did I win?

First of all, the test was divided into four major areas. One, misleading or "trick" questions. Two, questions of no import whatsoever. Three, "gimmes," or questions only an idiot could get wrong. And four, questions required under a preexisting contract with the fine folks at Expand-A-Belt fashions.

For example, question number 6, the one about hamburgers, was a dead giveaway. If you included "Jewish pickles" on your ideal burger, then give this book to a Methodist and go see *Yentl.* You'll learn a lot more about yourself than you will here. Suffice it to say that Barbra Streisand plays a young boy. That's all we're going to say. We don't want to spoil it for you.

Question number 7, however, was a trick question. If the first thing you notice about another's home is "how it smells," you were right. If the first thing you notice is "its resale value," you were also right. No matter what you answered, you were right, and well on your way to being White. Congratulations.

MERRILL MARKOE

MY PET, MYSELF

Merrill Markoe won an Emmy award as head writer for "Late Night with David Letterman." She is a contributing editor at New York Woman magazine and is one of an exploding list of new women humorists who are enriching what has for too long been a male-dominated field. But quite apart from gender, Markoe's is a unique viewpoint, to which the following perfectly attests.

I pick dogs that remind me of myself—scrappy, mutt-faced, with a hint of mange. People look for a reflection of their own personalities or the person they dream of being in the eyes of an animal companion. That is the reason I sometimes look into the face of my dog Stan (I have two) and see wistful sadness and existential angst, when all he is actually doing is slowly scanning the ceiling for flies.

We pet owners demand a great deal from our pets. When we give them the job, it's a career position. Pets are required to listen to us blithely, even if we talk to them in infantile and goofy tones of voice that we'd never dare use around another human being for fear of psychiatric observation. On top of that, we make them wear little sweaters or jackets, and not just the cool kind with the push-up sleeves, either, but weird little felt ones that say, "It's raining cats and dogs."

We are pretty sure that we and our pets share the same reality, until one day we come home to find that our wistful, intelligent friend who reminds us of our better self has decided a good way to spend the day is to open a box of Brillo pads. Unravel a few, distribute some throughout the house, and eat or wear all the rest. And we shake our heads in an inability to comprehend what went wrong here.

Is he bored or is he just out for revenge? He certainly can't be as stupid as this would appear. In order to answer these questions more fully, I felt I needed some kind of new perspective, a perspective that comes from really knowing both sides of the story.

Thus, I made up my mind to live with my pets as one of them: to share their hopes, their fears, their squeaking vinyl lamb chops, their drinking space at the toilet.

What follows is the revealing, sometimes shocking, sometimes terrifying, sometimes really stupid diary that resulted.

8:45 A.M. We have been lying on our sides in the kitchen for almost an hour now. We started out in the bedroom with just our heads under the bed. But then one of us heard something, and we all ran to the back door. I think our quick response was rather effective because, although I never ascertained exactly what we heard to begin with, I also can't say I recall ever hearing it again.

9:00 A.M. We carefully inspected the molding in the hallway, which led us straight to the heating duct by the bedroom. Just a coincidence? None of us was really sure. So we watched it suspiciously for a while. Then we watched it for a little while longer.

Then, never letting it out of our sight, we all took a nap.

10:00 A.M. I don't really know whose idea it was to yank back the edge of the carpet and pull apart the carpet pad, but talk about a rousing good time! How strange that I could have lived in this house for all these years, and never before felt the fur of a carpet between my teeth. Or actually bit into a moist, chewy chunk of carpet padding. I will never again think of the carpet as simply a covering for the floor.

11:15 A.M. When we all wound up in the kitchen, the other two began to stare at me eagerly. Their meaning was clear. The pressure was on for me to produce snacks. They remembered the old me—the one with the prehensile thumb, the one who could open refrigerators and cabinets. I saw they didn't yet realize that today, I intended to live as their equal. But as they continued their staring, I soon became caught up in their obsession. That is the only explanation I have as to why I helped them topple over the garbage. At first I was nervous, watching the murky fluids soak into the floor. But the heady sense of acceptance I felt when we all dove headfirst into the can more than made up for my compromised sense of right and wrong. Pack etiquette demanded that I be the last in line. By the time I really got my head in there, the really good stuff was gone. But wait! I spied a tiny piece of tin foil hidden in a giant clump of hair, and inside, a wad of previously chewed gum, lightly coated with sugar or salt. I was settling down to my treasure when I had the sense that I was being watched. Raising my head just slightly, I looked into the noses of my companions. Their eyes were glued to that hard rubber mass. Their drools were long and elastic, and so, succumbing to peer pressure, I split up my gum wad three ways. But I am not sure that I did the right thing. As is so often the case with wanting popularity, I may have gained their short-term acceptance. But I think that in the long run, I lost their real respect. No dog of reasonable intelligence would ever divide up something that could still be chewed.

11:50 A.M. Someone spotted a fly, and all three of us decided to catch him in our teeth. I was greatly relieved when one of the others got to him first.

12:20 P.M. Someone heard something, and in a flash, we were all in the back yard, running back and forth by the fence, periodically hooting. Then one of us spotted a larger-than-usual space between two of the fence boards, and using both teeth and nails, began to make the space larger. Pretty soon, all three of us were doing everything in our power to help. This was a case where the old prehensile thumb really came in handy. Grabbing hold of one of the splinters, I was able to enlarge the hole immediately. Ironically, I alone was unable to squeeze through to freedom, and so I watched with envy as the others ran in pointless circles in the lot next door. What was I going to do? All of my choices were difficult. Sure, I could go back into the house and get a hacksaw, or I could simply let myself out the back gate, but if I did that, did I not betray my companions? And would I not then be obligated to round us all up and punish us? No, I was a collaborator, and I had the lip splinters to prove it. So I went back to the hole and continued chewing. Only a few hundred dollars' worth of fence damage later, I was able to squeeze through that darn hole myself.

1:30 P.M. The extra time I took was just enough for me to lose sight of my two companions. And so, for the first time, I had to rely on my keen, new animal instincts. Like the wild creature I had become, I was able to spot their tracks immediately. They led me in a series of ever-widening circles, then across the lot at a forty-five-degree angle, then into a series of zigzags, then back to the hole again. Finally, I decided to abandon the tracking and head out to the sidewalk. Seconds later, I spotted them both across the street, where they were racing up and back in front of the neighbor's house. They seemed glad to see me, and so I eagerly joined them in their project. The three of us had only been running and hooting for less than an hour when the apparent owner of the house came to the front door. And while I admit this may not have been the best of circumstances for a first introduction, nevertheless I still feel the manner in which he threatened to turn the hose on us was both excessively violent and unnecessarily vulgar.

Clearly, it was up to me to encourage our group to relocate, and I was shocked at how easily I could still take command of our unit. A simple "Let's go, boys," and everyone was willing to follow me home. (It's such a power-packed phrase. That's how I met my last boyfriend!)

3:00 P.M. By the time we had moved our running and hooting activities into our own front yard, we were all getting a little tired. So we lay down on our sides on the porch.

4:10 P.M. We all changed sides.

4:45 P.M. We all changed sides again.

5:20 P.M. We all lay on our backs. (What a nice change of pace!)

6:00 P.M. Everyone was starting to grow restless. Occasionally, one of us would get up, scratch the front door, and moan.

I wrestled silently with the temptation simply to let us all in. But then I realized I didn't have any keys on me. Of course, it occurred to me that we could all go back through the new hole in the fence, but everyone else seemed to have forgotten about the entire fence incident by this time. As they say, "a word to the wise." And so, taking a hint from my friends, I began to forget about the whole thing myself.

6:30 P.M. The sound of an approaching car as it pulls into the driveway. The man who shares this house with us is coming home. He is both surprised and perplexed to see us all out in the front yard running in circles. He is also quickly irritated by the fact that no one offers any explanations. And once he opens the front door, he unleashes a furious string of harsh words as he confronts the mounds of garbage someone has strewn all over the house. We have nothing but sympathy for him in his tragic misfortune. But since none of us knows anything about it, we all retire to the coat closet until the whole thing blows over. And later, as he eats his dinner, I sit quietly under the table. As I watch him, a pleasant feeling of calm overtakes me as I realize just how much I have grown as a person. Perhaps that is why the cruel things he says to me seem to have no effect. And so, when he gets up to pour himself another beverage, I raise my head up to his plate, and, with my teeth, I lift off his sandwich.

LEWIS GRIZZARD

EDDIE HASKELL IS STILL A JERK

Anyone who watches the television show "Designing Women" will recognize Lewis Grizzard as the prodigal brother who longed to be a stand-up comedian and came to visit the Sugerbaker sisters after being released from a mental institution. In real life, Lewis Grizzard is a stand-up comedian, but even more impressively, he's the best-selling author of Elvis Is Dead and I Don't Feel So Good Myself, *and such other wonderfully titled books as* If Love Were Oil, I'd Be About a Quart Low *and* My Daddy Was a Pistol, and I'm a Son of a Gun.

Phil Donahue and his television show have been a great source of consternation for me. Five mornings a week, Donahue gets together with a crowd of women who live in Chicago and apparently have nothing better to do, and they discuss strange things.

One morning recently, for example, his guests were two homosexual women and a baby. The two homosexual women, who said they were very much in love, had decided they wanted a baby, so one of them was artificially inseminated with the sperm of the other's brother, and the baby on the program was the result.

One of the homosexual women was black and the other was white, and I think they named the baby something like "Joy" or "Mud." I only remember that the baby didn't have a regular

name like we used to give children—a name like Randy or
Arlene.

I frankly don't care if a black female homosexual and a white
female homosexual decide to love each other, but I do have
some concern for the offspring. Having been conceived in such
an unconventional manner and having been given a name that
would embarrass a dog, I wonder if the child will have the
desire or the opportunity to do the things that are important
to most children—such as playing Little League baseball, eating crayons in school, or laughing at a clown.

What bothers me about this situation in particular, and
about the Donahue show in general, is where all this might
lead. Television today is probably the greatest single influence
on the American public. A recent study showed that the average TV in this country is on six hours and fifty-five minutes
a day; that's almost forty-nine hours a week. In a ten-year
period, that's almost three years of watching TV! It's not sur-
prising, therefore, that in many cases society has become what
it watches.

So my question is this: Will all these televised discussions
of aberrant lifestyles eventually make such behavior completely acceptable, and will people start producing babies with
home chemistry sets and giving them names that will make
it difficult for them to survive when they enter the Marine
Corps?

Actually, my problems with television didn't begin with
Donahue. After my Aunt Jessie, who lived next door, brought
home the first television I could watch on a regular basis, it
took me a year to figure out that Howdy Doody was a puppet.
I presumed he had once suffered from some sort of crippling
disease, and that was why he walked funny. He also had a
strange mouth, which I attributed to not brushing regularly.
When Howdy talked, the entire bottom portion of his mouth
moved like he was trying to eat a large cantaloupe. Whole.

Finally I noticed the strings attached to him. It was like the
day I found out there is no Santa Claus and the day somebody
told me they heard Lash Larue was in a porno film. It broke

my heart. You know kids, though. I couldn't wait to tell everybody I knew of my discovery.

"Howdy Doody isn't real," I told one of my classmates at school.

"Yes, he is," he replied.

"No, he isn't. He's just a puppet. Somebody pulls his strings and that's what makes him walk and talk."

The kid started crying. I didn't dare tell him that Clarabelle's big red nose was probably fake, too.

Soon I discovered "Superman." I enjoyed watching "The Man of Steel," but I had some problems with him, too. In the first place, I never thought Superman's disguise as Clark Kent was all that clever. Lois Lane had to be a bigger dummy than Howdy Doody not to see right through it.

Whenever Superman decided to become Clark Kent, all he did was put on a coat and tie and a pair of glasses. That's a disguise? Superman and Clark Kent talked exactly the same, were the same height and weight, and if Lois had been any kind of reporter at all, she probably would have noticed that they had the same mole or freckle or other telltake body markings.

In retrospect, Lois Lane had no business working for *The Daily Planet*. She should have been on the obit desk in Topeka.

Something else used to bother me about the "Superman" show. Anytime "The Man of Steel" has a social misfit cornered, the crook would pull out a gun and fire six shots at Superman's chest. Of course, bullets just bounced off, because you couldn't hurt Superman.

Even as a kid, I knew what I would have done after that. I would have gone quietly. But not the crooks on "Superman." After watching their bullets bounce harmlessly away, they would throw their guns at him. Anybody knows you don't further rile a man whom six bullets couldn't stop by throwing your gun at him.

There were a lot of family shows on television in those early days. There was "The Donna Reed Show," for example. Donna was always so pleasant. I wonder why she never had that-time-of-the-month problems like other women?

"Father Knows Best," another great family show, was one of my favorites. Even so, I used to wonder why Robert Young never took his tie off. When he came home from a long day at the insurance office, he would keep his tie on and replace his jacket with a sweater. He did the same thing later as Marcus Welby, and remember that you never saw him without a tie on when he wound up selling Sanka. He may have been the only man in history to wear a tie more than Richard Nixon.

"Leave It to Beaver" was also a big hit. In fact, it still is. "Leave It to Beaver" reruns are on several cable stations today, and a fellow named Irwyn Applebaum has even written a book entitled *The World According to Beaver*. The book contains examples of the sort of dialogue that was featured on the show. Here's one between Wally and his friend, the ever-obnoxious Eddie Haskell.

EDDIE: Come on, Sam, time's a-wastin'.

WALLY: Look, Eddie, I can't go with you guys today. I've got to work out in the yard.

EDDIE: Work in the yard? Aw, come off it! We got . . . Oh, good morning, Mr. and Mrs. Cleaver.

JUNE: Hello, Eddie.

WARD: Good morning, Eddie.

EDDIE: Well, if you've got work to do, Wallace, I don't want to interfere. I was reading an article in the paper just the other day, and it said a certain amount of responsibility around the home is good character training. Well, good-bye, Mr. and Mrs. Cleaver.

WARD: *Good-bye*, Eddie.

EDDIE (whispering): Can I talk to you outside, Wally?

WALLY: Okay, Eddie, what's up?

EDDIE: Come on, Moe, drop the hoe. Lumpy's out in the car and we're ready to roll.

WALLY: I told you, Eddie. I can't. I got work to do.

EDDIE: Come on, Isabel, you gonna let your mother and father push you around? Why don't you read them the child labor law?

WALLY: Hey, Eddie, isn't it about the time of year you're supposed to shed your skin?

I take a certain amount of comfort in knowing that Eddie Haskell comes off as just as big a jerk today as he did twenty years ago. There are so few elements of life that have gone unchanged in that period.

"The Adventures of Ozzie and Harriet" was another classic of those timid times. There was Ozzie and Harriet and David and Ricky, and they lived in a big house and everybody was happy and problems were easy to solve. Television of the fifties rarely dealt with anything more intricate than a husband forgetting an anniversary or a wife burning dinner for the husband's boss.

In those days, Ozzie was always around to talk over problems with David and Ricky. As a matter of fact, I still don't know what Ozzie did for a living; I never recall his going to work. If they did "The Adventures of Ozzie and Harriet" today, Ozzie probably would be a dope dealer.

There are a lot of things I miss about television the way it used to be. I'll take John Cameron Swayze over Peter Jennings on a big story any day, and has there ever been a better detective than Sergeant Joe Friday on "Dragnet"?

Joe Friday didn't waste a lot of time keeping Los Angeles free of crime on his program. All he wanted was the facts. Today, television cops get involved in a lot of extracurricular activities, such as fooling around with women.

(Fact: Jack Webb, who played Joe Friday, died not long ago of a heart attack. Maybe he should have taken a few days off occasionally and gone to Pismo Beach with a girlfriend.)

"Amos 'n' Andy" was a favorite at my aunt's house. George "Kingfish" Stevens was always trying to con Andrew H. Brown, and sooner or later the Kingfish would end up in court with his lawyer, Algonquin J. Calhoun, representing him:

"Yo' Honor, it's easy for the prosecutor to talk that way about my client, George Stevens. It's easy 'cause my client is a crook, Yo' Honor!"

"Amos 'n' Andy" was classic humor, but unfortunately we can't watch it on television today. It's allegedly racist.

That's just another example of how confusing the modern world has become. I can't watch "Amos 'n' Andy" because it's racist, but it's okay to watch "Sanford and Son," which is filled with racist situations and remarks.

Remember the time Fred had to go to the dentist? He found out that the dentist was black and insisted on having a white man work on his mouth. And don't forget his classic line, "There ain't nothin' uglier than an old white woman."

There must be some big difference in the two programs, but I swear I can't see it. Maybe it's a matter of perspective.

I remember several years ago when I was working in Chicago, the nation's most segregated city, and caught a cab home one night after work. The cab driver was black, and we began to talk.

"Where you from?" he asked.

"Atlanta."

"Thought so," he said. "I'm from Mississippi."

Here it comes, I figured. A black cabbie is about to give me a lecture on how much better life is away from the racist jackals of the South.

"I'm going back one of these days," he said instead.

I was startled. "You don't like it here?"

"People ain't the same up here," he said. "In Mississippi, they always let you know where you stand. They put up signs down there that say, 'No Niggers Allowed.' Up here, they don't put up no signs. They just let you walk into a place and then tell you you can't stay. I liked it better when I knew ahead of time where I was wanted."

I guess that's how I feel about television these days. I liked it better when I knew what was okay to laugh at and what wasn't.

It is modern television, in fact, that has helped to foster the two most offensive Southern stereotypes—the racist redneck and the belligerent county sheriff. And nothing irritates me more than to see Southerners being portrayed on television by actors or actresses who can't speak the language.

Take *y'all*, for instance. Southerners never say *you all*, and even if we did, we wouldn't use it in the singular sense. The proper word, used when speaking to two or more others, is a contraction, *y'all*.

On television, however, some honey from the Bronx who has landed a part as a Southern belle inevitably says to her lover, "Why don't *you all* come ovuh heah and sit down by lil' o' me."

I doubt that "Amos 'n' Andy" was near the embarrassment to blacks that Yankees trying to portray Southerners are to Southern whites.

Television actually was responsible for my first encounter with discrimination, because it brought major league baseball into my life.

For the first time, I could *see* Mantle and Musial and Williams and Snider. I became a hardcore Dodger fan—they were still in Brooklyn then—and consequently developed a keen hatred for the Yankees.

I mentioned my love for the Dodgers one day to a cousin, who happened to be a Yankee fan. "The Dodgers!" he said, almost spitting out the words. "They're a nigger team!"

Perhaps I had overheard the older folks talking, or perhaps I had read something in the newspapers about Jackie Robinson, the first black man in major league baseball, but I never considered it when pledging my allegiance to the Dodgers. So when my older cousin made what was obviously a derogatory remark, I was hurt and confused. I pressed my cousin for more information, but all he would say was, "Niggers ain't got no business playing major league ball."

I decided to take the question to my mother. "Do niggers

have any business playing major league ball?" I asked her.

"The word," she said in her sternest schoolteacher voice, "is *knee-grow*. I don't ever want to hear you say that other word in this house."

Fine, but that didn't answer the question. Frankly, I was more interested in baseball than in race relations at the time.

"I don't know anything about baseball, son," she said, "but your daddy played with Negroes in the service."

That settled it. If my father had played with Negroes, then there was no problem with Jackie Robinson playing with the Dodgers. Besides, all I wanted Robinson to do was help beat the Yankees, which is exactly what he did in the 1955 World Series.

I was so thankful for the Dodger victory that I said a prayer in church, reasoning that God, in all his infinite wisdom, certainly must be a Dodger fan, too.

Parents today are concerned that their children see too much sex and violence on television. There wasn't any sex to speak of on TV when I was a child, unless you count watching lady wrestlers tumble around with one another in those tight-fitting outfits they used to wear.

There was violence, but the victims usually deserved the thrashings they got.

Johnny Mack Brown walks into a saloon on the Five O'Clock Movie and says, "Gimme a milk." Heroes in those days didn't drink liquor, you recall.

"Milk?" laughs an ornery galoot standing next to JMB at the bar. "Here, tenderfoot," he continues, pushing a drink toward Johnny Mack, "try a little of this red-eye. It'll put some hair on your chest."

Johnny Mack Brown, after gulping down his milk, of course, would proceed to beat laughing boy to within an inch of his life, and the saloon would be totally destroyed in the meantime. I never thought about it much back then, but now I wonder who paid for the damages after all those saloons were destroyed.

I watched so many westerns as a kid that I'm still an expert on who rode what horse. Try me.

Gene Autry? That's a throwaway. He rode Champion. Hopalong Cassidy? A little tougher, but no problem for an expert. His horse was Topper.

How about the horses of the sidekicks? Tonto rode Scout. Frog Millhouse's horse was named Ringeye. Festus Hagan's mule on "Gunsmoke" was Ruth.

What our parents should have worried about our seeing on television was not sex and violence, but rather a way of life that was totally unrealistic—one that we would never be able to emulate. Just as viewers today are influenced by the whackos on "Donahue," we were given a model of the way a family was supposed to work when we watched early television.

Ward and June never argued on "Leave It to Beaver," and Jim and Margaret knew their roles in "Father Knows Best." Jim sat in the den with his stupid tie and sweater on, while Margaret made dinner. And none of the kids ever got into any kind of trouble that couldn't be handled in a calm family conference.

One of the most unrealistic examples which television promoted was that of Roy Rogers and Dale Evans (who may have been the first feminist, now that I think about it. She kept her maiden name, and she never rode sidesaddle. Donahue would have loved her).

Roy went off every day and fought cattle thieves, while Dale stayed home and watched over the ranch. When Roy returned, Dale cooked him something to eat, and then they'd sit around singing "Happy Trails" together. For years, "Happy Trails" was my favorite song:

> Happy trails to you,
> Until we meet again.
> Happy trails to you,
> Keep smiling until then.
> Happy traaaaails to youuuuuu,
> 'Til we meeeeeet aaaaagain.

Of course, it didn't turn out that way at all. "Happy Trails" turned into "Forty Miles of Bad Road."

I came home after a hard day's work one evening and said to my then-wife, "Rustle up some grub, woman, and call me when it's ready. Me and ol' Bullet will be out in the backyard."

"Rustle your own grub, Roy," said my wife. "I'm taking Buttermilk and heading out for a few drinks with the girls."

I'm not certain when it was that I stopped watching television on a regular basis. I think it was soon after they took "Gunsmoke" and "Have Gun Will Travel" and "Peter Gunn" and "Perry Mason" off the air and replaced them with programs that gave me headaches.

I still search for the old shows—the ones that are being rerun, thank goodness. Give me Andy and Barney and Aunt Bea and Opie over "Hart to Hart" any day. And every time I flip through the channels looking for an old program and run across "Family Feud," I secretly hope that herpes can be contracted by kissing game show contestants.

I never liked "All in the Family." Everybody was always screaming at everybody else, and it made me nervous. Maude was a grumpy old bat, and that program where Tex Ritter's son John lived with those two air-brained women was horrible. Ol' Tex must still be twirling in his grave.

I don't like soap operas, because it's too hard to remember who is pregnant and by whom, and I always had a sneaking suspicion that Laverne and Shirley were gay. But then again, I don't remember ever seeing them on "Donahue."

The movies. They can get a little crazy, too. I'm all for realism, but the language they use in today's movies is atrocious. Henry Fonda and Katherine Hepburn even used dirty words in *On Golden Pond*. And if they ever made *Gone With the Wind* over again, I can't even imagine how Rhett would tell Scarlett to take a hike this time—"Frankly, my dear, I don't . . ."

When it comes to sex, movies are like everything else

today—overloaded. I enjoyed sex in movies more when you *thought* they were going to do it, but you were never quite sure.

In those days, when it became apparent that a couple had more on their minds than playing a few hands of canasta, the leading man and lady would embrace while doing-it music (violins and harps) played in the background. Then before they removed the first stitch of clothes, the camera faded off.

As a matter of fact, whenever you heard doing-it music in a movie, you knew it was safe to leave your seat and go buy a package of Milk Duds, because absolutely nothing was going to happen that you hadn't seen before. Today if you leave your seat for even a couple of minutes, you're liable to miss three gang rapes, two oral sex scenes, and enough skin to reupholster an entire Greyhound bus.

It doesn't have to be that way, of course. Great movies still can be made without having a nudist colony as the setting. Take *Tender Mercies*, for example: Robert Duvall won an Academy Award for his performance and never took off more than his shirt.

What we need is more movies like *The Natural* and *Patton*, my all-time favorite movie. George C. Scott was even better than his cousin Randolph. I also enjoy action movies where the villains gets theirs in the end—movies like *Walking Tall*, where Joe Don Baker took a stick and destroyed an entire Tennessee roadhouse and everybody inside it.

Unfortunately, I doubt that movies ever will be the same as they used to be. Back then we went for diversion and relaxation and Milk Duds, not for some deep, sensitive message; not to see people butchered with chain saws; not to see things you used to see only in the magazines your older brother brought home from the Navy.

I give credit to the brilliant Chicago columnist Mike Royko for putting today's movies in their proper perspective. Royko sensed that when John Wayne died, the movie industry changed forevermore.

In his tribute to the Duke, Royko cited the way he handled Dirty Ned Pepper in *True Grit,* and he wondered how John Travolta would have dealt with Dirty Ned in the same situation.

"He probably would have asked him to dance," wrote Royko.

ALAN COREN

ALL YOU NEED TO KNOW ABOUT EUROPE

Since the passing of S. J. Perelman, Alan Coren is, quite simply and in my opinion, the funniest man on earth. I have literally been unable to catch my breath laughing over certain Coren pieces—the following included. Coren was once an editor at the renowned humor magazine Punch *and has authored numerous books. He has also written for radio, television, and film, and has served as a broadcaster both in his native Britain and in the United States. Quite an impressive résumé for the funniest man on earth.*

GERMANY

THE PEOPLE

Germans are split into two broad categories: those with tall spikes on their hats, and those with briefcases. Up until 1945, the country's history was made by those with spikes. After 1945, it was made by those with briefcases. In common with the rest of Europe, its history is therefore now known as economics. Ethnically, the Germans are Teutonic, but prefer not to talk about it any more. This ethnos was originally triform, being made up of Vandals, Gepidae, and Goths, all of whom emigrated south from Sweden in about 500 B.C.; why they emigrated is not exactly clear, but many scholars believe it was because they saw the way Sweden was going, i.e., neutral.

Physically, Germans are tall and blond, though not as tall and blond as they sometimes think, especially when they are short, dark Austrians with a sense of destiny. When they sing, the Germans link arms and rock sideways; it is best described as horizontal marching.

THE LAND

The country, or *Lebensraum*, is extremely beautiful and situated in the very centre of Europe, thus lending itself to expansion in any direction, a temptation first succumbed to in the fifth century A.D. (the *Volkerwanderung*) when Germany embraced most of Spain, and regularly indulged in since. It is interesting to note that this summer there will be three million Germans in Spain, thus outnumbering the first excursion by almost a hundred to one.

THE HISTORY

For almost two thousand years, Germany was split into separate states that fought one another. In the nineteenth century, they combined and began fighting everyone else. They are currently split up again and once more fighting one another. If they combine, the result is anybody's guess. Having lost the last war, they are currently enjoying a *Wirtschaftswunder*, which can be briefly translated as "The best way to own a Mercedes is to build one." That is about all there is to German history, since no one has ever known what was going on, and if this is the case, then the Truth cannot be said to exist. Germany has, as you can see, provided many of the world's greatest philosophers.

BELGIUM

THE PEOPLE

Belgium is the most densely populated country in Europe, and is at the same time fiercely divided on the subjects of language and religion. This means that it is impossible to move anywhere in the country, which is packed with mobs standing chin to chin and screaming incomprehensible things at one another in the certain knowledge that God is on their side, whoever He is. That there has not been more bloodshed is entirely due to the fact that there isn't room to swing a fist. Consequently, what the Belgian authorities most fear is contraception: if it ever catches on, and the population thins to the point where rifles may be comfortably unslung from shoulders, the entire nation might disappear overnight.

THE LAND
The land is entirely invisible, except in the small hours of the morning, being for the rest of the time completely underfoot. It is therefore no surprise to learn that Belgium's largest industries are coal and mineral mining, as underground is the only place where there is room to work. Plans have been suggested for reclaiming land from the sea, on the Dutch pattern, but were always shelved as soon as it was realised that there was neither room for the water that would have to be removed from the sea, nor, alternatively, any spare land to spread to extend the coastline outwards.

THE HISTORY
Belgium has always suffered horribly at the hands of occupying forces, which, given the overcrowding, is only to be expected. The bayoneting of babies by Prussians, for example, was never intentional; it was simply that it was impossible to walk about with fixed bayonets in such confined spaces without finding something stuck on the end of them. For the same reason, the sprout was developed by Brussels agronomists, this being the largest cabbage a housewife could possibly carry through the teeming streets.

FRANCE

THE PEOPLE
The French are our closest neighbors, and we are therefore bound to them by bonds of jealousy, suspicion, competition, and envy. They haven't brought the shears back, either. They are short, blue-vested people who carry their own onions when

cycling abroad, and have a yard which is 3.37 inches longer than other people's. Their vanity does not stop there: they believe themselves to be great lovers, an easy trap to fall into when you're permanently drunk, and the natural heirs to Europe. It has been explained to them that there is a difference between natural heirs and legitimate heirs, but they cannot appreciate subtle distinctions, probably because French has the smallest vocabulary of any language in Europe.

THE LAND

France is the largest country in Europe, a great boon for drunks, who need room to fall, and consists of an enormous number of bars linked by an intricate system of serpentine cobbles. Exactly why France is so cobbled has never been fully explained, though most authorities favour the view that the French like to be constantly reminded of the feel of grapes underfoot. The houses are all shuttered to exclude light, as a precaution against hangovers, and filled with large lumpy beds in which the French spend 83.7 per cent of their time recovering from sex or booze or both. The lumpiness is due, of course, to the presence of undeclared income under the mattresses.

THE HISTORY

French history, or *gloire*, starts with Charlemagne, and ends with Charlemagne. Anything subsequent was in the hands of bizarre paranoiacs who thought they were God (Louis XIV) or thought they were Charlemagne (Napoleon) or thought they were God and Louis XIV and Charlemagne and Napoleon (de Gaulle). Like most other European nations, the French have fought everyone, but unlike the rest have always claimed that both victories and defeats came after opposition to overwhelming odds. This is probably because they always saw two of everything.

LUXEMBOURG

THE PEOPLE
There are nine people in Luxembourg, and they are kept pretty busy making stamps. It is not the smallest country in Europe: there are only eight people in Monaco, five in Andorra, and Herr J. F. Klausner in Liechtenstein, so as the fourth non-smallest country in Europe, it enjoys a rather unique position. The people are of middle height, with the small, deft fingers of master-perforators, and all look rather alike, except for their Uncle Maurice who lost an ear on the Somme. They are a rather arrogant people (they refer to World War I as the Battle of Maurice's Ear) but not unartistic: *My Day at the Zoo*, by the country's infant prodigy, ran into nine copies and won the Prix Maurice for 1969.

THE LAND
On a clear day, from the terrace of the Salon de Philatelie, you can't see Luxembourg at all. This is because a tree is in the way. Beyond the tree lies Belgium. The centre of the country is, however, very high, mainly because of the chimney on it, and slopes down to a great expanse of water, as they haven't got around to having the bathroom overflow pipe fixed. The climate is temperate (remember that ninety per cent of Luxembourg is indoors) and the local Flora is varied and interesting, especially on her favourite topic, the 1908 five-cent blue triangular.

THE HISTORY
Old Luxembourg (now the coal-cellar of the modern country), was founded in the twelfth century by King John of Bohemia, who wanted somewhere to keep the lawn-mower. It escaped most of the wars and pestilences that swept Europe in the subsequent eight centuries, often because the people were out when they called, and is therefore one of the most stable political and economic elements in the EEC: its trade balance is always favourable (imports come in at the back gate and leave by the front door as exports). Luxembourg is also the

oldest ally of Stanley Gibbons Ltd., although it is probably most famous as the birthplace of Horace Batchelor.

THE NETHERLANDS

THE PEOPLE

Like the Germans, the Dutch fall into two quite distinct physical types: the small, corpulent, red-faced Edams, and the thinner, paler, larger Goudas. As one might expect of a race that evolved underwater and subsisted entirely upon cheese, the Dutch are somewhat single-minded, conservative, resilient, and thoughtful. Indeed, the sea informs their entire culture: the bicycle, that ubiquitous Dutch vehicle, was designed to facilitate underwater travel, offering least resistance to waves and weed, the clog was introduced to weigh down the feet and prevent drifting, and the meerschaum pipe, with its characteristic lid, was designed expressly to exclude fish and the larger plankton. And those who would accuse the Dutch of overeating would do well to reflect on the notorious frangibility of dykes: it's no joke being isolated atop a flooded windmill with nothing to eat but passing tulips. You have to get it while you can.

THE LAND

Strictly speaking, the land does not exist: it is merely dehydrated sea, and concern was originally expressed when the EEC was first mooted that the Six might suddenly turn into the Five after a bad night. Many informed observers believe that this fear is all that lies behind the acceptance of Britain's membership, i.e., we are a sort of First Reserve in case Rain Stops Holland. Nevertheless, it is interesting country, sweeping up from the coastal plain into the central massif, a two-foot-high ridge of attractive silt with fabulous views of the sky, and down again to the valleys, inches below. Apart from cheese and tulips, the main product of the country is advocaat, a drink made from lawyers.

THE HISTORY

Incensed by poor jokes about the Low Countries, the Dutch, having emerged from the sea, became an extremely belligerent people, taking on Spain, France, England, and Austria in quick succession, a characteristic that has almost entirely disappeared from the modern Dutch temperament. It is now found only among expatriate Dutchmen, like Orangemen and Afrikaaners.

ITALY

THE PEOPLE

The median Italian, according to the latest figures of the Coren Intelligence Unit, is a cowardly baritone who consumes 78.3 kilometres of carbohydrates a month and drives about in a car slightly smaller than he is, looking for a divorce. He is governed by a stable conservative government, called the Mafia, who operate an efficient police force, called the Mafia, which is the official arm of the judiciary, called the Mafia. The Italians are an extremely cultivated folk, and will often walk miles to sell a tourist a copy of the Sistine Chapel ceiling made entirely from seashells. They invented the mandolin, a kind of boudoir banjo shaped like a woman's bottom, not surprisingly.

THE LAND

Italy is boot-shaped, for reasons lost in the mists of geology. The South is essentially agricultural, and administered by local land authorities, called the Mafia; the North is industrial, and run by tightly interlocked corporations, called the Mafia. The largest Italian city is New York, and is linked to the mainland by a highly specialised and efficient communications system, called the Mafia.

THE HISTORY

Italy was originally called Rome, which came to hold power over Europe by moving into new areas every week or so and threatening to lean on them if they did not fork out tithe (L.

protectio). It was run by a series of Caesars (Eduardus Gaius Robinsonius, Georgius Raftus, Paulus Munius, etc.) who held sway until the Renaissance, when Leonardo invented the tank and the aeroplane, and thus ushered in modern Italy (in World War II, the Italians, ever brilliant, possessed the only tank with a reverse gear). In the 1920s, the Caesars reasserted themselves in their two main linear branches, the Caponi and the Mussolini, whose symbol was the fasces, which signified "United We Stand," but they didn't.

JACK SCHMIDT, ARTS ADMINISTRATOR

Garrison Keillor was born in Minnesota, graduated from the University of Minnesota, and subsequently made Minnesota famous with his mainstay performances each Saturday evening on the radio show "A Prairie Home Companion." In addition, he has written an impressive body of work for The New Yorker *and other publications.*

He has also written pieces, naturally, for Twin Cities *magazine.*

It was one of those sweltering days toward the end of the fiscal year when Minneapolis smells of melting asphalt and foundation money is as tight as a rusted nut. Ninety-six, the radio said on the way in from the airport, and back at my office in the Acme Building I was trying to fan the memory of ocean breezes in Hawaii, where I had just spent two days attending a conference on midwestern regionalism.

It wasn't working. I was sitting down, jacket off, feet up, looking at the business end of an air conditioner, and a numb spot was forming around my left ear to which I was holding a telephone and listening to Bobby Jo, my secretary at the Twin Cities Arts Mall, four blocks away, reading little red numerals off a sheet of paper. We had only two days before the books snapped shut, and our administrative budget had sprung a deficit big enough to drive a car through—a car full of accountants. I could feel a dark sweat stain spreading across the back of my best blue shirt.

"Listen," I sputtered, "I still got some loose bucks in the publicity budget. Let's transfer that to administration."

"J.S.," she sighed, "I just got done telling you. Those loose bucks are as spent as an octogenarian after an all-night bender. Right now we're using more red ink than the funny papers, and yesterday we bounced three checks right off the bottom of the account. The budget is so unbalanced, it's liable to go out and shoot somebody."

You could've knocked me over with a rock.

"Sweetheart," I lied quickly, hoping she couldn't hear my heavy breathing, "don't worry about it. Old Jack has been around the block once or twice. I'll straighten it out."

"Payday is tomorrow," she sniffed sharply. "Twelve noon."

The Arts Mall is just one of the thirty-seven arts organizations I administer, a chain that stretches from the Anaheim Puppet Theatre to the Title IX Poetry Center in Bangor, and I could have let it go down the tubes, but hell, I kind of like the joint. It's an old Henny Penny supermarket that we renovated in 1976 when Bicentennial money was wandering around like helpless buffalo, and it houses seventeen little shops—mainly pottery and macramé, plus a dulcimer maker, a printmaker, a spatter painter, two sculptors, and a watering hole called The Barre. This is one of those quiet little bistros where you aren't driven crazy by the constant ringing of cash registers. A nice place to drink but you wouldn't want to own it.

I hung up the phone and sat for a few minutes eyeballing an old nine-by-twelve glossy of myself, trying to get inspired. It's not a bad likeness. Blue pin-striped suit, a headful of hair, and I'm looking straight into 1965 like I owned it, and as for my line of work at the time, anyone who has read *The Blonde in 204, Close Before Striking, The Big Tipper,* and *The Mark of a Heel* knows that I wasn't big on ballet.

I wasn't real smart at spotting trends, either. The private-eye business was getting thinner than sliced beef at the deli. I spent my days supporting a bookie and my nights tailing guys who weren't going anywhere anyway. My old pals in Homicide were trading in their wing tips and porkpie hats for Frye boots and Greek fisherman caps and growing big puffs of hair around their ears. Mine was the only suit that looked slept in. I felt like writing to the Famous Shamus School and asking what I was doing wrong.

"It's escapism, Mr. Schmidt," quavered Ollie, the elevator boy, one morning when I complained that nobody needed a snoop anymore. "I was reading in the *Gazette* this morning where they say this is an age of anti-intellectualism. A sleuth like yourself, now, you represent the spirit of inquiry, the scientific mind, eighteenth-century enlightenment, but heck, people don't care about knowing the truth anymore. They just want to have *experiences*."

"Thanks for the tip, Ollie," I smiled, flipping him a quarter. "And keep your eyes open."

I was having an experience myself at the time and her name was Trixie, an auburn-haired beauty who moved grown men to lie down in her path and wave their arms and legs. I was no stronger than the rest, and when she let it be known one day that the acting studio where she studied nights was low on cash and might have to close and thus frustrate her career, I didn't ask her to type it in triplicate. I got the dough. I learned then and there that true artists are sensitive about money. Trixie took the bundle and the next day she moved in with a sandal maker. She said I wasn't her type. Too materialistic.

Evidently I was just the type that every art studio, mime troupe, print gallery, folk-ballet company, and wind ensemble in town was looking for, though, and the word got around fast: Jack Schmidt knows how to dial a telephone and make big checks arrive in the mail. Pretty soon my outer office was full of people with long delicate fingers, waiting to tell me what marvelous, marvelous things they could do if only they had ten thousand dollars (minus my percentage). It didn't take me long to learn the rules—about twenty minutes. First rule: ten thousand is peanuts. Pocket money. Any arts group that doesn't need a hundred grand and need it *now* just isn't thinking hard enough.

My first big hit was a National Endowment for the Arts grant for a walk-up tap school run by a dishwater blonde named Bonnie Marie Beebe. She also taught baton, but we stressed tap on the application. We called the school The American Conservatory for Jazz Dance. A hundred and fifty thousand clams. "Seed money" they called it, but it was good crisp lettuce to me.

I got the Guild of Younger Poets fifty thousand from the Teamsters to produce some odes to the open road, and another fifteen from a lumber tycoon with a yen for haiku. I got a yearlong folk-arts residency for a guy who told Scandinavian jokes, and I found wealthy backers for a play called *Struck by Lightning*, by a non-literalist playwright who didn't write a script but only spoke with the director a few times on the phone.

Nobody was too weird for Jack Schmidt. In every case, I had met weirder on the street. The Minnesota Anti-Dance Ensemble, for example, is a bunch of sweet kids. They simply don't believe in performance. They say that "audience" is a passive concept, and they spend a lot of time picketing large corporations in protest against the money that has been given to them, which they say comes from illicit profits. It doesn't make my life easier, but heck, I was young once, too. Give me a choice, I'll take a radical dance group over a Renaissance-music ensemble any day. Your average shawm or sackbut player thinks the world owes him a goddamn living.

So I was off the pavement and into the arts, and one day Bobby Jo walked in, fresh out of St. Cloud State Normal and looking for money to teach interior decorating to minority kids, and she saw I needed her more. She threw out my electric fan and the file cabinet with the half-empty fifth in the third drawer and brought in some Mondrian prints and a glass-topped desk and about forty potted plants. She took away my .38 and made me switch to filter cigarettes and had stationery printed up that looks like it's recycled from beaten eggs. "Arts Consultant," it says, but what I sell is the same old hustle and muscle, which was a new commodity on the arts scene then.

"What your arts organizations need is a guy who can ask people for large amounts without blushing and twisting his hankie," I told her one day, en route to Las Palmas for a three-day seminar on the role of the arts in rural America. "Your typical general manager of an arts organization today is nothing but a bagman. He figures all he has to do is pass the hat at the board meeting and the Throttlebottoms will pick up the deficit. The rest of the time he just stands around at lawn parties and says witty things. But the arts are changing, Bobby Jo. Nowadays, everybody wants arts, not just the rich. It's big business. Operating budgets are going right through the ceiling. All of a sudden, Mr. Arts Guy finds the game has changed. Now he has to work for the money and hit up corporations and think box office and dive in and fight for a slice of the government pie, and it scares him right out of his silk jammies. That's when he calls for Schmidt."

She slipped her hand into mine. I didn't take her pulse or anything, but I could tell she was excited by the way her breath came in quick little gasps.

"Now anyone who can spell 'innovative' can apply for a grant, government or otherwise," I went on, "but that doesn't mean that the bozo who reads the application is necessarily going to bust into tears and run right down to Western Union. He needs some extra incentive. He needs to know that this is no idle request for funds typed up by somebody who happened to find a blank application form at the post office. He needs to know that you are counting on the cash, that you fully expect to get it, and that if you are denied you are capable of putting his fingers in a toaster. The arts are growing, Bobby Jo, and you and me are going to make it happen."

"You are a visionary, J.S.," she murmured. "You have a tremendous overall concept but you need a hand when it comes to the day-to-day."

"Speaking of ideas," I muttered hoarsely, and I pulled the lap blanket over our heads. She whispered my initials over and over in a litany of passion. I grabbed her so hard her ribs squeaked.

• • •

It was a rough morning. After Bobby Jo's phone call, I got another from the Lawston Foundry, informing me that Stan Lewandowski's sculpture, "Oppresso," would not be cast in time for the opening of the Minot Performing Arts Center. The foundry workers, after hearing what Lewandowski was being paid for creating what looked to them like a large gerbil cage, went out on strike, bringing the sculpture to a standstill. I wasted fifteen minutes trying to make a lunch date with Hugo Groveland, the mining heir, to discuss the Arts Mall. He was going away for a while, Groveland said, and didn't know when he'd be back, if ever. He hinted at dark personal tragedies that were haunting him and suggested I call his mother. "She's more your type," he said, "plus she's about to kick off, if you know what I mean."

On top of it, I got a call from the director of our dinner theatre in upstate Indiana. He had been irked at me for weeks since I put the kibosh on *Hedda Gabler.* He had been plumping for a repertory theatre. "Fine," I said. "As long as you make it *Fiddler on the Roof, The Sunshine Boys,* and *Man of La Mancha.*" Now he was accusing us of lacking a commitment to new writers. He said I was in the business of exploiting talent, not developing it.

"Listen, pal," I snarled. "As a director, you'd have a hard time getting people to act normal. So don't worry about me exploiting your talent. Just make sure you have as many people in the cast as there are parts. And tell your kitchen to slice the roast beef thin."

So he quit. I wished I could, too. I had a headache that wouldn't. And an Arts Mall with twenty-four hours to live.

"It's a whole trend called the New Naïveté," offered Ollie when I asked him why artists seemed to hate me, on the way down to lunch. "I was reading in the *Gazette* where they say people nowadays think simplicity is a prime virtue. They want to eliminate the middleman. That's you, Mr. Schmidt. Traditionally, your role has been that of a buffer between the individual and a cruel world. But now people think the world is kind and good, if only they could deal with it directly. They think if they got rid of the middleman—the bureaucracy, whatever you call it—then everything would be hunky-dory."

"Thanks, Ollie," I said as the elevator doors opened. "Let's have lunch sometime."

It reminded me of something Bobby Jo had said in a taxicab in Rio, where we were attending a five-day conference on the need for a comprehensive system of evaluating arts information. "It's simple, J.S.," she said. "The problem is overhead. Your fat cats will give millions to build an arts center, but nobody wants to donate to pay the light bill because you can't put a plaque on it. They'll pay for Chippewa junk sculpture, but who wants to endow the janitor?"

"Speaking of endowments," I whispered hoarsely, and I leaned over and pressed my lips hungrily against hers. I could feel her earlobes trembling helplessly.

The mining heir's mother lived out on Mississippi Drive in a stone pile the size of the Lincoln Monument and about as cheerful. The woman who opened the door eyeballed me carefully for infectious diseases, then led me to a sitting room on the second floor that could've gone straight into the Cooper-Hewitt Museum. Mrs. Groveland sat in a wing chair by the fireplace. She looked pretty good for a woman who was about to make the far turn.

"Mr. Smith, how good of you to come," she tooted, offering me a tiny hand. I didn't correct her on the name. For a few grand, I'm willing to be called a lot worse. "Sit down and tell me about your arts center," she continued. "I'm all ears."

So were the two Dobermans who sat on either side of her chair. They looked as if they were trained to rip your throat if you used the wrong fork.

Usually, my pitch begins with a description of the long lines of art-starved inner-city children bused in daily to the Arts Mall to be broadened. But the hounds made me nervous— they maintained the most intense eye contact I had ever seen from floor level—so I skipped ahead to the money part. I dropped the figure of fifty thousand dollars.

She didn't blink, so I started talking about the Mall's long-

range needs. I mentioned a hundred thou. She smiled as if I
had asked for a drink of water.

I crossed my legs and forged straight ahead. "Mrs. Groveland," I radiated. "I hope you don't mind if I bring up the
subject of estate planning."

"Of course not," she radiated back. "The bulk of my estate,
aside from the family bequests and a lump-sum gift to the
Audubon Society, is going for the care of Luke and Mona here."
At the word "estate," the Dobermans seemed to lick their
chops.

I had to think fast. I wasn't about to bad-mouth our feathered
friends of the forest, or Mrs. Groveland's family, either, but I
thought I just might shake loose some of the dog trust. I told
her about our Founders Club for contributors of fifty thousand
or more. Perhaps she could obtain *two* Founderships—one for
each Doberman. "Perhaps it would take a load off your mind
if you would let us provide for Luke and Mona," I said. "We
could act as their trustees. We just happen to have this lovely
Founders Club Kennel, way out in the country, where—"

At the mention of a kennel, the beasts lowered their heads
and growled. Their eyes never left my face.

"Hush, hush," Mrs. Groveland scolded gently. "Don't
worry," she assured me, "they don't bite."

They may not bite, I thought, but they can sue.

Then Mona barked. Instantly, I was on my feet, but the dogs
beat me to it. The sounds that came from their throats were
noises that predated the Lascaux Cave paintings. They were
the cries of ancient Doberman souls trying to break through
the thin crust of domestication, and they expressed a need
that was far deeper than that of the Arts Mall, the arts in
general, or any individual artist whom I would care to know.
The next sound I heard was the slam of a paneled oak door
closing. I was out in the hallway and I could hear Mrs. Groveland on the other side saying, *"Bad* Luke, *naughty* Mona!"
The Woman who had let me in let me out. "They're quite
protective," she informed me, chuckling. If a jury had been
there to see her face, I'd have altered it.

When I got back to the office, I gathered up every piece of

correspondence in our National Arts Endowment file and threw it out the window. From above, it looked like a motorcade was due any minute. I was about to follow up with some of the potted plants when the phone rang. It rang sixteen times before I picked it up. Before Bobby Jo could identify herself, I'd used up all the best words I know. "I'm *out*," I added. "Through. Done. Kaput. The End. Cue the creditors. I've had it."

"J.S.," she began, but I was having none of it.

"I've had a noseful of beating money out of bushes so a bunch of sniveling wimps can try the patience of tiny audiences of their pals and moms with subsidized garbage that nobody in his right mind would pay Monopoly money to see," I snapped. "I'm sick of people calling themselves artists who make pots that cut your fingers when you pick them up and wobble when you set them on a table. I'm tired of poets who dribble out little teensy poems in lower-case letters and I'm sick of painters who can't even draw an outline of their own hand and I'm finished with the mumblers and stumblers who tell you that if you don't understand them it's *your* fault."

I added a few more categories to my list, plus a couple dozen persons by name, several organizations, and a breed of dog.

"You all done, J.S.?" she asked. "Because I've got great news. The Highways Department is taking the Arts Mall for an interchange. They're ready to pay top dollar, plus—you won't believe this—to sweeten the deal, they're throwing in six point two miles of Interstate 594."

"Miles of what?" Then it clicked. "You mean that unfinished leg of 594?" I choked.

"It's been sitting there for years. There are so many community groups opposed to it that the Highways Department doesn't dare cut the grass that's growing on it. They want us to take them off the hook. And if we make it an arts space, they figure it'll fulfill their beautification quota for the next three years."

"We'll call it The Arts Trip!" I exclaimed. "Or The ArtStrip! The median as a medium! Eight-lane environmental art! Big, big sculptures! Action painting! Wayside dance areas! Living poetry plaques! Milestones in American music! Arts parks and Arts lots! A drive-in film series! The customized car as American genre! The customized van as Artsmobile! People can have an arts experience without even pulling over onto the shoulder. They can get quality enrichment and still make good time!''

"Speaking of making time—" Her voice broke. She shuddered like a turned-on furnace. Her breath came in sudden little sobs.

I don't know what's next for Jack Schmidt after the Arts Highway is finished, but, whatever it is, it's going to have Jack Schmidt's name on it. No more Mr. Anonymous for me. No more Gray Eminence trips for yours truly. A couple of days ago, I was sitting at my desk and I began fooling around with an ink pad. I started making thumbprints on a sheet of yellow paper and then I sort of smooshed them around a little, and one thing led to another, and when I got done with it I liked what I saw. It wasn't necessarily something I'd hang on a burlap wall with a baby ceiling-spot aimed at it, but it had a certain *definite* quality that art could use a lot more of. I wouldn't be too surprised if in my next adventure I'm in a loft in SoHo solving something strictly visual while Bobby Jo throws me smoldering looks from her loom in the corner. In the meantime, good luck and stay out of the dark alleys.

CHET WILLIAMSON

GANDHI AT THE BAT

Chet Williamson, creator of the marvelous New Yorker *piece below, is the author of numerous horror and mystery novels and short stories. He lives somewhere in Pennsylvania, and must have a very odd mind indeed to juggle three specialties so adeptly.*

History books and available newspaper files hold no record of the visit to America in 1933 made by Mohandas K. Gandhi. For reasons of a sensitive political nature that have not yet come to light, all contemporary accounts of the visit were suppressed at the request of President Roosevelt. Although Gandhi repeatedly appeared in public during his three-month stay, the cloak of journalistic silence was seamless, and all that remains of the great man's celebrated tour is this long-secreted glimpse of one of the Mahatma's unexpected nonpolitical appearances, written by an anonymous press-box denizen of the day.

Yankee Stadium is used to roaring crowds. But never did a crowd roar louder than on yesterday afternoon, when a little brown man in a loincloth and wire-rimmed specs put some wood on a Lefty Grove fastball and completely bamboozled Connie Mack's A's.

It all started when Mayor John J. O'Brien invited M. K. ("Mahatma") Gandhi to see the Yanks play Philadelphia up at "The House That Ruth Built." Gandhi, whose ballplaying experience was limited to a few wallops with a cricket bat, jumped at the chance, and 12 noon saw the Mayor's party in the Yankee locker room, where the Mahatma met the Bronx Bombers. A zippy exchange occurred when the Mayor introduced the Lord of the Loincloth to the Bambino. "Mr. Gandhi," Hizzoner said, "I want you to meet Babe Ruth, the Sultan of Swat."

Gandhi's eyes sparkled behind his Moxie-bottle lenses, and he chuckled. "Swat," quoth he, "is a sultanate of which I am not aware. Is it by any chance near Maharashtra?"

"Say," laughed the Babe, laying a meaty hand on the frail brown shoulder, "you're all right, kiddo. I'll hit one out of the park for you today."

"No hitting, please," the Mahatma quipped.

In the Mayor's front-row private box, the little Indian turned down the offer of a hot dog and requested a box of Cracker Jack instead. The prize inside was a tin whistle, which he blew gleefully whenever the Bambino waddled up to bat.

The grinning guru enjoyed the game immensely—far more than the A's, who were down 3–1 by the fifth. Ruth, as promised, did smash a homer in the seventh, to Gandhi's delight. "Hey, Gunga Din!" Ruth cried jovially on his way to the Yankee dugout. "Know why my battin' reminds folks of India? 'Cause I can really Bangalore!"

"That is a very good one, Mr. Ruth!" cried the economy-size Asian.

By the top of the ninth, the Yanks had scored two more runs. After Mickey Cochrane whiffed on a Red Ruffing fastball, Gandhi remarked how difficult it must be to hit such a swiftly thrown missile and said, "I should like to try it very much."

"Are you serious?" Mayor O'Brien asked.

"If it would not be too much trouble. Perhaps after the exhibition is over," his visitor suggested.

There was no time to lose. O'Brien, displaying a panache that would have done credit to his predecessor, Jimmy Walker, leaped up and shouted to the umpire, who called a time-out. Managers McCarthy and Mack were beckoned to the Mayor's side, along with Bill Dinneen, the home-plate umpire, and soon all of Yankee Stadium heard an unprecedented announcement:

"Ladies and gentlemen, regardless of the score, the Yankees will come to bat to finish the ninth inning."

The excited crowd soon learned that the reason for such a breach of tradition was a little brown pinch-hitter shorter than his bat. When the pin-striped Bronx Bombers returned to their dugout after the last Philadelphia batter had been retired in the ninth, the Nabob of Nonviolence received a hasty batting lesson from Babe Ruth under the stands.

Lazzeri led off the bottom of the stanza, hitting a short chop to Bishop, who rifled to Foxx for the out. Then, after Crosetti fouled out to Cochrane, the stadium became hushed as the announcer intoned, "Pinch-hitting for Ruffing, Mohandas K. Gandhi."

The crowd erupted as the white-robed holy man, a fungo bat propped jauntily on his shoulder, strode to the plate, where he remarked to the crouching Mickey Cochrane, "It is a very big field, and a very small ball."

"C'mon, Moe!" Ruth called loudly to the dead-game bantam batter. "Show 'em the old pepper!"

"I will try, Mr. Baby!" Gandhi called back, and went into a batting stance unique in the annals of the great game—his sheet-draped posterior facing the catcher, and his bat held high over his head, as if to clobber the ball into submission. While Joe McCarthy called time, the Babe trotted out and politely corrected the little Indian's position in the box.

The time-out over, Grove threw a screaming fastball right over the plate. The bat stayed on Gandhi's shoulder. "Oh, my," he said as he turned and observed the ball firmly ensconced in Cochrane's glove. "That *was* speedy."

The second pitch was another dead-center fastball. The Mahatma swung, but found that the ball had been in the Mick's glove for a good three seconds before his swipe was completed. "Stee-rike two!" Dinneen barked.

The next pitch was high and outside, and the ump called it a ball before the petite pundit made a tentative swing at it. "Must I sit down now?" he asked.

"Nah, it's a ball," Dinneen replied. "I called it before you took your cut."

"Yes. I *know* that is a ball, and I did swing at it and did miss."

"No, no, a ball. Like a free pitch."

"Oh, I see."

"Wasn't in the strike zone."

"Yes, I see."

"So you get another swing."

"Yes."

"And if you miss you sit down."

"I just *did* miss."

"Play ball, Mister."

The next pitch was in the dirt. Gandhi did not swing. "Ball," Dinneen called.

"Yes, it is," the Mahatma agreed.

"Two and two"

"That is four."

"Two balls, two strikes."

"Is there not but one ball?"

"Two balls."

"Yes, I see."

"And two strikes."

"And if I miss I sit down."

Ruth's voice came booming from the Yankee dugout: "Swing early, Gandy baby!"

"When is early?"

"When I tell ya! I'll shout 'Now!' "

Grove started his windup. Just as his leg kicked up, the Bambino's cry of *"Now!"* filled the park.

The timing was perfect. Gandhi's molasses-in-January swing met the Grove fastball right over the plate. The ball shot downward, hit the turf, and arced gracefully into the air toward Grove. *"Run,* Peewee, *run!"* yelled Ruth, as the crowd went wild.

"Yes, yes!" cried Gandhi, who started down the first-base line in what can only be described as a dancing skip, using his bat as a walking stick. An astonished Grove booted the high bouncer, then scooped up the ball and flung it to Jimmie Foxx at first.

But Foxx, mesmerized by the sight of a sixty-three-year-old Indian in white robes advancing merrily before him and blowing mightily on a tin whistle, failed to descry the stitched orb, which struck the bill of his cap, knocking it off his head, and, slowed by its deed of dishabille, rolled to a stop by the fence.

Gandhi paused only long enough to touch first and to pick up Jimmie's cap and return it to him. By the time the still gawking Foxx had perched it once more on his head, the vital vegetarian was halfway to second.

Right fielder Coleman retrieved Foxx's missed ball and now relayed it to Max Bishop at second, but too late. The instant Bishop tossed the ball back to the embarrassed Grove, Gandhi was off again. Grove, panicking, overthrew third base, and by the time left fielder Bob Johnson picked up the ball, deep in foul territory, the Tiny Terror of Tealand had rounded the hot corner and was scooting for home. Johnson hurled the ball on a true course to a stunned Cochrane. The ball hit the pocket of Cochrane's mitt and popped out like a muffin from a toaster.

Gandhi jumped on home plate with both sandalled feet, and the crowd exploded as Joe McCarthy, the entire Yankee squad, and even a beaming Connie Mack surged onto the field.

"I ran home," giggled Gandhi. "Does that mean that I hit a run home?"

"A home run, Gandy," said Ruth. "Ya sure did."

"Well, technically," said Umpire Dinneen, "it was a single and an overthrow and then—"

"*Shaddup*," growled a dozen voices at once.

"Looked like a homer to me, too," the ump corrected, but few heard him, for by that time the crowd was on the field, lifting to their shoulders a joyous Gandhi, whose tin whistle provided a thrilling trilling over the mob's acclaim.

Inside the locker room, Manager McCarthy offered Gandhi a permanent position on the team, but the Mahatma graciously refused, stating that he could only consider a diamond career with a different junior-circuit club.

"Which club would that be, kid?" said the puzzled Bambino.

"The Cleveland Indians, of course," twinkled the Mahatma.

An offer from the Cleveland front office arrived the next day, but India's top pinch-hitter was already on a train headed for points west—and the history books.

LEWIS BURKE FRUMKES

THE FRUMKES BOOK OF RECORDS

Lewis Burke Frumkes is a free-lance writer whose work has appeared in Harper's, Punch, The New York Times, Self, Cosmopolitan, Redbook, *and many other major publications. He is the author of* How to Raise Your IQ by Eating Gifted Children, The Mensa Think Smart Book, *and* Name Crazy.

HEAVIEST MAN

The heaviest medically weighed human was the Eskimo Ezuk Kazook who weighed 22,000 pounds. Kazook died in 1926 at the age of twenty-three when he was accidentally harpooned to death while taking a late afternoon swim. The Scandinavian whaler responsible for the harpooning was so overcome by the error of what he had done that he sold the blubber back to the Eskimos at half price.

PROLIFIC DENTIST

The world's most prolific dentist is Dr. Orion Schtumpf of Pasadena, California, who holds the record for the most tooth extractions made in one year. In 1976 Dr. Schtumpf extracted no fewer than 2,020 teeth over a period of just two months. The woman from whom the teeth were extracted says she feels fine and is allowed to eat anything she wants as long as it is in the form of a gas. The teeth are displayed prominently in Dr. Schtumpf's office and in his trophy room at home.

FASTEST HUMAN

For many years it was supposed that Jesse Owens or perhaps a modern day gold medal Olympic sprinter could be called the world's fastest human. But officially the fastest human turns out to be R. Bernie Allen of East Islip, Long Island, who was clocked by his wife at over 70 mph going from the living room to the bathroom during a severe case of stomach cramps. Mr. Allen was 46 years old at the time.

SMALLEST WOMAN

The smallest full-grown woman who ever lived was Olivia Rose Humstutter born in Suffolk, England, April 1, 1932. At birth Ms. Humstutter was so small she was practically invisible and had to be verified with an electron microscope. By the time she was 21 she stood 6 ins. tall and weighed just under 4 oz. Attractive to look at, Ms. Humstutter studied acting in London and entered the legitimate theatre where she won acclaim for her roles as Tinkerbell in *Peter Pan* and a Munchkin in *The Wizard of Oz*. In later years she gave up a promising stage career to become the mistress of Rumpelstiltskin.

MOST SHOTPUTS CAUGHT

Hubert C. Dinkle of Nebraska holds the record for having caught the most sixteen-pound shotputs dropped from an airplane. In December 1975 Mr. Dinkle, surrounded by photographers in an open target field, caught one of the ten shotputs dropped from a B-52 bomber. Despite the fact that he was wearing a specially constructed catcher's mitt at the time, Mr. Dinkle caught the shotput with his head and was driven fifteen feet into the ground. To memorialize the feat, his widow had the shotput cleaned and sold it to a local sports shop.

MOST SUCCESSFUL MATADOR

The most successful matador of all time, measured by bulls killed, was Juan "The Butcher" Del Pingo of Madrid, Spain, whose lifetime total was seventeen thousand.

Early in his career Del Pingo discovered that bulls were especially susceptible to the .44 magnum which he kept hidden under his cape. Del Pingo met his Waterloo when a bull called "El Braino" (The Smart One) entered the ring wearing a bullet-proof vest and chased him into the second-tier bleachers. His nerve gone, Del Pingo spent his remaining years fighting chickens at a local poultry farm.

MOST UNUSUAL ACCIDENT

The most unusual accident took place on September 5, 1972; a Mr. Tony "The Canary" La Rocca was found at Kennedy International Airport with his head lodged in the tailpipe of a Boeing 747 bound for Okinawa.

At the time close friends speculated that La Rocca may have been depressed after having spilled his guts to a grand jury.

OLDEST LIVING THING

Some reputable scientists claim that the oldest recorded living thing is a bristlecone pine (Pinus Longalva) designated WPN-114, growing at 10,750 feet above sea level on the northeast face of Wheeler Peak (13,063 feet) in eastern Nevada, which according to studies is about 4,900 years old. Others say George Burns.

LONGEST JELLYFISH

The longest jellyfish ever recorded was *Cyanea arctica*. One specimen washed up on shore in Florida had a bell 7½ feet in diameter and tentacles 120 feet long, thus giving a theoretical tentacular span of some 245 ft. It was eventually popped by a ten-year-old boy walking along the beach with a stick and yielded twelve quarts of grade A unrefined raw marmalade.

DENSEST TERRITORY

The most densely populated territory in the world is the Portuguese province of Macau (or Macao), on the southern coast of China. It has an estimated population of 314,000 (in 1970) in an area of 6.2 square miles, giving a density of about 50,645 per square mile. In graphic terms this is somewhat denser than a subway car and somewhat less dense than a black hole. For the last twenty years Macau has been the first choice of pharmaceutical companies when testing new underarm deodorants.

BRUCE JAY FRIEDMAN

LET'S HEAR IT FOR A BEAUTIFUL GUY

Author of the plays Steambath *and* Scuba Duba, *the novels* Stern *and* A Mother's Kisses, *the screenplays for the films* Splash *and* Stir Crazy, *and numerous short stories for* Playboy, The New Yorker, New York, *and* Rolling Stone, *Bruce Jay Friedman has been called a "masterly humorist of American angst," and I certainly won't disagree.*

Sammy Davis is trying to get a few months off for a complete rest.
—*Earl Wilson, February 7, 1974.*

I have been trying to get a few months off for a complete rest, too, but I think it's more important that Sammy Davis get one. I feel that I can scrape along and manage somehow, but Sammy Davis always looks so strained and tired. The pressure on the guy must be enormous. It must have been a terrific blow to him when he switched his allegiance to Agnew and Nixon, only to have the whole thing blow up in his face. I was angry at him, incidentally, along with a lot of other fans of his, all of us feeling he had sold us down the river. But after I had thought it over and let my temper cool a bit, I changed my mind and actually found myself standing up for him, saying I would bet anything that Agnew and Nixon had made some secret promises to Sammy about easing the situation of blacks—ones that the public still doesn't know about. Otherwise, there was no way he would have thrown in his lot with that crowd. In any case, I would forgive the guy just about anything. How can I feel any other way when I think of the pleasure he's given me over the years, dancing and clowning around and wrenching those songs out of that wiry little body? Always giving his all, no matter what the composition of the audience. Those years of struggle with the Will Mastin Trio, and then finally making it, only to find marital strife staring him in the face. None of us will ever be able to calculate what it took out of him each time he had a falling-out with Frank. Is there any doubt who Dcan and Joey sided with on those occasions? You can be sure Peter Lawford didn't run over to offer Sammy any solace. And does anyone ever stop to consider the spiritual torment he must have suffered when he made the switch to Judaism? I don't even want to talk about the eye. So, if anyone in the world does, he certainly deserves a few months off for a complete rest.

Somehow, I have the feeling that if I met Sammy, I could break through his agents and that entourage of his and convince him he ought to take off with me and get the complete rest he deserves. I don't want any ten percent, I don't want any glory; I just feel I owe it to him. Sure he's got commitments, but once and for all he's got to stop and consider that it's one time around, and no one can keep up that pace of his forever.

The first thing I would do is get him out of Vegas. There is absolutely no way he can get a few months' rest in that sanatorium. I would get him away from Vegas, and I would certainly steer clear of Palm Springs. Imagine him riding down Bob Hope Drive and checking into a hotel in the Springs! For a rest? The second he walked into the lobby, it would all start. The chambermaids would ask him to do a chorus of "What Kind of Fool Am I?" right in the lobby, and, knowing Sammy and his big heart, he would probably oblige. I think I would take him to my place in New York, a studio. We would have to eat in, because if I ever showed up with Sammy Davis at the Carlton Delicatessen, where I have my breakfast, the roof would fall in. The owner would ask him for an autographed picture to hang up next to Dustin Hoffman's, and those rich young East Side girls would go to town on him. If they ever saw me walk in with Sammy Davis, that would be the end of his complete rest. They would attack him like vultures, and Sammy would be hard put to turn his back on them, because they're not broads.

We would probably wind up ordering some delicatessen from the Stage, although I'm not so sure that's a good idea; the delivery boy would recognize him, and the next thing you know, Sammy would give him a C note, and word would get back to Alan King that Sammy had ducked into town. How would it look if he didn't drop over to the Stage and show himself? Next thing you know, the news would reach Jilly's, and if Frank was in town—well, you can imagine how much rest Sammy would get. I don't know if they're feuding these days, but you know perfectly well that, at minimum, Frank would send over a purebred Afghan. Even if they were feuding.

I think what we would probably do is lay low and order a lot of Chinese food. I have a hunch that Sammy can eat Chinese takeout food every night of the week. I know I can, and the Chinese takeout delivery guys are very discreet. So we would stay at my place. I'd give him the sleeping loft, and I'd throw some sheets on the couch downstairs for me. I would do that for Sammy to pay him back for all the joy he's given me down through the years. And I would resist the temptation to ask him to sing, even though I would flip out if he so much as started humming. Can you imagine him humming "The Candy Man"? *In my apartment!* Let's not even discuss it.

Another reason I would give him the sleeping loft is that there is no phone up there. I would try like the devil to keep him away from the phone, because I know the second he saw one he would start thinking about his commitments, and it would be impossible for the guy not to make at least one call to the Coast. So I'd just try to keep him comfortable for as long as possible, although pretty soon my friends would begin wondering what ever happened to me, and it would take all the willpower in the world not to let on that I had Sammy Davis in my loft and was giving him a complete rest.

I don't kid myself that I could keep Sammy Davis happy in my loft for a full couple of months. He would be lying on the bed, his frail muscular body looking lost in a pair of boxer shorts, and before long I would hear those fingers snapping, and I would know that the wiry little great entertainer was feeling penned up and it would be inhuman to expect him to stay there any longer. I think that when I sensed that Sammy was straining at the leash, I would rent a car—a Ford LTD (that would be a switch for him, riding in a Middle American car)—and we would ride out to my sister and brother-in-law's place in Jersey. He would probably huddle down in the seat, but somehow I have the feeling that people in passing cars would spot him. We'd be lucky if they didn't crash into telephone poles. And if I know Sammy, whenever someone recognized him he wouldn't be able to resist taking off his shades and graciously blowing them a kiss.

The reason I would take Sammy to my sister and brother-in-law's house is because they're simple people and would not hassle him—especially my brother-in-law. My sister would stand there with her hands on her hips, and when she saw me get out of the Ford with Sammy, she would cluck her tongue and say, "There goes my crazy brother again," but she would appear calm on the surface, even though she would be fainting dead away on the inside. She would say something like "Oh, my God, I didn't even clean the floors," but then Sammy would give her a big hug and a kiss, and I'm sure that he would make a call, and a few weeks later she would have a complete new dining-room set, the baby grand she always wanted and a puppy.

She would put Sammy up in her son's room (he's away at graduate school), saying she wished she had something better, but he would say, "Honey, this is just perfect." And he would mean it, too, in a way, my nephew's bedroom being an interesting change from those one-thousand-dollar-a-day suites at the Tropicana. My brother-in-law has a nice easygoing style and would be relaxing company for Sammy, except that Al does work in television and there would be a temptation on his part to talk about the time he did the "Don Rickles Show" and how different and sweet a guy Don is when you get him offstage. If I know Sammy, he would place a call to CBS—

with no urging from any of us—and see to it that Al got to work on his next special. If the network couldn't do a little thing like that for him, the hell with them, he would get himself another network. Sammy's that kind of guy.

One danger is that my sister, by this time, would be going out of her mind and wouldn't be able to resist asking Sammy if she could have a few neighbors over on a Saturday night. Let's face it, it would be the thrill of a lifetime for her. I would intercede right there, because it wouldn't be fair to the guy, but if I know Sammy he would tell her, "Honey, you go right ahead." She would have a mixed group over—Italians, an Irish couple, some Jews, about twelve people tops—and she would wind up having the evening catered, which of course would lead to a commotion when she tried to pay for the stuff. No way Sammy would let her do that. He would buy out the whole delicatessen, give the delivery guy a C note, and probably throw in an autographed glossy without being asked.

Everyone at the party would pretend to be casual, as if Sammy Davis weren't there, but before long the Irish space salesman's wife (my sister's crazy friend, and what a flirt *she* is) would somehow manage to ask him to sing, and imagine Sammy saying no in a situation like that. Everyone would say just one song, but that bighearted son of a gun would wind up doing his entire repertoire, probably putting out every bit as much as he does when he opens at the Sands. He would do it all—"The Candy Man," "What Kind of Fool Am I?" tap-dance, play the drums with chopsticks on an end table, do some riffs on my nephew's old trumpet and work himself into exhaustion. The sweat would be pouring out of him, and he would top the whole thing off with "This Is My Life" ("and I don't give a damn"). Of course, his agents on the Coast would pass out cold if they ever got wind of the way he was putting out for twelve nobodies in Jersey. But as for Sammy, he never did know anything about halfway measures. He either works or he doesn't, and he would use every ounce of energy in that courageous little show-biz body of his to see to it that my sister's friends—that mixed group of Italians, Irish, and Jews—had a night they'd never forget as long as they lived.

. . .

Of course, that would blow the two months of complete rest, and I would have to get him out of Jersey fast. By that time, frankly, I would be running out of options. Once in a while, I pop down to Puerto Rico for a three- or four-day holiday, but, let's face it, if I showed up in San Juan with Sammy, first thing you know, we would be hounded by broads, catching the show at the Flamboyan, and Dick Shawn would be asking Sammy to hop up onstage and do a medley from *Mr. Wonderful*. (He was really something in that show, battling Jack Carter tooth and nail, but too gracious to use his bigger name to advantage.)

Another possibility would be to take Sammy out to see a professor friend of mine who teaches modern lit at San Francisco State and would be only too happy to take us in. That would represent a complete change for Sammy, a college campus, but as soon as the school got wind he was around, I'll bet you ten to one they would ask him to speak either to a film class or the drama department or even a political science group. And he would wind up shocking them with his expertise on the Founding Fathers and the philosophy behind the Bill of Rights. The guy reads, and I'm not talking about *The Bette Davis Story*. Anyone who sells Sammy Davis short as an intellectual is taking his life in his hands.

In the end, Sammy and I would probably end up in Vermont, where a financial-consultant friend of mine has a cabin that he never uses. He always says to me, "It's there, for God's sake—use it." So I would take Sammy up there, away from it all, but I wouldn't tell the financial consultant who I was taking, because the second he heard it was Sammy Davis he would want to come along. Sammy and I would start out by going into town for a week's worth of supplies at the general store, and then we would hole up in the cabin. I'm not too good at mechanical things, but we would be sort of roughing it, and there wouldn't be much to do except chop some firewood, which I would take care of while Sammy was getting his complete rest.

I don't know how long we would last in Vermont. Frankly,

I would worry after a while about being able to keep him entertained, even though he would be there for a complete rest. We could talk a little about Judaism, but, frankly, I would be skating on thin ice in that area, since I don't have the formal training he has or any real knowledge of theology. The Vermont woods would probably start us batting around theories about the mystery of existence, but to tell the truth, I'd be a little bit out of my depth in that department, too. He's had so much experience on panel shows, and I would just as soon not go one-on-one with him on that topic.

Let's not kid around, I would get tense after a while, and Sammy would feel it. He would be too good a guy to let on that he was bored, but pretty soon he would start snapping those fingers and batting out tunes on the back of an old *Saturday Evening Post* or something, and I think I would crack after a while and say, "Sammy, I tried my best to supply you with a couple of months of complete rest, but I'm running out of gas." He would tap me on the shoulder and say, "Don't worry about it, babe," and then, so as not to hurt my feelings, he would say he wanted to go into town to get some toothpaste. So he would drive in, with the eye and all, and I know damned well the first thing he would do is call his agents on the Coast and ask them to read him the "N.Y. to L.A." column of a few *Variety*s. Next thing you know, I would be driving him to the airport, knowing in my heart that I hadn't really succeeded. He would tell me that any time I got to the Coast or Vegas or the Springs, and I wanted anything, *anything*, just make sure to give him a ring. And the following week, I would receive a freezer and a videotape machine and a puppy.

So I think I'm just not the man to get Sammy Davis the complete rest he needs so desperately. However, I certainly think someone should. How long can he keep driving that tortured little frame of his, pouring every ounce of his strength into the entertainment of Americans? I know, I know—there's Cambodia and Watergate, and, believe me, I haven't forgotten our own disadvantaged citizens. I know all that. But when you think of all the joy that man has spread through his night-club appearances, his albums, his autobiography, his video specials and even his movies, which did not gross too well but were a lot better than people realized, and the things he's done not only for his friends but for a lot of causes the public doesn't know about—when you think of all that courageous little entertainer has given to this land of ours, and then you read that he's trying, repeat *trying*, to get a few months off for a complete rest and he can't, well, then, all I can say is that there's something basically rotten in the system.

BUT SOFT . . . REAL SOFT

Woody Allen, of whom it has been written that "His only regret in life is that he is not someone else," is doing just fine as Woody Allen. His multiple careers have included comedy writer, stand-up comedian, playwright, script writer, television star, movie star, film director, and . . . let's see . . . oh, yes, author.

Ask the average man who wrote the plays entitled *Hamlet, Romeo and Juliet, King Lear,* and *Othello,* and in most cases he'll snap confidently back with, "The Immortal Bard of Stratford on Avon." Ask him about the authorship of the Shakespearean sonnets and see if you don't get the same illogical reply. Now put these questions to certain literary detectives who seem to crop up every now and again over the years, and don't be surprised if you get answers like Sir Francis Bacon, Ben Jonson, Queen Elizabeth, and possibly even the Homestead Act.

The most recent of these theories is to be found in a book I have just read that attempts to prove conclusively that the real author of Shakespeare's works was Christopher Marlowe. The book makes a very convincing case, and when I got through reading it I was not sure if Shakespeare was Marlowe or Marlowe was Shakespeare or what. I know this, I would not have cashed checks for either one of them—and I like their work.

Now, in trying to keep the above-mentioned theory in perspective, my first question is: if Marlowe wrote Shakespeare's works, who wrote Marlowe's? The answer to this lies in the fact that Shakespeare was married to a woman named Anne Hathaway. This we know to be factual. However, under the new theory, it is actually Marlowe who was married to Anne Hathaway, a match which caused Shakespeare no end of grief, as they would not let him in the house.

One fateful day, in a jealous rage over who held the lower number in a bakery, Marlowe was slain—slain or whisked away in disguise to avoid charges of heresy, a most serious crime punishable by slaying or whisking away or both.

It was at this point that Marlowe's young wife took up the pen and continued to write the plays and sonnets we all know and avoid today. But allow me to clarify.

We all realize Shakespeare (Marlowe) borrowed his plots from the ancients (moderns); however, when the time came to return the plots to the ancients he had used them up and was forced to flee the country under the assumed name of William Bard (hence the term "immortal bard") in an effort to avoid debtor's prison (hence the term "debtor's prison"). Here Sir Francis Bacon enters into the picture. Bacon was an innovator of the times who was working on advanced concepts of refrigeration. Legend has it he died attempting to refrigerate a chicken. Apparently the chicken pushed first. In an effort to conceal Marlowe from Shakespeare, should they prove to be the same person, Bacon had adopted the fictitious name Alexander Pope, who in reality was Pope Alexander, head of the Roman Catholic Church and currently in exile owing to the invasion of Italy by the Bards, last of the nomadic hordes (the Bards give us the term "immortal bard"), and years before had galloped off to London, where Raleigh awaited death in the tower.

The mystery deepens for, as this goes on, Ben Jonson stages a mock funeral for Marlowe, convincing a minor poet to take his place for the burial. Ben Jonson is not to be confused with Samuel Johnson. He was Samuel Johnson. Samuel Johnson was not. Samuel Johnson was Samuel Pepys. Pepys was actually Raleigh, who had escaped from the tower to write *Par-*

adise Lost under the name of John Milton, a poet who because of blindness accidentally escaped to the tower and was hanged under the name of Jonathan Swift. This all becomes clearer when we realize that George Eliot was a woman.

Proceeding from this then, *King Lear* is not a play by Shakespeare but a satirical revue by Chaucer, originally titled "Nobody's Parfit," which contains in it a clue to the man who killed Marlowe, a man known around Elizabethan times (Elizabeth Barrett Browning) as Old Vic. Old Vic became more familiar to us later as Victor Hugo, who wrote *The Hunchback of Notre Dame*, which most students of literature feel is merely *Coriolanus* with a few obvious changes. (Say them both fast.)

We wonder then, was not Lewis Carroll caricaturing the whole situation when he wrote *Alice in Wonderland?* The March Hare was Shakespeare, the Mad Hatter, Marlowe, and the Dormouse, Bacon—or the Mad Hatter, Bacon, and the March Hare, Marlowe—or Carroll, Bacon, and the Dormouse, Marlowe—or Alice was Shakespeare—or Bacon—or Carroll was the Mad Hatter. A pity Carroll is not alive today to settle it. Or Bacon. Or Marlowe. Or Shakespeare. The point is, if you're going to move, notify your post office. Unless you don't give a hoot about posterity.

DELIA EPHRON

CAR TALK

Delia Ephron, best-selling author of How to Eat Like a Child *and* Teenage Romance, *is also the author of* Funny Sauce, *a sort of update of* Please Don't Eat the Daisies—*with all the differences that that entails, as witness the following.*

I back the car out of the driveway and head down the block.

"Oooooo, look at those guys."

"Foxyyyyy!"

The two twelve-year-olds are in the back seat. This is the way we always ride. Lisa and her friend Kim in the back, me in the front. Them talking, me listening.

"If you had all the children you could have from now until you couldn't have any more, you'd have forty children."

"Every year?"

"No! Altogether."

"Wow, think of all the Christmas presents you'd have to buy."

I never correct their inaccuracies. I suppose I could say, "Girls, the maximum number of children a woman can have varies from woman to woman," and leave it at that. But even if I could bring myself to speak that sentence, setting them straight on the facts of life, even a fact as silly as this, is an exercise in futility. No sooner do you do it than they mix up what they are told with what they fear, hope, or imagine. The real choice a parent has is this: Do you tell a child the facts and then watch her make hash of them, or do you let her get an already cockeyed version from her friends? Either way, the result is the same.

So I stay out of it. Besides, if I say something—anything—Lisa and Kim might realize I'm listening. And they might stop talking. I make a right turn onto Wilshire Boulevard.

"Michael Jackson doesn't take female hormones anymore. Now he takes pills—steroids. But that's all. He doesn't drink, take drugs, or smoke."

"Thank God. I'd die if he smoked. I'd absolutely die."

"He's not gay anymore either."

"I know. He stopped when he was fourteen."

"Yeah, but the thing is, he tried to kill himself. He slit his wrists 'cause he found out his father's gay."

Lisa: *"That is dumb. Look, I love my dad. Nobody knows how much I love my dad. But I wouldn't slit my wrists if he were gay."*

"Yeah, but Michael Jackson's dad started him in show business."

I do not dwell on the logic of this. I do not dwell on the fact that this information (and almost all the information these girls exchange) sounds like it came from the *National Enquirer.* I find their conversation about Michael Jackson comforting, confirming my stepdaughter's stability. Think of it—my stepdaughter is too sensible to commit suicide if her father were homosexual. Never mind that it's my husband she's talking about. Never mind that it's a sensibleness of a limited sort. With any child entering adolescence, one hunts for signs of health, is desperate for the smallest indication that the child's problems will never be important enough for a television movie. I want to believe that, of course, I will be driven crazy when Lisa is a teenager, but only in a cute way.

So I rejoice in Lisa's practicality as I pull into the left lane and pass a car going too slowly.

"Kim, you know that guy I was going with, Robert?"

"Yeah."

"He was arrested for attempted murder."

"What?" I scream.

Lisa: *"Delia, just forget I mentioned it. Forget it, okay?"*

I slam on the brakes, realizing in the nick of time that the car in front of me has stopped for a light.

"Who is Robert?"

Lisa sighs. "He's the guy who lives in Ashley's building."

"I don't want you to speak to him again."

"It wasn't murder—it was just attempted murder."

"Lisa!"

Lisa sighs again.

"Now tell me exactly what happened."

"Well, Robert—he was really nice, too—got into a fight with an old lady and took a twenty-two and shot through her window."

"Is this the truth?"

"Ashley says so. Ashley never lies."

"Lisa, listen. If you know anyone who does anything criminal like that, you do not speak to him again. Ever! Do you understand? I don't want you hanging around with anyone who's violent."

"Duh," says Lisa.

Duh? I ignore the charm of this response. I suddenly feel ridiculous. Somehow sucked in. I remember that Ashley is also twelve. We ride in silence for a few blocks. Then:

Lisa, very excited: "Kim, let's say I was walking down the street and I saw Robert, okay. I wouldn't look at him. I'd just pretend I didn't see him and hold my head kinda sideways."

"Oooooo, neat," says Kim.

Girls, I want to scream, this is real life! But I don't. I shut up. It serves me right for listening. If you listen, you might hear. If you hear, you might mix up what they say with what you fear or imagine. It's a lot smarter and safer, if you want the news, to buy the *Enquirer*.

We are now five blocks from the department store. I move into the left lane to get there faster.

"Remember Vincent, the boy I got married to in recess in the fourth grade?"

I start humming. That's what I always did at the movies when I was a child. To block the sound, I hummed during the scary parts.

RICHARD MELTZER

THE ARMENIAN SHOW (NOT TO BE MISSED)

If there were an award for National Curmudgeon, Richard Meltzer would surely be in the running. Since moving from New York to Los Angeles, he has become a master of uninhibited diatribes against his adopted city. He is the author of, among other books, Richard Meltzer's Guide to the Ugliest Buildings in Los Angeles *and* L.A. Is the Capital of Kansas.

Fred Astaire special on the occasion of the AFI folks figgered he's due to croak so let's honor him before the worms get their turn was real reet and a half from the wd. go—one of them Great Moments In Nothin'-type events that nothin' fans are fond of and will *kick themselves* for missing when they do (it happens). Me, I kicked the nothin' habit a longgg time ago but the guy does have the same birfday as me (May 10) so shoot if I did not watch. Watched and watched and watched—till my eyes were blue in the face—but did not find the answer I have long longed for, ans. to what is the goddam APPEAL of Frederick anyway?

Appeal COULD BE: he is harmless (cannot, will not HARM YOU). In mod-rin terms: not macho (won't stick his hand up your dress). Also possible: dances about as good as EVERY-MAN (you remember *him*). And: sings no better than Dom DeLuise (so you don't get dazzled into heart attacks or anything). Plus: man is a SUAVE motherfuh (for all the suaveness fans). OTHER THAN THAT his qualifications for the coveted

AFI whatsis were: dunno. Walked: not especially gimpy (considering).

From the 37th floor of 2029 Century Park East I look down on HUNDREDS OF TINY LITTLE ANTS partying, lunching, & having a goodtime while *The Incredible Hulk* has been *canceled*. They are sitting at CUTE LITTLE TABLES OF YELLOW, PINK, & GREEN out front of the Century Plaza celebrating their merry rumps off at the ABC Affiliates Convention while meanwhile *The Hulk* is *gone*. Hey I know it's on CBS and all that but FUGGA WUGGA you'd think networks *everywhere* would be mourning, instead of sunning themselves over frosty cold piña coladas and Long Island ice tea. *You'd think*—but the *is* is scarcely ever the *ought* so boo hoo hoo hoo hoo. A fanntasstic show—I watched it twice— is no mo' . . .

Commercial for Off! with the $100 bill in the bug tank is DIRTY, FILTHY, SMUTTY—dirtier than pee'd-on doo-doo on *Peyton Place*. Woman sticks her arm in a den of mosquitoes to *get the Ben Franklin* (i.e. hoor herself like a common garden-variety FIVE-DOLLAR TART) and then the Off! guy tells her "GET OFF!" (i.e. have a real major thunderhump of a-louder-than-life MULTIPLE ORGAZ). As this advert is just *loaded* with genuwine GOOD STUFF like you only find in torrid, stimulating, suggestive FRENCH MAGAZINES, I suggest you tell your friends to watch it real quick, before the Moral Maj. gets wind o'things and they turn it into *Lassie* . . .

Two on the Town temporarily ABANDONED THE TOWN for Ulster, and in so doing co-hosts Steve & Melody SHED MUCH LIGHT on the Northern Ireland QUESTION. "Life goes on," explained Steve, "as it has for centuries"—beautif'ly put. Furthermore, UNEMPLOYMENT is kinda high BUT (Steve again, he had all the good lines) "many *do* work, contributing *many things* to the world"—hey that's WONDA-FUL. Thanx Steve, thanx Melody even tho you didn' say diddleypoot, WE SURE THANK YOU f'r takin' time out from your Brit Isle stay to 'splain us what we di'n't know about the IRISH PART . . .

"Pete Ellis Dodge, Long Beach Freeway, Firestone exit, Southgate" is a jingle that is *not half bad.* Very tuneful.

Sunday, 3:30 P.M., channel 22—*The Armenian Show.* Guy in a tan suit, brown plaidish tie, black shirt, conventional non-square haircut (black), black beard, & moviestar specs with one of those horizontal THINGS over the nose, hands in front of him like a *gentleman,* intristing delivery in a non-anglo tongue that could be, yes, it could be ARMENIAN. Pale blue backdrop w/ dark blue rectangle in upper lefthand corner, AS-BAREZ DAILY (213) 380-7646 in white letter-over toward the bottom. You will enjoy this enjoyable show—not to be missed.

SPEAKING OF foreign type UHF shows do not be a-scared of *Sumo Digest,* ch. 18, 9:30 P.M., three Mondays every other month. Have no fear as the voice-over of Gordon Berger (this word jockey's fave UHF'er of all time) supplies commentary in queen's eng. over jap-o-nese from the original tapes so if you're one or t'other you'll get plenty o' verbal drift to accompany your sumo entrancement. Last month it was Chiyonofuji losing to Kitanoumi on senshuraku by tsuridashi, and the whole shebang'll be back next with the NATSU BASHO which if y'don't watch hang your head as it is the GREATEST SHOW IN ALL OF L.A. (true).

Brenda Vaccaro for Playtex tampons is one big face filling THE ENTIRE SCREEN. She is wearing lipstick. "Double-layered design" is what she prefers. Fine, ok, rooty toot. But then a kind wart is given to Playtex DEODORANT tampons, at which time you kind of gotta take INVENTORY on her credibility and not even waste your time on Playtex *regular:* WHO WITH THE INTELL. & TOLERANCE OF MS. VAC-CARO WOULD WANNA DEODORIZE THE FINE BOU-QUET OF FRESH MENSTRUE?????

Moving from tampies to nappies the ANTI-MOISTURE BRI-GADE must be stopped. Ad for Light Days sez make 'em part of your "morning routine." Inotherwords keep yer region DRY even when the droplets ARE NOT red. Tell me this: whose wool're they tryin' to pull with that one?!?!

Doing some good . . . channel 9 went & did some rilly fine GOOD with *Just Like All of Us,* wherein it was showed—for the whole-wide-whirl to see—that RETARDS CAN ANSWER PHONES, write down (if you spell it out for them) names like Smith and Jones, load machinery on a truck, make amorous physical whoopy w/ others of their KIND, get a degree from jr. college, and (even) be neurotic like everybody else! (Another 10–11 stereotypes bit the dust . . .)

Don Wilson—it turns out—IS NOT DEAD AFTER ALL. No Candy-Gram ads for the last three yrs. had us imagining otherwise, but now he's back pushing various prod with that special flair for touching over-the-hilless that is HIS & HIS ALONE. Appears he's lost a couple lbs. in the interim as well. WELCOME BACK, y'old dogface!

WISH-I'D-SAID-THAT DEPT.—"When the day comes that there's no sportsmanship in golf, there'll be no sportsmanship left." (Stu Nahan at the L.A. Open.)

A SICK SHOW AND GOOD THING IT'S NO LONGER ON—*Private Benjamin.* Grownup boys and girls calling each other "sir" is sick sick SICK, that went out with the '49 Studebaker. Not quite as sick but certainly UP THERE is this drink they invented for the final show: a "pinky suprise" (lots of fizz or foam on top which Eileen Brennan fingers out with her pinky & says *mmm mmm good*). Sicker than the rest of it put together: "Liebestraum" or something playing in the background as she "puts on something a little more comfortable" in her PRIVATE SUITE . . .

Mrs. Salvador Boapadoap writes: "I would like to know if any stars of local televicion [sic] are of the Roman Catholic faith. Please tell me because I must got to know." To tell you the truth Mrs. B, none of my many contacts inside the industry have been able to come up with such admittedly essential info, altho it is RUMORED on the network front that Robert Walden of *Lou Grant* once attended Mass on an occasional basis. ANYONE WHO KNOWS MORE'N THAT PLEASE DROP US A CARD . . .

What's green and skates (and sez "Trident is recommended by moms like me")? PEGGY PHLEGM.

Newly unearthed anagrams for television: EVIL ON SITE; I STONE LIVE. Newer still (just did 'em this sec): VILE ION

SET; LEVI TESION (y'know, the *big jean tease* on account there's no designer type ads for Levis but probably *some day soon*); TENSIO. "E" I.V. ("E" type *tension* that you get *intravenous*); STENO VEIL I (the *world's first* thing for stenos to wear over their face so the x-citement of daytime shows won't distract them from their *work*); NO ELEV. IS IT (teevee explained in terms of sea level); NITE IS LOVE (that's true); NO LITE SIEV. (a sieve has *not been developed* that'll skim off *all remaining calories* in Miller Lite); LE VIN 'TIS O.E. (the wine is *only ethyl*, i.e., ethyl alc. is *why you drink it*—Orson Welles is *not the reason*); SEE, VOIT NIL (= do not buy a football from the principal sponsor of *Pro Bowlers Tour*). Fun with spelling & letters!

Speaking of fun, the author's only regret, now that Cyndy Garvey's flown the coop at *AM Los Angeles*, is she never showed us (at least a foto of) her CLITORIS.

If you can read this sentence you can read a book. GO READ *Richard Dawson and Family Feud* by Mary Ann Norbom (Signet, 150 pp., $1.95), the type will not rub off on yer hands nor the nifty pixture of R.D. with former mirage partner DIANA DORS and their ugly offspring GARY . . .

A number to reckon with: 186 HMR. License # on a powder blue VW being driv by a bearded fellow with "ABC-TV" plastered on the rear. Could THIS HIPPIE be the ex-mastermind behind Battlestar Galactica?

Steve Allen, Friday nite, NBC. What I wanna know is izzit a SPECIAL or izzit a SHOW? Not on every week and t' make things rough *TV Guide* duz not say SPECIAL under the HEADING. So it must be a SHOW. A truly HORRIBLE show. One of the POORER shows in the HISTORY OF MAN and his kind. He sends out Billy Crystal and his new lame PUNCH-DRUNK BOXING routine and tells you "No, this is not really comedy but a *plaintive portrayal* of an ex-pug." He—no that's all I watched, 10 seconds of Steverino and 15 of Billy C—I turned it off it was just too NAUSEATING. So all I wanna know is whud they do with Steve-o's JOWLS and SENILITY, both of which he sure as fug HAD for it musta been 10–15 years so really WHUD THEY *DO* WITH 'EM???????

They finally got something RIGHT—Host Larry Carroll of *Where Were You?*, on the controversial subject of 1974. "In all, it was a pretty good year" and that's no lie: The annum that gave us the abolition of pneumonia, the death of Eisenhower, the Plymouth Bobcat, and the election of Buddy Hackett as mayor of Hartford could not be *all bad*.

1, 2, 3, 4, 5, 6, 7, 8, 9, 11, sorry, 10, 11, 12, 13, 14, 16, oops, 15, 16, 17, 18, 19, 20, 21, 22, 23, 24, 25, 26, 27, 28, 29, 210, that's wrong, 30, 31, 32, 33, 34, 35, 36, 37, 38, 39, 40, 41, 42, 43, 44, 54, no, 45, 46, 47, 48, 49, 50, 51, 512, wait I got it, 52, 53, 54, 55, 56, 57, 58, 59, 60, 61, 62, 63, 64, 65, 66, 67, 68, 69, 70, 71, 72, 73, 74, 75, 76, 77, 78, 79, 80, 81, 82, 28, no, 83, 84, 85, 86, 87, 88, 89, 90, 91, 92, 93, 94, 95, 96, 97, 98, 99, 100, 1001, 1002 . . . (Proof that TV does *not* impair your ability to count!)

ART BUCHWALD

TWO MODEST PROPOSALS

Art Buchwald, a syndicated columnist whose comically jaundiced eye has been cast on Washington politics for the past two and a half decades, and whose books include While Reagan Slept *and* You Can Fool All of the People All the Time, *claims to be neither a Democrat nor a Republican, but against whoever happens to be in office.*

In the world of nuclear arms, missiles do not kill people, nations kill people.

Therefore at the start of the new arms negotiations it's time both the Soviet Union and the United States take a new approach to the question of disarmament.

Instead of working for the reduction of offensive and defensive nuclear weapons, we should negotiate limits on how many times each superpower may kill a person in the event of an all-out war.

At the moment it is believed that the U.S. and the Soviets have stockpiled enough weapons to destroy each other's citizens ten times over.

The first step then is to produce an agreement that would reduce the nuclear arsenals in both countries to the point where they could only kill every American and Soviet citizen *five* times.

Cutting the KR (Kill Ratio) in half won't be easy, but it is possible to persuade the superpowers to agree to it, particularly when it can be argued that you only have to kill a person *twice* to make your point in an all-out holocaust. With a Kill Ratio of five, both sides would still have a margin of safety in case their missiles malfunction or fail to hit their targets.

The U.S. military will argue that the Soviets may sign a treaty agreeing to kill every American only five times, and then cheat, by stashing away enough weapons to kill them seven times.

The Soviet military could balk at cutting the KR in half on the grounds that while the U.S. might reduce its weapons, they are still at a disadvantage because if we refuse to include West European warheads in the count, each U.S.S.R. citizen could still be killed eight times.

At this point the negotiators in Geneva would have to resort to compromise.

The Americans could address thc U.S. military fears by insisting on on-site inspection of both nuclear stockpiles. If it were found that the Soviet weapons on hand had enough power to kill the Americans more than the agreed upon KR of five, the U.S. could abrogate the treaty and proceed to build new weapons that would kill every Soviet citizen fifteen times.

In exchange for on-site inspection, we would include the West European nukes in our KR, and reduce American stockpiles until both the U.S. and West European KR came out to five.

If the Kill Ratio formula is unacceptable, there is no reason for the superpowers to leave the bargaining table.

Another solution might be to work out a fair agreement on how many people each side may be permitted to wipe out in the event of a war. Neither country would have to reduce its arsenal, but would be limited to firing only enough missiles to waste one hundred million people on the other's territory.

The obvious question is, who would monitor the pact to see that the superpowers did not bag more than their limit? This could be done by the International Red Cross, who would have access to all the stricken areas. If either side went over the one-hundred-million ballpark figure, the other would then be permitted to match them body for body.

With the limits set by the treaty, it would not only be a

waste of money for the superpowers to continue the arms race, but there would be an incentive to reduce their nuclear arsenals accordingly.

I have no illusions that either the Kill Ratio reduction proposal, or the one-hundred-million limit on casualties can be successfully negotiated overnight.

I'm throwing them on the table as a starting point in the new discussions. When it comes to serious disarmament talks you have to start somewhere.

HOWARD MOHR

EATING IN MINNESOTA

Howard Mohr, like Garrison Keillor, has been intimately involved in "A Prairie Home Companion," creating more than two hundred scripts for that program. He has also made frequent appearances on the show playing Bob Humde, inventor of The Cow Pie Key Hider, among other characters. The following was culled from his book, How to Talk Minnesotan.

HOTDISH

On your visit to Minnesota, you will sooner or later come face to face with Minnesota's most popular native food, *hotdish*. It can grace any table. A traditional main course, *hotdish* is cooked and served hot in a single baking dish and commonly appears at family reunions and church suppers. *Hotdish* is constructed on a base of canned cream of mushroom soup and canned vegetables. The other ingredients are as varied as the Minnesota landscape. If you sit down to something that doesn't look like anything you've ever seen before, it's probably *hotdish*.

As of the November 1986 state hotdish survey, there were 3,732 different hotdish recipes in Minnesota, up twelve from the previous November. Here are eight hotdishes taken at random from that survey.

Spaghetti-Tuna Hotdish
Garbanzo Bango Hotdish
Velveeta-Hamburger Hotdish
Ketchup Surprise Hotdish
Back of the Refrigerator Hotdish

> Doggone Good Hotdish
> Turkey Wiener Doodah Hotdish
>   (1985 Winner of La Grande Prix de Hotdish)
> Organ Meat—Cashew Hotdish

If you're visiting Minnesota in late August, the Hotdish Pavilion at the Minnesota State Fair is quite the deal. You have to see it to believe it. You'll get your fill of hotdish and hotdish-style entertainment.

The three-volume *Official State Hotdish Cookbook* can be ordered from the Hotdish Institute, Mendota Heights. Major credit cards accepted. If you order before the end of 1987, you will also receive the beautiful album (cassette or eight-track) of the most loved hotdish songs, with baritone Ernie "Hotdish" Johnson and his Mushroom Band. Order before Memorial Day and you will also receive *Hotdish on the Prairie*, a collection of poems by Minnesota's best-known food poets.

If you want to try experimenting at home with hotdish before your visit, here's a generic recipe. Roughly speaking, anything goes.

GENERIC HOTDISH (for 4)
Mix together in a large bowl:
>   *Two cans cream of mushroom soup*
>   *1 pound cooked pulverized meat*
>   *2 cans of vegetables.*

Stir.
Salt to taste.
Pour into baking dish.
Sprinkle with canned french-fried onion rings
>   *or chow mein noodles.*
Bake at 400 degrees until a brown crust forms.

Barbecues

The *barbecue* is a Minnesota sandwich consisting of boiled ketchup and hamburger served on a white buttered bun. It is commonly eaten with a spoon.

—*"Hand me another napkin, please, this barbecue is not too bad, but it's running down my arm."*

The *barbecue* should not be confused with the Minnesota *taco*, pronounced *tack-oh*. The Minnesota *taco* consists of ketchup and hamburger served inside a folded tortilla (pronounced *tore-till-a*) and topped with Cheese Whiz. Many cooks substitute pickled herring for the hamburger and use cream of mushroom soup instead of Cheese Whiz as a topping. Lettuce is optional. Buttered and folded white bread can be substituted for the tortillas. It is commonly eaten with a spoon.

—*"Hand me another napkin, please. This taco is not too bad, but it's running down my arm. It sort of reminds me of the barbecues we had yesterday."*

The Minnesota Salad

The *Minnesota salad* is an appetizing complement to any hotdish and is composed of Jell-O in any flavor, miniature colored marshmallows, canned fruit cocktail, and a generous dollop of Cool Whip on top. A common variant is to mix the Cool Whip with the Jell-O and sprinkle the marshmallows on top and omit the fruit.

—*"Boy, pass me some more of that salad. I love marshmallows with my pork chops."*

Don't make the mistake of calling the Minnesota salad *dessert* or saving it until the end of the meal.

The Minnesota tossed salad consists of a few leaves of iceberg lettuce floating on a sea of French dressing. It is acceptable to drink the dressing when you finish the lettuce.

THE THREE SQUARES

BREAKFAST
Breakfast occurs in the morning and is very close to the national standard. You get up and sit in your bathrobe and stare

until the coffee is done. Maybe you have a doughnut with your second cup. When the other members of your household wander in, you don't speak unless spoken to. Your radio is on. The announcers themselves got up early in the morning and had a cup of coffee before they drove to the station in their bathrobes. They sound happy, but it is a dog's life, getting paid to sound happy in the morning.

DINNER
The Minnesota *dinner* is served at twelve noon sharp and is the major meal of the day. In smaller towns the fire whistle goes off right on the money so everybody can stop at once.

SUPPER
The Minnesota *supper* is served after 5 but before the 6 o'clock news on TV—which is announced with another blast on the fire whistle—and typically consists of leftovers from dinner, although many people fry up a few potatoes for extra bulk in the winter.

LUNCH AND A LITTLE LUNCH
In Minnesota, lunch is typically eaten three times a day. Lunch is situated before, after, and between breakfast, dinner, and supper. The mid-afternoon lunch occurs between 3 and 3:30. The morning lunch occurs at 10, or shortly thereafter.

If a Minnesotan says:

—*"Do you want lunch?"*

Your reply should not be:

—*"Lunch? In the middle of the morning? I think I'll just wait till noon like an ordinary human being."*

Lunch commonly consists of a drink—coffee, punch, or Kool-Aid—and a large tray of meat sandwiches on snack buns, fresh-baked cinnamon rolls, and several varieties of the native dessert called *bars.*

—*"Oh, boy,* lunch, *it's been over two hours since* dinner *and I'm real hungry again."*

A LITTLE LUNCH

Lunch can also occur at other odd times of the day. It is then called "a little lunch."

—*"Well, what do you say, shall we have a little lunch?"*

Little has no more to do with size and variety in the phrase "a little lunch" than it does when you say "I had a little trouble" after the parking brake fails on your car and it rolls through the wall into the No Smoking section of the Perkins Family Restaurant.

Wherever two or three are gathered together, a little lunch will be forthcoming: at 4-H, poker games, Lutheran Circle, piano recitals, town council, funerals, weddings. The little lunch is always larger than the mid-morning and mid-afternoon lunch, with a better selection of bars and meat sandwiches. You can easily make a meal out of it.

A WORD ABOUT GRADUATION NIGHT IN MINNESOTA

On the night the local high school has graduation, the parents of the graduates each put on a little lunch. This is the biggest little lunch of the year. If you've lived in the same area most of your life, then you could be invited to as many as twenty graduation lunches. We call it the "night of the long lunch." You are expected to drive around to every lunch site and not only put in an appearance, but load up your plate with mints, ham sandwiches on snack buns, bars, and potato salad. Wear loose clothing as you begin the journey, or you might need professional help undressing when you get home after midnight.

Several times during your visit with Minnesotans you will be asked if you want a little lunch. In Minnesota a person is never left sitting without a plate of food for long. The good host will offer food every two hours and keep it in plain view between offers. Never refuse lunch when it is offered, although you can request smaller portions without penalty.

ACCEPTING FOOD ON THE THIRD OFFER

Abrupt and eager acceptance of any offer is a common mistake made by Minnesota's visitors. If a Minnesotan says:

—*"Can I get you a cup of coffee?"*

You should not say:

—*"Yeah, that would be great, thanks, with a little cream and sugar. And how about one of those cookies?"*

We never accept until the third offer and then reluctantly. On the other hand, if a Minnesotan does not make an offer three times, it is not serious. Besides, those aren't cookies on the tray, they're bars, as you can see from their rectangular shape and the thickness of the Rice Krispie center.

BASIC PHRASES
I really couldn't.
I can't let you.
I shouldn't.

DIALOGUE
—"Want a cup of coffee before you go?"
—"No, I wouldn't want to put you out. I'll get by."
—"You sure? Just made a fresh pot."
—"You didn't have to go and do that."
—"How about it, one cup?"
—"Well, if it's going to hurt your feelings, but don't fill it full."
—"How about a bar with that?"
—"I appreciate it, but no, really, I shouldn't."
—"They're Double Crispie Foghorn Bars."
—"I can't. I got my mind made up. I'm not gonna let you give me one."
—"There's one already cut with your name on it."
—"Whatever."
—"Cream for that coffee?"
—"No, no, no. That's okay, I can drink it black."
—"No problem. I'll get you some cream."
—"No, stay put. I don't need it."

—"You sure? It's just right out there in the refrigerator."
—"Well, if you're going that way anyway. I don't want you to make a special trip."
—"Sugar?"
—"I don't have to have sugar in my coffee . . ."

(Continue the above dialogue, adding other food items for practice.)

Special Note: In some non-food situations, Minnesota offers and refusals can be speeded up, as, for example, if you have lost your footing while removing snow from the roof of your house and are hanging by your feet from the rain gutter. Use your best judgment.

—*"Want some help?"*
—*"No, that's okay, I've got one foot worked loose."*
—*"No problem. I'm right here."*
—*"I got into this, I'll get out of it."*
—*"You look uncomfortable."*
—*"Well, maybe you could hold my shoulders while I twist around."*

DESSERT NEGOTIATION

In this lesson you learn how to get all the dessert you want and deserve without appearing to want or desire it. That's the way we do it: It's okay to want something, we just don't believe in showing it.

PHRASES
Just a sliver.
About half that.
If you insist.
I'm trying to cut down.
Boogie Beat Bongo Bar?

DIALOGUE
(Two Minnesotans at the Sunday dinner dessert table. The hostess speaks first.) Here's your motivation: When you line up for Minnesota dessert, you are only helping out the people

who went to all the trouble to make that sea of sweets. If you don't eat their dessert it's like a slap in the face. So even if you don't want dessert, you should take some, or suffer the consequences. There is little difference between refusing dessert in order to get all you want and refusing dessert because you don't want any. It comes to the same thing: a plate full of dessert.

HOSTESS: How about some pie?

GUEST: I don't need it, really, I'm sort of on a diet, but maybe just a sliver of the coconut creme.

H: How about the Dutch apple?

G: Well, I shouldn't, but go ahead. Just a taste, though, and leave off the ice cream.

H: It's homemade. Ralph cranked it up this morning.

G: Homemade ice cream. It'd be a crime to pass that up, wouldn't it?

H: Silver Doodle Velvet sheet cake? I know Darlene brought it especially for you.

G: About half of what you gave Bill there. I'm trying to cut down.

H: There's one Roll Me Over caramel nougat bar left. Why don't you eat it? Go ahead. Then we can wash the pan.

G: It's the least I can do, I guess. But then I'm gonna have to go lie down awhile.

H: Can you get it all on that plate?

G: No problem, I can stack up a couple of things and pile it in the middle there.

SUNDAY DINNER

Some Minnesotans insist that Sunday dinner start at 12 noon sharp like the other six dinners of the week, but the standard is closer to 1 P.M., and can be as late as 1:30 if the sermon was long or if the oven did not go on automatically at 9:30 while you were deep in the examination of the first chapter of Romans in Sunday School.

If you are invited to Sunday dinner in Minnesota, don't make plans for later in the day. After you eat you are obligated to move into the living room for conversation conducted through yawns. If there's no football game on TV or you can't hold your eyes open any longer or you are listing in the lounger more than forty-five degrees, you should go someplace where you can lose consciousness without drawing attention to yourself with unusual body noises.

—"After a meal like that a guy gets logy."

—"Why don't you take that back bedroom. There's a comforter in the closet behind the card table."

By 3:45, everybody will be strung around the house sawing logs. Don't just lie down and read magazines or snoop in the drawers. Take off your shoes and go to sleep. You should have crease marks on your face from the bedspread when you come back out around 5:30 or 6.

Many Minnesotans feel more comfortable napping on top of their own beds. They excuse themselves and drive home—if it's less than twenty miles—for a snooze. But when it's time to haul out the leftovers at the meal site, they drive back and complete their Sunday obligation.

Out of bed, dress for church, Sunday dinner, nap, leftover supper, coffee and bars, and back in bed. It's a complete Sunday package. Bailing out at any point would be a mistake without a legitimate reason or two.

—"Johnnie's throwing up. We better head out."

—"The headlights bit the dust on the way down. We gotta get home before dark. I think it's a short."

—"I'm not sure I shut the gate on the cattle yard."

When you leave early, you will be given a bag of leftovers. Don't refuse it.

THE CODE OF HAMMURABI

Doug Kenney, whose flame burned short but bright, was a charter luminary on the National Lampoon *magazine staff, and contributed brilliant material to this remarkable humor magazine (which, in its way, spurred the current Golden Age of Humor much as* The New Yorker *had spurred the last). You may remember Kenney as the wrong-way "majorette" in the movie* National Lampoon's Animal House.

I Hammurabi the Just, true son of King Zestab-pez-necco and conqueror of the evil tyrant Ashur-du-smelbad, by this stela set in the marketplace do set down my Code.

Let it be known throughout all Mesopotamia, both to Assyria and Babylonia, that these laws will make the flesh of the people glad, and are not to be leaned on.

—If two oxcarts meet at a crossroad, the oxcart on the right has the right-of-way.
—If an oxcart meets a war chariot at a crossroad, the vehicle equipped with bows, arrows, spears, slings, and scythe-blade hubs has the right-of-way.
—If traveling in congested cities, charioteers shall set melons on the points of their scythes.

—If a man split the ear of his wife, the ear of his favorite dog shall be split.

—If a man split the ear of his slave girl, his first and second wife shall split the sewing.

—If a man deflower another's slave girl, he shall pay one-half mina of silver and the cost of new sheets.

—If a woman in a quarrel damages the testicles of a man, her testicles shall be damaged.

—If a man damages the testicles of a eunuch, he shall inform the eunuch.

—If a man flog his wife, pluck out her hair, or smite and damage her nose, she shall have been flogged, had her hair plucked out, been smote, and had her nose damaged.

—If a temple prostitute refuses the silver coin of an undiseased freeman, she shall be made to lie with his ox in the square, and miniature bas-reliefs of the event may be sold to adult males above the age of fourteen.

—If a slave strikes his master's son, the slave's hand shall be cut off.

—If a son kills his father's slave, his allowance shall be cut off.

—If a son says to his father, "You are not my father," he shall be sent upstairs without supper and smothered.

—If a freeman kills a tax collector of the King, he shall be sent on in his place, swordless, to Palestine.

—If a house of mud brick collapses, killing the owner, the mason shall be pressed under every tablet relating to building codes.

—If a surgeon, using a bronze instrument, blinds, kills, or cripples a slave, his fee must be drastically reduced.

—If a royal physician prescribes to a King a strict regimen of diet and exercise, he shall be set on stakes.

—If a teacher kills a student for whispering, a note must be obtained from the parents.

—If, in the course of building a great ziggurat tall enough to reach Heaven, the workers suddenly lay down their tools claiming they no longer understand each other, the usual Jews shall be rounded up for questioning.

—If a man copulates with an ape, the child must be exposed or apply for Egyptian citizenship.

—If a man's orchard bears fruit, but at harvest time the fruit is found on the neighbor's side of the wall, and the neighbor accounts for this with a tale of a great wind in the night, the windfall fruit belongs to the neighbor and the neighbor's testicles belong over the first man's fireplace.

—If a merchant measures with false weights in the market, his weight shall be guessed by his customers, and he shall before them consume ox droppings in this amount.

—If a man in the King's game reserve slays a spotted lion under ten spearpoints in length, he has slain a hyena.

—If a man unlawfully enters a ziggurat and defaces the walls with vile cuneiforms, he shall inscribe on a stone tablet, "I will not deface ziggurat" one thousand times with his nose and be put to death.

—If a man be overheard telling impure tales concerning the goddess Ishtar, his tongue shall be torn out and put to death.

—If I find out who keeps singing popular songs under my window, he shall be thrown in the Holy River.

—If a man's brother-in-law lives under his roof, and does no work and stirs not, after four years he may be considered furniture and sold.

—If a man damage the eye of another man's horse, the first man shall be responsible for future moving violations.

—If a wet nurse substitutes a changeling for a freeman's son, and the real son returns years later by accident as part of a traveling acrobatic troop and is immediately recognized by the father by means of a distinctive ring or birthmark, the rights to any resulting poem, song, or bas-relief shall belong to the King.

—If a scribe makes an error in the transcription of a royal edict, he shall be [text unintelligible].

BILL COSBY

ALMOST AS SMART AS NEANDERTHALS

What the heck can I say about Bill Cosby? I still remember discovering, as a child, his record "I Started Out as a Child," and any television fan knows his backhand intimately from "I Spy." There have also been, of course, his stand-up comedy appearances, movie acting, and hit television series, "The Bill Cosby Show." And in his two best-sellers, Fatherhood *and* Time Flies, *Cosby proves that he can be as funny on paper as he is on stage.*

Before we had children, my wife and I felt educated. She was a college graduate, a child psychology major with a B-plus average, which means, if you ask her a question about a child's behavior, she will give you eighty-five percent of the answer. And I was a physical education major with a child psychology minor at Temple, which means if you ask me a question about a child's behavior, I will advise you to tell the child to take a lap.

Because we were college graduates, we studied things that people have always done naturally, like have children; and so, we decided to have our first child by natural childbirth. Childbirth, of course, *is* a natural thing: the pains come automatically, the muscles contract and push down, and all you need, as they say, is hot water. Neanderthals delivered children without training manuals.

At any rate, these classes give the father a diploma so that he can attend the birth. And what the classes teach him is how to be a cheerleader in the delivery room: how to say, "Push! Push! Push 'em out, shove 'em out, waaay out!"

My wife's job was to keep breathing, but she had studied how to do this in the course, so she was breathing at the top of her class. By the time we had finished the class, we were well prepared for natural childbirth, which means that no drugs can be given to the female during delivery. The father, however, can have all he wants.

One day near the end of the ninth month, my wife came running to me, breathing rapidly, and she cried, "Bill!"

"Push!" I said.

But then I remembered something from the class: You have to go to a hospital. And so we did, at 120 miles an hour, with my wife moaning all the way. When we got to the hospital, we went right to the delivery room, where I put the booties on my shoes. Her legs went up into the stirrups, while the obstetrician sat awaiting the delivery, like Johnny Bench.

When the first big pain hit her, I merrily said, "Push!"

Like every man, of course, I had no understanding of how a labor pain really feels. Carol Burnett said, "If you want to know the feeling, just take your bottom lip and pull it over your head."

When the second big pain hit, she cried out and stood up in the stirrups.

"Morphine!" she said. "I want morphine!"

"But dear," I sweetly replied, "you *know* that morphine—"

"*You* shut up! You did this to me!"

And at the next contraction, she told everyone in the delivery room that my parents were never married. Then she continued breathing while I continued cheering from the sidelines: "Push! Push! Push!"

"I don't *want* to push anymore," she said. "Bill, tell them to give me something."

"No, dear, the class forbids—"

"I'm dropping out of *school!*"

"But you can *do* it!"

Meanwhile, Johnny Bench was still sitting there, waiting for the delivery.

"Look!" I suddenly said. "Isn't that the head?"

"I believe it is," he replied.

"Well, go *get* it."

"It's stuck."

"Then get the salad spoons, man."

So he got the salad spoons, the baby came out, and my wife and I were suddenly sharing the greatest moment in our lives. This was what we had asked God for; this was what we wanted to see if we could make. And I looked at it lovingly as they started to clean it off, but it wasn't getting any better.

And then I went over to my wife, kissed her gently on the lips, and said, "Darling, I love you very much. You just had a lizard."

MERLE KESSLER

PERFECT PITCH

Early in his career, Merle Kessler collaborated with Duck's Breath Mystery Theatre, but he is probably best known, under the alias "Ian Shoales," for his commentaries on "Nightline" and on National Public Radio's "All Things Considered." Two volumes of Shoales's work have been published so far, I Gotta Go *and* Ian Schoales' Perfect World.

Commercial; 60 seconds (CONVERGENCE AIRLINES)

VIDEO	AUDIO
A SLEEK SILVER AIRPLANE HANGS IN A SILVER SKY. IT BLURS AT THE EDGES, THEN ZOOMS OUT OF FRAME.	CHORUS OF VOICES Arise! Arise and fly! FX: SONIC BOOM
EMPTY SILVER SKY	ANNOUNCER You can hurtle through time and space at incredible speeds.
CUT TO: A SLEEK SILVER AIRPLANE HANGS IN A SILVER SKY, MOTIONLESS.	Or you can take your time. FX: WHISTLING WIND At Convergence Airlines, the choice is yours.

CUT TO:

INTERIOR OF SLEEK AIR-
PLANE, PASSENGERS
STRAPPED IN, FACES CON-
TORTED FROM THE PULL
OF MANY G-FORCES.

New York to Paris in five
minutes.

CUT TO:

INTERIOR OF SLEEK AIR-
PLANE. THE WINDOWS ARE
OPEN. PASSENGERS ARE LEAN-
ING OUT. SOME ARE WAVING
TO PEOPLE FAR BELOW.

ANNOUNCER
Or New York to Paris in
five days.

At Convergence Airlines,
the choice is yours.

CUT TO:

ATTRACTIVE FLIGHT AT-
TENDANT READING A
THICK NOVEL. PASSENGER
APPROACHES. FLIGHT AT-
TENDANT DOESN'T LOOK
UP.

We won't pamper you.

PASSENGER
Can I get a cup of coffee?

FLIGHT ATTENDANT
Go ahead. I'm not your
servant, sir. I'm a trained
professional.

CUT TO:

OPEN WINDOW. A PASSEN-
GER LEANS TOO FAR OUT
AND FALLS. A SECOND PAS-
SENGER GRABS A FLIGHT
ATTENDANT.

ANNOUNCER
At Convergence Airlines,
every choice is yours.

SECOND PASSENGER
Miss, that man fell out the
window!

FLIGHT ATTENDANT
He was an adult, who
chose not to wear his seat
belt. You must live with
the choices you make in
life. Or die with them.
The choice is always yours.

SLEEK SILVER PLANE
HANGING FIRE IN THE SKY.

ANNOUNCER
Dance on the wing under
the stars or cling to your
seat for dear life. At Convergence, you make the
choices. Don't blame us.
Try us.

CHORUS OF VOICES
Arise! Arise and fly with
me!

ED McCLANAHAN

ROUSE UP, O YOUNG MEN OF THE NEW AGE!

Kentucky-born Ed McClanahan's first book, The Natural Man, *has become something of a minor classic. His second book,* Famous People I Have Known, *expounds, in autobiographical detail, on the greats and not-so-greats he has rubbed elbows with, and includes the following story of the 1960s—an era which now seems, at least through McClanahan's mildly nostalgic eyes, to have happened on Mars.*

In the latter 1960s, on a corner in downtown Palo Alto scarcely a brickbat's throw from the Stanford campus, there stood an aged, derelict, three-story brick office building, the first floor of which was occupied by a fish 'n' chips 'n' rock 'n' roll establishment called the Poppycock. Upstairs, the sweaty-hatband gents who managed the building had rented out the old offices, formerly the domain of perfectly respectable doctors, realtors, and accounting firms, to an assortment of artists, writers, sex therapists, filmmakers, and anarcho-syndicalist organizations dedicated to the violent overthrow of whatever wasn't nailed down.

And I was a primary ingredient of this unsavory mélange, having rented, on the very day the sweaty hatbands took over in 1967, for the speaks-for-itself sum of twenty-five dollars a month, the second-floor office directly above the Poppycock's bandstand. In this grimy, scrod-scented aerie, with the jackhammer syncopations of Big Brother and the Holding Company or the early Grateful Dead rattling the floorboards at my feet, I composed my rhapsodic odes to the revolutionary spirit of the times, for publication in *The Free You*, of which I was a fearless editor.

Beneath my window, meanwhile, the beat went on day and night; the sidewalks swarmed with rock 'n' roll riffraff, adolescent acidheads and swiftly aging speedsters, motorcycle madmen and wilted flower children, slightly unhinged outpatients from the nearby VA hospital, spare-changers and affluent musicians and plainclothesmen and nouveau riche dealers, all the myriad varieties of California white trash. Street-corner preachers and peace-movement pitchmen harangued the passersby; in the shadows, furtive retail and wholesale transactions were negotiated by shifty-eyed entrepreneurs and consumers. Now and then, there was a peace march on University Avenue; once, a riot. The Poppycock corner was where It was indisputably At in Palo Alto. If ever an old would-Beat had found his little piece of heaven, I'd found mine.

Nonetheless, late in the fall of '68, when with the chilly weather the street people began to invade the upstairs of the building, prowling the dim, scabrous hallways like vermin in the hide of some mangy old mutt, holding court in the unoccupied offices, performing their unholy rituals in the toilets, the mellow vibes started to ring a little sour. One November night in the darkened hall, I stumbled over an astonishingly pungent wino, who roused himself just long enough to announce that he was the new night watchman, before he crashed again. Another time, someone stole the padlock right off my office door while I was inside working. Several times my doorway was employed as a *pissoir*. Finally, in December, someone jimmied my new padlock and made off with an antiquated thesaurus and a packet of Pearly Gates morning-glory seeds.

All of which is why, late one night during the Christmas holidays, I went out of my way to swing by the Poppycock and check out my office as I drove home after a party. The weather had turned decidedly nippy during the past few days, and as a consequence the traffic in the halls had been especially heavy; only that afternoon I'd been interrupted at my inflammatory scribblings by a door-to-door acid salesman, then by a pair of giggling fourteen-year-old androgynes who were *buying* acid door-to-door, and finally by the aromatic night watchman, who put the arm on me for fifty cents as a reward for keeping such a sharp eye on things. So I was apprehensive.

Sure enough, I'd had more callers. This time they'd busted the door clear off its hinges and appropriated my radio and my brand-new, nifty little hundred-dollar Hermes portable typewriter, which at the time I treasured above all things except, possibly, my mustache. The radio was an elderly, malfunctioning table model with an intolerable frog in its throat; if the counterculture was that hard up for a radio, I wouldn't begrudge it. But the typewriter was an altogether other matter. Why, stealing the tools of a writer's trade is a counterrevolutionary act, it's positively reactionary, a crime against humanity itself! And to add insult to injury, the barbarians had strewn my manuscripts and papers about the premises in a manner suggesting a profound disrespect for Art. So I did what any reasonable, responsible apostate would do under the circumstances: I called the cops.

They came immediately, two grave, businesslike young patrolmen who strode in right past the spray-painted OFF THE PIGS! legends with which one of the building's unofficial tenants had thoughtfully decorated the hallways, strode into my office and looked around, and strode right back out again. Nothing they could do, they said, unless I had the serial number of the typewriter and it happened to turn up in a pawnshop. But surely there was *something*, I fumed. How about fingerprints? Nope, the patrolmen said, not a chance—for hadn't I myself already poked about the room in search of clues like Dick Tracy's inept rookie in "The Crimestopper's Textbook," smudging fingerprints wherever I touched?

"I tell you what, Mr. Lannieham," mused one of the cops on his way out, "if I was writing *me* a book in this place, I believe I'd use a pencil."

So, finally, deep in the middle of the night, I battened down the hatches as best I could and grumbled my way home to bed, where I fell into an uneasy sleep and dreamed grumpy cartoon dreams in which my lovely little Hermes sprouted wings and blithely flew away, as I groaned into my pillow. In the morning, rather earlier than I might have chosen, I was awakened by . . .

. . . the phone. "Ed?" a dimly familiar voice inquires, rather tentatively. "This is Whitey." A pause, while I ruminate on that. Then: "You know. Whitey? That used to be in your writing class?"

"Um, um, oh, yeah. Whitey. Right, right." And slowly a face emerges out of the recent past: Whitey, a Stanford grad student in another department, who'd taken my creative-writing course last spring; a long-haired, semi-serious radical from Texas, a little older than most of my students, and a pretty fair country writer when it came to that. "How you making it, Whitey? What's new?" I am polite but wary; I can feel a request for a letter of recommendation coming on, and I'm not in a real accommodating frame of mind just now. If Whitey wants me to write a recommendation for him, I'll tell him I can't because some damn long-haired Commie hippie ding-dong stole my damn typewriter, that's what I'll tell him.

But Whitey graciously overlooks my lack of warmth. "Listen, Ed," he is already saying, "lemme ask you a question, and if the answer's no, then just forget I asked it, okay?"

Uh-oh, sounds like the old letter-of-recommendation song and dance, all right. "Yeah, sure," I tell him, barely suppressing a grouchy sigh. "Go ahead, I guess."

"Well then, tell me: did you get ripped off last night?"

Say what? Suddenly I am sitting bolt upright in bed, with my ear socked like a suction cup to the receiver. "Yeah, I did, I sure did!"

"A typewriter and a radio, maybe?"

"Yeah, right!"

"Well, listen"—Whitey is speaking almost in whispers now, and hastily—"listen, if you can come over to my place right away, I think I can get it back for you, the typewriter anyhow. The guys that took it are friends of this chick I live with, see, and they came by and tried to sell it to me. When I found out they ripped it off from upstairs in the Poppycock, I sort of thought it might be yours. One of them is still here, and I think he'll give it back, if you ask him for it. You better hurry, though. I don't know how long I can keep him here."

Hey hey, a freaking miracle! I nearly garrote myself with the phone cord getting together a pencil and paper to take down Whitey's address, and within minutes I have scooped up my writer friend Wig, who's visiting from back East and has evinced an unwholesome desire to experience the California Thing to the fullest, and we are zipping across town in my—you guessed it—VW Microbus, the McClanavan, and I am blithering merrily away about how this is, after all, the Christmas season, and I am, after all, a generous, large-spirited sort who'll probably let bygones be bygones as long as I get my typewriter back, blah-blah-blah. It will be a while yet before it occurs to me that such generosity as has been displayed so far has been entirely on the part of Whitey, and of the thief himself. By the time we reach Whitey's east Palo Alto neighborhood—a semi-genteel ghetto shared by working-class blacks and white Stanford students—I have once again persuaded myself that I am the hero of my own life story.

As we curb the McClanavan before a shabby old gray stucco house with the window shades all pulled, so that it looks out upon the world with a blank, noncommittal stare, I note that squarely in the middle of the tiny, blighted front yard there stands, for all the world like one of those little cast-iron jockeys that grace the front yards of Southern manses, a middle-aged gentleman of color, regarding us with baleful eye from beneath the bill of an improbably spiffy-looking golf cap. Could this be our man? Suddenly it occurs to me that I may be dealing here not with some trifling amateur but with genuine, grown-up criminals, second-story men, hardened

Hermes-nappers. Black Panthers, even. If they demand a ransom, how high can I go before I meet my lofty revolutionary principles coming down?

"Yawl huntin' Whitey?" this striking fixture demands as I alight before him. And when, quailing inwardly, I confirm our mission with a nod, it is as if I have popped the cork on a Neal Cassady genie, another Talking Dervish.

"Me too!" he cries, hurrying to join us at Whitey's doorstep. "Me too, I was jis goin' to see ole Whitey my*seff*, I was down at the A & *Pee* sto' this mornin', see, and that sto' guy, he say, Jabbers, yawl want this here trash, I gone th'ow hit out if you don't want hit? And dog if he don't gimme a whole gret big ole *bag* of rotten p'*taters*, and t'*maters*, and *squarsh* and all, you never see the like, *vedgibles* y'see. So I taken hit home wimme, and my ole woman she say, Jabbers, you blame ole fool you, I ain't eatin' no sich damn ole rubbage as that, hee hee hee; she say you gwan crost the street to that ole hippie's house and axe him does *he* want this ole stuff. So I'm gonna axe ole Whitey could he use 'em, they jis what he *need* y'see, ole skinny long-hair thing, he make him some good vedgible *soup* y'see . . ."

Jabbers indeed. It is the first wash of a floodtide of words that seem to flow from him ceaselessly and effortlessly, an aimless torrent that begins nowhere and goes nowhere and ends nowhere, as if his tongue has somehow come unfastened at both ends and blithers on of its own free will and accord, cut loose from its last flimsy moorings to his mind. Right away I detect the breath of Sneaky Pete upon the air, and I understand that this here is no doped-up desperado, no cat burglar, no fiery black Maoist bent upon the radical restructuring of the social order by appropriating the equipment of capitalist-road writers. This here is the neighborhood lush, is who this is; Uncle Remus's long-lost no-'count nephew.

Now Jabbers is rapping briskly at the door, still talking like a teapot: "That Whitey, he all *right*, by God, he tole me he *fo'* the black man, he even got him a big ole pitcher of a Neegrow right on his wall in there, one of these Black Pampher boogers holdin' him a big ole *gun*, look mean as *hell*, by God!

So I gonna give ole Whitey all the rotten vedgibles he can *eat*, y'see, cause he good to Jabbers, him and that Miss Mercy, that li'l girly of his'n, she gimme a li'l taste of po't *wine* one time, so I . . ."

The door opens, and Whitey is standing in the hallway, looking pretty much the same as when I'd last seen him, back in the early autumn. He's got a little more hair, I suppose, but then for that matter so do I. Who, in fact, does not, these days?

"Hey, come in," he says amiably. "Where'd you find old Jabbers?"

He does not wait for an answer, giving Wig and me to understand that we might have found Jabbers almost anywhere. Whitey is friendly, but as we enter I notice that he keeps peering anxiously over my shoulder to the street, as though he is expecting someone to slip in behind us. Later I am to discover that his anxiety has to do with some utterly unrelated negotiations he has going with yet another set of people, who are due to arrive momentarily—but just now I have no way of knowing that, so Whitey's uneasiness is making me uneasy too. As he leads us down the darkened hall toward the kitchen, I feel as jittery as an overwound windup toy; at any moment I might disintegrate in a small explosion of tiny springs and cogwheels.

". . . got t'maters over there *this* big, by God; some of 'em ain't got no rotten places a-*tall*, hardly. Yawl wouldn' have a li'l taste of sweet po't *wine* fo' ole Jabbers, I don't reckon? I sho' could use me a . . ."

Then we are in the kitchen, and there, sitting at a table piled high with dirty dishes, pots and pans, old newspapers, books, manuscripts—in short, the kind of kitchen table no self-respecting graduate student would be without—sitting there at one end of the table is a very pretty girl—Miss Mercy? Was that what Jabbers called her?—with a blond baby on her lap, and across from her sits what has to be the scruffiest hippie west of Marrakesh. I recognize him right off. He's a Poppycock regular, just a kid, maybe seventeen or eighteen, a barefoot psychedelic waif with a pale, pinched, meager little face beneath a wild snarl of dark, matted hair that reaches halfway

down his back, and a wispy little-boy goatee, and a meticulously filthy old plaid flannel shirt with the sleeves half rotted
away, and about a dozen greasy leather pouches, stuffed with
who-knows-what insalubrious substances, dangling from the
belt loops of his crusty jeans. As we file into the room Whitey
says to him, "This is Ed," and through the hanging veil of hair
he looks up at me, me and my eighteen-dollar Mod Squad coif
and my eighty-dollar granny glasses, looks up at me with the
sweetest, saddest, shyest, most winning smile, an exquisitely
lovely *gift* of a smile, and holds out his hand for me to shake,
and says, softly and with perfect ingenuousness:

"Hey, man, meet the cat that ripped off your typewriter!"

"That's Yogurt," Whitey says. "I already told him you were
coming."

Then we, Yogurt and I, are shaking hands and giggling and
clapping each other on the back like long-lost Oddfellows, and
I am charmed beyond measure, and utterly won over.

". . . I b'lieve I better give ole Yogurt some good rotten
t'maters *too*, look to me like he need somethin' to clean hisself
out, them t'maters be jis the trick . . ."

I am beginning to realize that Jabbers's gibberish is to social
intercourse what the tamboura is to Indian music, a kind of
liquid atonal drone that rushes along just beneath the surface
of the conversation, bubbling up like a wellspring whenever
there's the smallest silence.

"Listen, man," Yogurt is imploring me, "I mean, I got to
tell you, man, like, we wouldn't *never*'ve ripped off your shit
if we would've known you were a hip dude!"

Me? A hip dude? Me, this aging Peter Pan in pointy boots?
Surely he can't mean it, surely he's setting me up for some
awful put-down. But his voice and hangdog expression are so
freighted with earnest apology that finally I'm unable to harbor
the slightest doubt of his sincerity. It is perhaps the grandest
compliment I've been paid in my whole life . . . so grand that
it completely crowds out of my consciousness the fact that,
however much it distresses him to have to confess to having
ripped off a hip dude, Yogurt is not the least bit abashed at
admitting he's a thief.

"Oh, that's all right," I hear myself reassure him, half-apologetically. "In fact, I don't really care at all about the radio, you all can keep that if you want to. I would kind of like to have the typewriter back, though, if you could see your way clear to . . ."

"Hey, no problem, man!" Yogurt reassures *me*. "It's cool, it's cool! The only thing is, I ain't got it with me right now. Who's got it right now is Wheatgerm and the Beast."

Wheatgerm? The Beast? Uh-oh.

". . . now, you gonna make you some mash p'taters, you jis mash up them little rotten parts right in, you won't never hardly know they in there . . ."

"Yeah, Wheatgerm and the Beast took it all with them, see. But I'll go find them, man, and score it back for you! Hey, man, I'll go right now, yeah, hey!" In a sudden burst of zeal he leaps up from the table, and I see all over again how pitifully frail he is. A rag, a bone, a hank of hair, that's Yogurt. "Hey, why don't *everybody* come, shit yeah, let's go find this dude's shit for him!"

Almost at once he has the whole roomful of people—remember now, there's Whitey and the girl and the baby and Jabbers (". . . I bet ole Beast'd *love* to have some nice squarsh . . .") and Wig and me and, oh yeah, Yogurt's big black dog, who as I recall was under the table until Yogurt stood up and brought the dog up with him, like some kind of strangely malformed shadow—all of us suddenly swirling about this cramped little kitchen in the wake of Yogurt's enthusiasm, which is already propelling Yogurt himself out of the kitchen and down the hall toward the front door. And now somehow the entire mass has packed itself like a school of compliant sardines into a space about one-third as large as the kitchen we've just escaped, and Jabbers is babbling and Yogurt is inviting us to go with him and we are declining and the baby is babbling hardly less coherently than Jabbers, and the dog—whose neck, it develops, is bound by a length of twine to Yogurt's wrist—is barking gaily; and then there is a knock at the door and Whitey opens it and admits two guys who are obviously the ones he has been expecting, two long-haired, beady-eyed types with their collars turned up and their hands jammed into their coat pockets, one of them with a package under his arm that doubtless contains a variety of vedgible matter that Whitey really has been pining for.

Whitey coughs nervously and asks the newcomers if they've come to look at the room, heh heh, and they cough nervously and say, Oh yeah, the room, heh heh, and Whitey shuffles his feet anxiously, making ready to lead them off, but before they can get mobilized, Yogurt parts the assembled multitudes by leaping to the little peephole window in the door, and peers out and giggles and announces, "Uh-oh, this is gonna get interestin'! Here comes Wheatgerm and the Beast!"

The door swings open and somebody yells, Hey, Wheatgerm! and in bops a Chaplinesque little bundle of rags and bone and hair who could be Yogurt's double and is, in fact (someone tells me later), his first cousin. The two of them fling themselves into each other's arms, embracing and crying out each other's name—"Yogurt baby!" "Wheatgerm!"—as joyously as if they haven't crossed paths in years and years; and I relax a little, thinking, If this is the biggest size they come in, I guess I'll be okay.

Until the door swings open one more time, and into the melee strides a great, slab-shouldered, scowling ogre wearing biker's leathers and cycle boots and a thick chain for a belt, and the most remarkable head of hair I've ever seen, a dense yellow shock the shape and color and texture of a haystack, with a short, ropy queue that swings loose from the crown of his skull; and within this strange hummock of hair are these pale, cold, blue eyes glowering, darting furiously from face to face in the sullen half-light of the hallway. A griffin with a lion's mane and the fierce eye of an eagle; a very Caliban. Behold, the Beast!

And the dog is yipping and Jabbers is yapping and the baby is yowling and Yogurt and Wheatgerm are whooping and Whitey and his colleagues are mumbling conspiratorially behind their hands, and we are all milling around, treading on one another's feet—all of us, that is, except the Beast, who stands motionless and silent in the midst of all this clamor, savagely glaring straight at me.

But before I can give more than passing consideration to Wig's and my chances if we were to bolt for the door, Yogurt wraps one arm around Wheatgerm's shoulders and the other around the Beast's waist and draws them through the burgeoning assemblage to where I'm standing and cries above the din:

"Hey, you guys, meet the cat that we ripped the typewriter off of!"

". . . or you could squeeze you some of them t'maters and make you some nice *jewce*, which that reminds me, I don't reckon you all would have a li'l sip or two of . . ."

The Beast is squinting into the gloom, his ice-blue eyes just inches from my own, his small mouth working slowly, as if he savors the taste of the rage that's rising in his gorge. Our eyes stay locked that way until, after the longest possible time, he reaches out and grabs my hand and pumps it vigorously, exclaiming:

"Aw, no shit, man, was that your place? Hey, listen, man, we wouldn't *never*'ve ripped you off if we knew you was a hip dude!"

"Right, man!" Wheatgerm concurs enthusiastically, pumping my other hand and breaking into an ecstatic little dance of mock dismay. "Right, we wouldn't *never* rip off a hip dude!"

"We gotta get this dude's shit, man!" cries Yogurt. "Where's it at, man?"

"The typewriter's over at the other place, man," Wheatgerm offers.

"Yeah," the Beast says, turning back to me. "We can get the typewriter right now, man, no sweat. It's over at this place where we slept at last night. But listen, man, I ain't so sure about your radio. Because the thing is, see, the Spirit's got that."

The Spirit?

". . . I tell yawl what, I jis let yawl have that whole big ole *bag* of truck, if somebody jis gimme *one li'l ole half pint* of . . ."

"Right!" Yogurt pipes. "Let's go get the dude's typewriter, before the Spirit gets it! This here's a good dude, man, let's go get his shit for him!"

"Yeah!" Wheatgerm chimes in, and "Shit yes!" bellows the Beast, and the dog yelps something that sounds a lot like "Fucking-A!" And Yogurt flings open the door, and to my astonishment the four of them split, vanish, evaporate before my very eyes!

Watching the door swing shut behind them, I am once again beset by doubts. Have I stood here and watched my three yeggs stroll out the door scot-free and never fired a shot? Has my Hermes really spread its little wings and flown the coop for good?

Meanwhile, the congestion in the hall is easing as quickly as it had set in. Whitey waves me an indifferent farewell, and he and his misanthropic associates, still growling among themselves, slouch off toward the rear of the house (that will be the last we'll see of them, by the way; they never reappeared while Wig and I were there), and the baby toddles through a doorway off the hall, and Jabbers toddles after him (". . . you wait up there, li'l buddy, ole Uncle Jabbers gonna git you some nice squarsh . . ."), and the girl follows them and Wig follows her and I follow Wig. We find ourselves in the living room, which is pretty thoroughly littered with the baby's toys, but otherwise rather barren, except for a couple of worn, over-stuffed chairs and a rump-sprung couch, beneath which skulks what at first appears to be some species of rodent, but soon turns out instead to be a very small Chihuahua, hairless as a jalapeño, and not a great deal larger.

"Come on out, Thor," the girl languidly summons this un-comely quadruped, as she gathers up the baby and settles her-self on the couch. "That big old doggy's all gone now. But don't you worry, man," she adds, turning to me, "they'll be right back, I betcha. They'll bring back your typer thingy too, you see if they don't."

Thor, after assuring himself that the coast is really clear, creeps out from under the couch and prances like a rat on stilts across the floor to Wig's chair, where he throws himself upon Wig's ankle and begins making ardent love to his desert boot.

I slump wearily onto the couch beside the girl. "Sure," I am halfheartedly declaring, "I believe it, I know they will."

Wig, to the vast amusement of Jabbers, is striving desperately to scrape the amorous Thor off his foot on the leg of his chair. "Hee hee!" Jabbers exults. "I jis wisht you'd looky here at ole Thor humpin' on this ball-headed boy!"

The girl has heard the way my voice sagged beneath the weight of disbelief. "*Truly* they will, man," she assures me serenely. "They're beautiful dudes!"

I try to say "They are!" But despite my best effort it comes out "They are?" Guiltily, I cover it with another question: "Your name is . . . ?"

"Mercy," she says. "I, you know, go by that. I started using it last year when I was dancing topless. Miss Mercy, they called me. Hey, c'mon, Thor! Leave the dude's shoe alone, man! Thor's kind of, you know, horny," she explains apologetically to Wig. "The lady dogs around here are all sort of too tall for him. He keeps tryin' to ball the cat, but she's like you, she's not too crazy about it either."

If Wig is wounded by the discovery that he is not the sole object of Thor's affection, he is too preoccupied just now to say so, what with trying to fend off both Thor's attentions to his foot and Jabbers's attentions to his bald noggin. "I jis wisht yawl'd looky here at the *head* on this ole boy, I b'lieve I never did see no ball-head hippie before, Yogurt and Whitey and them has got *plenny* hair but this here ole boy ain't got but jis that little ole *fuzz* around the *edge*, if you'd jis set *still* a minute and let ole Jabbers *rub* that head a little, we might could make hit *grow*, hee hee hee . . ."

"So," I inquire of Miss Mercy, "how long have you known these . . . beautiful dudes?"

"Oh, a *long* time, two or three months at *least*. They used to come in this place where I was a waitress. The Beast is from around here, I think. He's, like, a dropout. Yogurt and Wheatgerm are runaways from back East somewheres. Okaloma or somewheres."

Okies. The mind boggles.

"The thing is," Mercy goes on, "they're really penny-stricken, see. They live on just whatever they can hit people up for, and sleep just, you know, wherever they happen to crash, with a chick sometimes, or in the Beast's car. So like whenever I run into them I bring them home with me and feed them. I really love those three dudes, man, *truly* I do. I mean, they wouldn't've done anything like, you know, ripping off your shit or anything like that if they hadn't've been, you know, drunk."

"Drunk?" I am taken aback. "I thought they were . . . hippies."

"Oh, I guess they, you know, get stoned now and then, same as everybody else. But what they're really *into* is wine. They're juiceheads, mostly."

Despite my surprise, I have to concede, upon reflection, that this is actually one of the more cogent facts I've managed to glean about them—for I too have harkened upon occasion to the call of the wild grape. But I've been sort of reluctantly assuming, of recent years, that us juiceheads are a dying breed; and the shock of learning that we've merely been underground, just waiting to be rediscovered by the avant-garde, is almost too much for me. At last! A cultural revolution worth laying the old bod upon the line for!

"How about the Spirit?" I ask Miss Mercy. "Who's he?"

"I don't know too much about him," she says vaguely. "I think he's, like, a colored dude or something, maybe." She leans back and peers around the window shade and exclaims, "Hey, there they are, they're back!"

The door crashes open out in the hall, Thor scrabbles hastily back under the couch, and in the blinking of an eye they have materialized before me, Yogurt and Wheatgerm and the Beast and the dog, all four of them grinning broadly and the dog wagging his tail besides, and dangling from the Beast's big right hand, which he is holding out to me, is my Hermes portable typewriter!

"Hey, far out, thanks, I . . ."

"Now, you ole Beasty, I don't reckon yawl would've brung ole Jabbers a li'l taste of Sneaky *Pete*, by any . . ."

"But it don't look so good for the radio, man," Wheatgerm is telling me, shaking his head sorrowfully. "Because the Spirit's got that, see."

What Wheatgerm is saying is, the Spirit ain't got quite as much respect for hip dudes as we do, see, so don't sit up nights waiting for him to bring your radio back. But so delighted am I to have made the grade as a hip dude, to have actually won admission to the august company of these splendid fellows, that at this point I couldn't possibly care less about the wretched radio. What's one radio more or less among us hip dudes? To hell with the radio! Let the radio go wherever the Spirit moves it!

"So tell me," I inquire of them, chuckling as merrily as if nothing in the world gratifies me quite as much as a good burglary at my own expense, "how'd you all break in my door?"

"Be damn if I can remember," the Beast admits, scratching his haymow reflectively. "We were drunk as dog shit, man."

"You *kicked* it down, you dumb fuck!" Wheatgerm crows. "You were so drunk you kicked the fucker right down, and can't even remember you did it!"

"Oh, yeah, that's right, I did," the Beast muses, blushing modestly at the gargantuan proportions of his drunk.

"Hey listen, man," Yogurt says to me, "we really gotta get shakin', see. Because we have to get to this chick's house that said she'd ball us if we get there before her old man comes home from work. So we better split. We're sorry about your radio, though, man, we really are."

". . . I reckon this here's about the first ball-head hippie ever I run into . . ."

We are all on our feet now, and the Beast is shaking my hand again, and Wheatgerm and Yogurt are sort of plucking at my sleeves, imploring me one last time to forgive them for ripping off such a hip dude. And I, of course, am doing so with all my heart, trailing them halfway down the front hall dispensing absolution, feeling guilty as sin for stealing back my typewriter. For want of something better to offer them in recompense for the injustice of it all, I mention that I just might try to write something about them sometime.

"Good fucking deal, man," the Beast says heartily. "You can write anything you want to about me. 'Cause I can't read anyhow."

"Hey, Mercy," Yogurt calls back from the front door, "thanks a lot for the breakfast, man."

"Sure," she coos as the door slams after them. "Any time, man!"

I go back into the living room to gather up my typewriter and rescue Wig from Jabbers, who is again imploring permission to rub his pate ("... it so *shiny*, jis lemme feel of it *one time*, hee hee hee ..."), and from Thor, who is again putting the moves on the seductive desert boot. We are just maneuvering ourselves into position to make a break for it, when we hear the front door open, and suddenly the Beast is framed once more in the hall doorway.

"Hey listen, man," he says to me, "you ain't got any spare change you could lend us, have you?"

I come up with thirty-five or forty cents, which I'm half ashamed to offer him. But the Beast seems perfectly content with the donation.

"Thanks, man," he says cheerfully. "Later."

"... hey, you ole Beasty you, if yawl gonna git some wine you won't forgit ole Jabbers, would you now, yawl 'member how ole Jabbers give yawl some Sweet Lucy the other day, you 'member that, don't you, Beasty ..."

But Jabbers is too late, for the Beast is long gone once again. And this time Wig and I are close behind him.

"Bye bye," Miss Mercy calls sweetly as we slip out the door. "You dudes hurry back, now."

"... shore, yawl come back I git you some nice vedgibles too, my ole woman she likes to see a ole ball-head hippie, I take yawl home wimme ..."

Wig and I reach the stoop just in time to see an old Ford ragtop pull away in a great cloud of blue exhaust. The dog is

hanging half out of the gaping hole that used to be the back
window, barking his head off, and the Beast and Yogurt are
waving good-bye from the far side of the car, above the tattered
top, and Wheatgerm is leaning out the window on the near
side, his hands cupped to his mouth to make himself heard
above the roar of the engine.

"Hey," he yells, "do you cats realize how *weird* all this shit
is?"

"Sure we do," Wig says as the old car, listing and yawing,
careens around the corner and out of sight. "We're in California, aren't we?"

So that afternoon I dropped in at the Palo Alto police station—
the Pork Works, we local *illuminati* were fond of calling it—
to report that, faced with the appalling incompetence of our
appointed constabulary, I had conducted my own private investigation, had swiftly apprehended the typer-nappers with
my bare hands, and, having discerned them to be, not unlike
myself, members in good standing of the oppressed and voice-
less masses, had liberated them to go forth and do the People's
work. Or words to that effect. The impassive functionary behind the desk took down this intelligence without comment,
and I left feeling, all things considered, enormously satisfied
with myself. The hip dude had closed the case.

And I continued to feel pretty mellow right up until, late
the same evening, as Wig and I were sitting up enjoying one
last midnight pipe of Acapulco moonshine, the telephone rang
and it was a Lieutenant Badger of the PAPD, who demanded
to know, What means this nonsense in this report, Mr. Mick-
elhan, and wouldn't I like to clear up the record on this matter,
and didn't I understand that after all a felony had been com-
mitted here, a *felony*, Mr. Monahan, and I'm sure you understand that you can't just walk in here and halt an investigation
of a felony, sir, merely because you personally happened to be
fortunate enough to get your property back, don't you realize
that there have been other burglaries of a similar nature in
that neighborhood, and do you think it fair, Mr. Moneyhon,
that your property should be returned to you whereas other

persons have no hope of regaining theirs, don't you realize that the burglaries will continue until these people are brought to justice, it's too bad you don't feel you can cooperate with us, it's irresponsible citizens like you who make police work difficult, good evening, Mr. Asshole, click.

Unmanned by the rigor of the lieutenant's reproaches and the iron logic of his argument, I never even managed to get my defense mechanisms into gear; my end of the dialogue sputtered along as if my plugs were damp: Well, yessir, but . . . Yes, that's so, but . . . I can understand that, but . . . I see, but . . . Yes, but . . . Yes, but . . . Yes, but . . .

He's right! I told Wig after I'd recounted Lt. Badger's dressing-down. He's dead right; why should I be immune from harm when my neighbors are getting ripped off night after night?

"So," Wig ventured to interject, "you're going to turn them in, then?"

What? Turn them in? Hand those beautiful dudes over to the cops, after they trusted me enough to confess their little indiscretion to me? C'mon, Wig!

"Well, maybe you should look them up and give the typewriter back to them. Or"—Wig was grinning now—"maybe you should just take an ax to the typewriter and clear up the whole business once and for all."

Then at last I got the point. Which is simply that as long as there's a need to choose between love and duty, there will be those who agonize that they cannot fully commit themselves to either. And their hand-wringing shall become, in the end, itself a kind of commitment. And they shall be called—among other things, such as sophists, equivocators, cavilers, fucken punks, and even, now and then, hip dudes—they shall sometimes be called writers.

And that made me feel a little better about the whole deal—if only because it reminded me what I was supposed to do with the damned typewriter.

HOW NOT TO MARRY A MILLIONAIRE: A GUIDE FOR THE MISFORTUNE HUNTER

Fran Lebowitz, the author of two very successful collections of essays, Metropolitan Life *and* Social Studies, *may be the most lauded humorist of the past decade. The New York Times has called her "a sort of Edwin Newman for the chic urban decay set . . . the satire is principled, the taste impeccable—there is character here as well as personality."*

I couldn't have said it better myself.

The marriage of a well-known Greek shipping heiress and an unemployed Russian Communist has given rise to the speculation that we may, in fact, be witnessing an incipient trend. It is not unlikely that working your way down may shortly become the romantic vogue among the truly rich—with interest ranging from the merely less fortunate to the genuinely poor. Should this become the case, our more affluent brethren will undoubtedly be in need of some practical advice and careful guidance. Thus I offer the following course of instruction:

I. WHERE POORER PEOPLE CONGREGATE

Meeting the poorer person is a problem in itself, for the more conventional avenues of acquaintance are closed to you. The poorer person did not prep with your brother, form a racehorse syndicate with your broker, or lose to you gracefully in Deauville. He does not share your aesthetic interest in pre-Columbian jewelry, your childhood passion for teasing the cook, or your knowledge of land values in Gstaad. Therefore, it is not probable that the poorer person is someone whom you are just going to run into by chance. He must be actively sought. In seeking the poorer person, one must be ever mindful of both his habits and his daily routine:

a. The very backbone of the mass-transit system *is* the poorer person, who when he must go somewhere will usually avail himself of the vivid camaraderie to be found on buses and subways. Should you choose this method, take special care that you do not give yourself away by an awkward and superfluous attempt to hail the E train or by referring to the bus driver as "the captain."

b. The poorer person performs most personal services for himself. Thus he can commonly be found in the acts of purchasing food, laundering clothing, shopping for hardware, picking up prescriptions, and returning empty bottles. These tasks can be accomplished at locations throughout the city and are all open to the public, which can, if you like, include yourself.

c. Generally speaking, the poorer person summers where he winters.

d. Unless he's an extremely poorer person (i.e., a welfare recipient) he will spend a substantial portion of each day or night at work. Work may occur in any number of places: stores, offices, restaurants, houses, airports, or the front seats of taxicabs. With the possible exception of the last, you yourself have easy and frequent access to all such locales—a circumstance that can often be used to advantage, as it affords you the opportunity of making that crucial first gesture.

II. BREAKING THE ICE WITH POORER PEOPLE

In approaching the poorer person, one can employ, of course, the same tactics that one might use in approaching someone on more equal footing with oneself. Charm, wit, tact, direct eye contact, simple human warmth, the feigning of interest in his deeper feelings—all of these may be beneficial in establishing rapport. Such strategies are, however, not without risk, for they are every one open to misinterpretation and most certainly cannot be counted upon for immediate results. Poorer people, being, alas, not only poorer but also people, are quirky; they too have their little moods, their sore spots, their prickly defenses. Therefore their responses to any of the above might well be erratic and not quite all that one has hoped. Do not lose heart, though, for it is here that your own position as a richer person can best be exploited and can, in fact, ensure you of almost instantaneous success in getting to know the poorer person more intimately.

Buy the poorer person an expensive present: a car; a house; a color television set; a dining room table. Something nice. The poorer person, without exception, loves all these things. Buy him one of them and he will definitely like you enough to at least chat.

III. WHAT NOT TO SAY TO POORER PEOPLE

It is at this juncture that the utmost care be exercised lest you lose your hard-won toehold. For it is in actual conversation with the poorer person that even the most attentive and conscientious student tends to falter.

Having been softened up with a lavish gift, the poorer person will indeed be in an expansive, even friendly, frame of mind. He is not, however, completely and irrevocably yours yet; it is still possible to raise his hackles and make as naught all of your previous efforts. A thoughtless remark, an inopportune question, an unsuitable reference—any of these may offend the poorer person to the point where you may totally alienate him. Below are some examples of the sort of thing one really must strive to avoid.

a. Is that your blue Daimler blocking the driveway?
b. . . . and in the end, of course, it's always the larger stockholder who is blamed.
c. I'll call you around noon. Will you be up?
d. Who do you think you are, anyway—Lucius Beebe?
e. Don't you believe it for a minute—these waiters make an absolute fortune.
f. Oh, a uniform. What a great idea.

IV. A SHORT GLOSSARY OF WORDS USED BY POORER PEOPLE

sale—An event common to the retail business, during the course of which merchandise is reduced in price. Not to be confused with *sail*, which is, at any rate, a good word not to say to poorer people.

meatloaf—A marvelously rough kind of pâté. Sometimes served hot.

overworked—An overwhelming feeling of fatigue; exhaustion; weariness. Similar to jet lag.

rent—A waste of money. It's so much cheaper to buy.

MARY WOLLSTONECRAFT SHELLEY

What can I say about a book like Instant Lives & More *when it has "advance comments" on the back from people like Goethe, Flaubert, and Virginia Woolf ("Leonard and I stayed up half the night. It took us hours to burn it.")*

Howard Moss was also the author of several volumes of poetry and criticism and edited and introduced The Nonsense Books of Edward Lear.

"**S**till asleep, Percy Bysshe?" she asked softly. The bedroom held the light from the hills; dawn was rising rapidly. Her candle dripped a bit of wax onto his magnificent hair, but the slow suspiration of his breath—musical and cadenced, as if, even asleep, he were composing a poem—made her heart stir. But she had work to do, work she could not let even *him* know of. For she was tampering with life itself, up in the attic. She had forbidden anyone to come near it, pretending that she was repairing her "dolls," and in a funny way—she laughed—she *was*.

Outside, it was cold. Stone-castle cold, she said to herself, taking the broad steps quickly, until she reached the top of the north tower. There he was, standing in the doorway, an extension cord wrapped around his left ankle. Behind him, the tubes bubbled and the electrodes spit their bluish sparks.

"What are you do . . . ?"

"Ughffph," the monster said.

She realized she'd made the head too small in relation to the body. But synthetic flesh wasn't as easy to get, these days, as people imagined. She'd had to do with bits and pieces. He looked a little like a protoplasmic patchwork quilt.

He tried to take her hand. She recoiled.

He grabbed a pad and pencil and wrote, "Oi . . . luff . . . ooo . . ."

How ghastly! And yet how miraculous! He had learned to read and write overnight! All by himself! And she had made him up out of . . . wholecloth.

"I don't think we'd be . . ."

"Unghk," he said, the faint blush of anger beginning to douse the patched-up "features" that passed for a "face."

"Would you like some cranberry juice?" she asked, desperate to amuse him while she secretly filled a hypodermic needle with 1,000 ccs. of phenobarbital, her favorite drug.

"Suture . . . self," he said. The remark left no narrow chink for a rejoinder. She tried.

"A walk? How about a walk?"

He smiled, ivory showing through the integuments she had stretched above the few bits of whalebone she had been able to purloin.

"Ye . . . ess . . . wor . . . war . . . auk."

Where could they go? she wondered. There was a pounding at the door. My God! Could it be Percy Bysshe? If he found out she'd been "experimenting" again, it would kill him.

"Just one moment, please," she said, trying to shove the monster back into the darkness of the attic.

"Get back into a recess . . . back! . . . back!" Mary whispered hoarsely.

The monster looked at her. "That's easier Sade than Donne . . ."

Even in this intolerable moment of panic, Mary could not resist a tiny rush of pride. Whatever she had created, it was far more literate than she had guessed . . .

ANDREW A. ROONEY

SATURDAYS WITH THE WHITE HOUSE STAFF

Instantly recognizable as the nasal, mildly exasperated commentator on television's "Sixty Minutes," Andy Rooney, who began his career as a correspondent for Stars and Stripes, *writes a column that appears three days a week in over 250 newspapers. He is the author of six books, including two best-selling collections of his newspaper work,* A Few Minutes with Andy Rooney *and* And More by Andy Rooney.

Every Saturday morning I make a list of Things to Do Today. I don't *do* them, I just make a list. My schedule always falls apart and I realize that what I need is the kind of support the President gets. Here's how Saturday would go for me if I had the White House staff home with me:

7:15–7:30—I am awakened by one of the kitchen staff bringing me fresh orange juice, toast, jam, and coffee.

7:30–7:45—The valet lays out my old khaki pants, a clean blue denim shirt, and my old work shoes. I dress.

7:45–8:00—The newspaper is on my desk, together with a brief summary of it prepared overnight by three editors.

8:00–8:15—My mail has been sorted with only the interesting letters left for me to read. Checks for bills have been written and stamps put on envelopes. All I have to do is sign them. The Secretary of the Treasury will make sure my checks don't bounce.

8:15–8:30—Staff maintenance men have left all the right tools by the kitchen sink, together with the right size washers. I repair the leaky faucet.

8:30–8:45—While I repaired the faucet, other staff members got the ladder out of the garage and leaned it against the roof on the side of the house. While two of them hold it so I won't fall, I clean out the gutters. They put the ladder away when I finish.

8:45–9:00—Manny, my own barber, is waiting when I get down from the roof and he gives me a quick trim.

9:00–9:15—Followed by four Secret Service operatives, I drive to the car wash, where they see to it that I go to the head of the line.

9:15–9:30—On returning from the car wash, I find the staff has made a fresh pot of coffee, which I enjoy with my wife, who thanks me for having done so many of the little jobs around the house that she'd asked me to do. Two insurance salesmen, a real estate woman, and a college classmate trying to raise money call during this time, but one of my secretaries tells them I'm too busy to speak with them.

Long before noon, with my White House staff, I've done everything on my list, and I can relax, read a book, take a nap or watch a ballgame on television.

I'm dreaming, of course. This is more the way my Saturdays *really* go:

6:00–7:30—I am awakened by a neighbor's barking dog. After lying there for half an hour, I get up, go down to the kitchen in my bare feet, and discover we're out of orange juice and filters for the coffeemaker.

7:30–8:30—I go back upstairs to get dressed, but all my clean socks are in the cellar. They're still wet because they weren't taken out of the washing machine and put in the dryer. I wait for them to dry.

8:30–9:30—Now that I have my shoes on, I go out to the driveway to get the paper. Either the paperboy has thrown it into the bushes again or he never delivered it. I drive to the news store and get into an argument about why the Raiders beat the Eagles.

9:30–10:30—The mail has come and I sit down in the kitchen to read it. The coffee was left on too high and is undrinkable. The mail is all bills and ads. I don't know how much I have in the bank, and I don't have any stamps. I don't feel like doing anything. I just sit there, staring.

10:30–11:30—I finally get up and go down to the cellar but can't find the right wrench for the faucet in the kitchen sink, and I don't have any washers anyway. I try to do it with pliers and string but finally give up.

11:30–12:30—I don't feel like digging the ladder out from behind the screens so I drive to the car wash, but there are twenty-three cars in front of me. Later, at the barbershop, Manny can't take me today.

I go home, get out of the car, and find the left front tire is soft. I go into the house and sit down to stare again as my wife comes in and complains that I never do anything around the house.

HENRY BEARD AND BRIAN McCONNACHIE

NATIONAL SCIENCE FAIR PROJECTS

Henry Beard and Brian McConnachie were both stalwarts for a time of National Lampoon *magazine. Beard, along with Doug Kenney and Rob Hoffman, founded the magazine in 1970. They also collaborated on some of the funniest material the magazine has ever printed.*

Ever since the first Stone Age man was left behind when everyone else went out on the hunt because he had a high voice and couldn't do fifty push-ups, and while they were gone, he invented the bow and arrow, and then when they came back, he gave them all horrible infected wounds (he had invented poison, too, probably just a smear of bison dung on the points), and they died after suffering for many days, ever since then science has been a very important part of our world. In fact, our whole world is built on science, and scientists are the most important people in it, and if you don't believe me, the next time you want to know how to limit ion diffraction in a solid-state optical collimator, go ask Tony Franks and his friends on the football team! What do they know?

Science in high school is very important, too. And this is why science fairs are important. If we spent all our time in Mr. Smethurst's drug store drinking cherry cokes and talking with those girls in the tight sweaters so tight you can see their thrusting breasts, why we wouldn't have rockets, and atom bombs, and jet planes, and hydrogen bombs, now would we? No, we certainly wouldn't.

They'll laugh at you. Oh, yes. They laughed at us, too. They called us names like "foureyes," and "fairy," and "wonk," and "geek," and "nurd." I remember. (It is very important for a scientist to have a good memory.) They made fun of our pencil holsters and our slide rules and our baby clothes that our parents made us wear instead of the clothes we wanted to wear. They were all down in the old wrestling room with Mary Vincenzo, and she had her shirt unbuttoned and her bra off, and they were looking right at her thrusting breasts, and we were upstairs in the chem lab looking right at guppies and mice.

Well, let them laugh. I remember one time I was walking back from the library with Phillip Snell, and Tony Franks and his hoody friends started pushing us, and they tripped Phil, and he just picked himself up and opened up his book bag and took out a petri dish with a culture in it that he had been working on for the Science Fair, and he threw it at Bill Dorn, and the next day Dorn's hair started falling out and his face looked like chipped beef, and three days later he died and they had to bury him in a vat of quicklime.

There's an important lesson in this. You think anybody likes spending 500 hours in a smelly basement classifying moths by the number of little brown spots on their anterior wings? No, we'd rather be at the multiplication dance, but Mary Vincenzo and her friends won't dance with us. They can tell. There's some way they can always tell. Well, so all right.

But look out, Tony Franks. One day when you're married to Mary Vincenzo and you have sixteen kids and you're working late at your stupid gas station to make ends meet, I'll come driving up in my car that can go around the world five times on a half a can of unsalted peanuts, and I'll say, "Remember me? I'm Brian Milley," in my high voice, and you'll recognize me, and then I'll take a long black tube out of the glove compartment and push a button, and then, Tony Franks, you'll spend the rest of your life sucking glucose out of a catheter in the wet end of a gym bag.

Brian Milley
Senior Coordinator
International Science Fair

FEAR IN MICE

BY RODNEY PURWISS
I did this project to find out if mice get scared the same way we do when someone bigger than us gives us "a hard time." I chose mice because they are much smaller than I am, and so it is very easy to scare them, and they don't scare me at all, because if they get "out of line" I just step on them with a track shoe.

I tried many ways of scaring my mice, and I found that all of them worked. These were a few of the ways I used: banging trash can lids together next to their tiny heads; singeing their fur with hot matchheads; throwing burnt-out lightbulbs at their cages; serving them into sofa cushions with my brother's badminton racket; putting them in an Osterizer and turning it to "Puree."

I tested all of these methods because I thought the mice might be "faking it." I discovered that they weren't because a lot of them died.

The next thing I did was to make a scientific test with many mice and I refined my ways of scaring them. These are the results:

BURNING	STICKING	STABBING	POKING
Made a bad smell	Good. Drives them nuts	Good. Squeals	Takes too long

CRUSHING WITH PLIERS	DROWNING	REMARKS
Made a big mess	Too quick	Mice died

Since mice cost money, I had to find a way to scare them without killing them. I finally decided on a method which requires a hammer. I hit the table hard very close to the mouse, and it runs around very fast. It is very scared. It tries to escape, but there is nowhere to go. Finally, it stops running, because it is exhausted, and just sits and cringes. I hate mice. They are so puny. Sometimes I accidentally hit the mice with the hammer—accidentally on purpose, ha ha.

I learned a lot from this project. It cost me fifteen dollars for the hammer and some knives and awls and things, and ninety dollars for all the mice. It was worth it. Now I am experimenting with pets from the local pound. They are bigger and harder to scare, but I have learned a lot about electricity and acid in my science classes this year, and I am putting my knowledge to good use.

WHERE ROCKS COME FROM

BY WINSTON BRESSALEW

Since I walk by myself with my head down a lot, I see a great many interesting things that the average person misses, and what I mostly see is rocks. There certainly are a lot of them around! This is how I became interested in rocks, and why I decided to do my Science Fair project on them.

Rocks are our friends! You can talk to them, and they are very polite, and they don't care what you look like or anything. They're swell. They make excellent pals.

I have only a few rocks here in my collection because I didn't want to take too many rocks so far away from home. Many of the rocks I especially thought were nice have pebbles. You shouldn't take a rock away from its pebbles.

There are many different kinds of rocks, and different sizes. There are no two alike, just like people, but unlike people there are no bad rocks. Rocks are born inside the earth. Most of them were born a long time ago and are very old and have quite a "story" to tell about what the earth was like before there were so many noisy people around pushing and shoving.

I think if people were more like rocks the world would be a better place. Rocks stay put, and don't fight with each other. The more time you spend with rocks the more you get to like them. They aren't very good at card games and stuff, but who cares? They don't mind if you sit on them. They are very quiet, but I think this is because things go too fast for them.

But people should be careful of rocks, too. Once someone was chasing me after school, and he tripped on a rock and fell and hit his head on another rock. It's funny, I'd walked over that place before and I never saw those rocks. Maybe they were just visiting. Anyway, this person got a bad concussion, and now he drools and blinks, and he pronounces words like he had a dish of cole slaw in his mouth.

DEVELOPMENT OF A PRACTICAL DEATH RAY

BY MARK GOTT

There were many reasons why I chose this project. I have always been interested in ultra-klystronic projection and electromorbidity effects in the transuranium elements, particularly in their possible utilization as demolecularizers in a theoretical photodestruction process.

This led me to experiment with instantaneous total-voltage release in dry cell batteries, and to the perfection of a workable flux conversion cycle based on the principle of phased electromagnetic pulses at the wavelength of hydrogen with resultant catastrophic elimination of hydrogen bonds.

I think that a death ray could come in very handy some day. We do not know what we may find in outer space, and I think just to be on the safe side, we ought to have a few tricks up our sleeve. Also, the communists are bad people and may want to do something to us one of these days; it would be nice if we could fry a couple of them to teach them to lay off and stop making fun of us and bumping into us in hallways just to impress their girlfriends.

I have tested my death ray. Here are some results:

Bugs—Total vaporization.
Mice—Total vaporization.
Dogs—Vaporization. Some ashy residue.
Birds—No traces found. Some smoke when hit.
Goldfish—Vaporization. Some slime on top of water.

I have not completed penetration and range tests yet, but here are a few tests which I have made:

Four Feet of Concrete—No noticeable reduction of power.
Test with Target Cat on Golf Course at Range of 500 Yards—No noticeable difference in effect achieved at point blank range.

These are all the tests I made. I did not test my death ray on Doug Ransome. I don't know where he is. Maybe he went off and joined the Army. Why would I do a thing like that? People say I didn't like him because he made me cry a lot. Maybe so, but just because you don't like someone doesn't mean you go and use your death ray on him.

HOMO SAPIEN REPRODUCTION

BY MINTON DE FOLLEY
I know this is a dirty subject, but sometimes it is necessary to undertake a dirty subject in the name of science. It is also a difficult subject, because it is hard to get any information about it, since everyone you ask thinks you're being "funny" or "dirty."

I used a number of scientific methods for my project, including investigation and observation. None of them worked very well, and I didn't find out very much. Basically, what seems to happen is, a man and a woman get together somewhere, like in a bed or outside or in the mop closet in the basement of the East Wing, just outside of the locker room, and something happens. I am not too sure what happens, but what I think happens is, a woman has a hole somewhere, maybe where men have belly buttons, and the man does number one into her hole. I know that is disgusting, but a good scientist doesn't judge Nature.

I don't think the woman likes to do this much, because when I have been able to observe this process, the woman is usually groaning and once one of them screamed. Also, when you ask women about it, they usually get angry, unlike men, who usually laugh at you.

I was able to make some observations. This is what I found:

	I	II	III
	Back seat of car, night	In the mop closet, day	Shrubs near field house, day
Noise:	Moans, like at dentist	Breathing hard. Doing exercises first necessary?	Breaking twigs, groans. Fighting?
Action:	Same as dancing, only closer and lying down	Couldn't see	Couldn't see
Results:	None observed	Girl left school to visit sick grandmother; never came back	None observed
Remarks:	Had to run, lost flashlight	Beat up	Beat up

I also did researches in available publications. This is what I learned:

Hot Wind in Havana: Action compared to waves, pounding surf. Must refer to #1.
Nugget: Women have big things in front. Is this where babies grow?
Roller Derby Girls: Women sometimes do this with other women. Why? Practice?

Finally, I attempted to verify my basic conclusions with other sources. This attempt was not successful.

Information
Sister Mary Louise: God will put you in a barbecue pit for forty thousand years.
Mr. Lenders (biology teacher): I'm retiring in two years. Do me a favor and go study sphagnum moss.

I still don't know how this process produces babies. Something is needed from a drug store, I think. Also, it is supposed to be more fun than collecting stamps. Someday I hope to find out more about this subject.

This subject cost me $14.50, including $2.00 for the flashlight. Also 300 Hail Marys, if that counts.

MICE IN ORBIT

BY NEVIL KRAUS

Four of my mice are gone. When I set up this exhibit, I had twelve mice. I don't think this is fair. I spent six months on this project. I did flight parabolas. I tested the mice for osteoporosis. I could have been holding the bats for the baseball team or counting the number of seed pods on the maple tree in our back yard or learning the multiplication tables up to 500 times 500 or something, but instead I was doing this project.

You can't leave anything out around here, that's what I learned from this project. Next time I do something for a science fair, I'm going to put a lot of electricity in it, and if anyone gloms any of my stuff, they're going to end up with a pair of baked potatoes on the ends of their arms.

GROWING HIGH NUTRIENT BACTERIAL CULTURES AND FEEDING THEM TO BUGS

BY ANN DITZENBERGER

For my project, I took many different kinds of protein-rich bacteria, including some new strains of cocci I bred, and mushed them up in Clark bars and fed them to a lot of different bugs.

The bugs here are just a few of the ones which I have been able to grow. At home in my cellar I also have a moth the size of a tennis racket, a seven-pound chigger, some silverfish larger than cocker spaniels, and a spider as big as a number seven frying pan, but they don't like coming out in the day-time.

Many people don't like bugs, but I think this is silly. Bugs help mankind in many ways, and they are very loyal. They make very good watch "dogs," and if someone tried to break into our house, my wasps would sting him silly before he got five feet, and my spider would wrap him up like a mummy and suck him dry.

ESTABLISHING COMMUNICATION WITH THE CENTER OF THE EARTH

BY JED HIBBS

I think it must be nice in the center of the earth. It is very dark and no one can see you there. I am sure there are people down there and they are nice people. I spent many hours in my basement with the light off to test what it is like, and it seemed fine. At first, I planned as my project to try to get down to the center of the earth and go there for a visit over summer vacation, but when I dug a hole, I could only get down about nine feet before it filled up with water, so I gave up this idea and decided instead to talk with the people in the center of the earth.

To accomplish this, I put a microphone in the hole I dug, and then I waited and listened. After about three or four months I was about to give up and that's when I heard something. It sounded very far off but I could make out some of the words. It was a bunch of middle-earth dwellers in trouble. They said, "Help me Rhonda help me something something my heart." And then it went dead. I couldn't get anything for two years and then it came back as mysteriously as it went away. They were louder this time. It was the same voices and they said that they wished they all could something something California girls. Then it went dead just like the first time. I think they want all our California girls and we're supposed to drop them down a volcano to them.

EXTORTIONAL UTILIZATION OF A THEORY OF ENTROPIC DEGRADATION

BY EDMUND WILTING

In the course of experiments aimed toward evolving a practical means of measuring the acceleration of the entropy quotient in subatomic particles which I conducted during my junior year, I discovered that

$$E \times 4/R^2 + (i \frac{V_1 + V_2 + Vn)}{Ft^8} - (3i \frac{Xn - V)}{\pi 2x^\circ} < Mhv \text{ and}$$

$$E^2 = \frac{m \times iC \div A.}{i - 1 \cdot F}$$

I also found that if I combined $.9k + x\frac{iF}{pr^\circ}$ with $V^9 +$

$\frac{(x^2 - x!)}{P} + F^\circ$ then $E = m - c^2$.

I figure I can maybe make myself about $10 \times \$100^4$ by not using it. It'll be interesting to see what happens.

DAVE BARRY

DAZE OF WINE
AND ROSES

If you read just about any newspaper, you probably know Dave Barry's work. Winner of the Pulitzer Prize for commentary, Barry has become one of the best known columnists in America. Aside from his two essay collections, Bad Habits *and* Dave Barry's Greatest Hits, *he is also the author of* Babies and Other Hazards of Sex, Stay Healthy Until You're Dead, *and* Dave Barry's Guide to Marriage and/or Sex.

I have never gotten into wine. I'm a beer man. What I like about beer is you basically just drink it, then you order another one. You don't sniff at it, or hold it up to the light and slosh it around, and above all you don't drone on and on about it, the way people do with wine. Your beer drinker tends to be a straightforward, decent, friendly, down-to-earth person who enjoys talking about the importance of relief pitching, whereas your serious wine fancier tends to be an insufferable snot.

I realize I am generalizing here, but, as is often the case when I generalize, I don't care.

Nevertheless, I decided recently to try to learn more about the wine community. Specifically, I engaged the services of a rental tuxedo and attended the Grand Finale of the First Annual French Wine Sommelier Contest in America, which was held at the famous Waldorf-Astoria hotel in New York. For the benefit of those of you with plastic slipcovers, I should explain that a "sommelier" is a wine steward, the dignified person who comes up to you at expensive restaurants, hands you the wine list, and says "Excellent choice, sir," when you point to French writing that, translated, says "Sales Tax Included."

Several hundred wine-oriented people were on hand for the sommelier competition. First we mingled and drank champagne, then we sat down to eat dinner and watch the competition. I found it immensely entertaining, especially after the champagne, because for one thing many of the speakers were actual French persons who spoke with comical accents, which I suspect they practiced in their hotel rooms ("Zees epeetomizes zee hrole av zee sommelier sroo-out eestory . . . ," etc.) Also we in the audience got to drink just gallons of wine. At least I did. My policy with wine is very similar to my policy with beer, which is just pretty much drink it and look around for more. The people at my table, on the other hand, leaned more toward the slosh-and-sniff approach, where you don't so much *drink* the wine as you frown and then make a thoughtful remark about it such as you might make about a job applicant ("I find it ambitious, but somewhat strident." Or: "It's lucid, yes, but almost Episcopalian in its predictability.") As it happened, I was sitting next to a French person named Mary, and I asked her if people in France carry on this way about wine. "No," she said, "they just drink it. They're more used to it."

There were twelve sommeliers from around the country in the contest; they got there by winning regional competitions, and earlier in the day they had taken a written exam with questions like: "Which of the following appellations belong to the Savoie region? (a) Crepy; (b) Seyssel; (c) Arbois; (d) Etoile; (e) Ripple." (I'm just kidding about the Ripple, of course. The Savoie region would not use Ripple as an insecticide.)

The first event of the evening competition was a blind tasting, where the sommeliers had to identify a mystery wine. We in the audience got to try it, too. It was a wine that I would describe as yellow in color, and everybody at my table agreed it was awful. "Much too woody," said one person. "Heavily oxidized," said another. "Bat urine," I offered. The others felt this was a tad harsh. I was the only one who finished my glass.

Next we got a nonmystery wine, red in color, with a French name, and I thought it was swell, gulped it right down, but one of the wine writers at my table got upset because it was a 1979, and the program said we were supposed to get a 1978. If you can imagine. So we got some 1978, and it was swell, too. "They're both credible," said the wine writer, "but there's a great difference in character." I was the only one who laughed, although I think Mary sort of wanted to.

The highlight of the evening was the Harmony of Wine and Food event, where the sommelier contestants were given a menu where the actual nature of the food was disguised via French words ("Crochets sur le Pont en Voiture," etc.), and they had to select a wine for each of the five courses. This is where a sommelier has to be really good, because if he is going to talk an actual paying customer into spending as much money on wine for one meal as it would cost to purchase a half-dozen state legislators for a year, he has to say something more than, "A lotta people like this here chardonnay."

Well, these sommeliers were good. They were *into* the Harmony of Wine and Food, and they expressed firm views. They would say things like: "I felt the (name of French wine) would have the richness to deal with the foie gras," or "My feeling about Roquefort is that . . ." I thought it was fabulous entertainment, and at least two people at my table asked how I came to be invited.

Anyway, as the Harmony event dragged on, a major issue developed concerning the salad. The salad was Lamb's-Lettuce with—you are going to be shocked when I tell you this—Walnut Vinaigrette. A lot of people in the audience felt that this was a major screw-up, or "gaffe," on the part of the contest organizers, because of course vinaigrette is just going to fight any wine you try to marry it with. "I strongly disagree with the salad dressing," is how one wine writer at my table put it, and I could tell she meant it.

So the contestants were all really battling the vinaigrette problem, and you could just feel a current of unrest in the room. Things finally came to a head, or "tete," when contestant Mark Hightower came right out and said that if the rules hadn't prevented him, he wouldn't have chosen any wine at all with the salad. "Ideally," he said, "I would have liked to have recommended an Evian mineral water." Well, the room just erupted in spontaneous applause, very similar to what you hear at Democratic Party dinners when somebody mentions the Poor.

Anyway, the winning sommelier, who gets a trip to Paris, was Joshua Wesson, who works at a restaurant named Huberts in New York. I knew he'd win, because he began his Harmony of Wine and Food presentation by saying: "Whenever I see oysters on a menu, I am reminded of a quote. . . ." Nobody's ever going to try buying a moderately priced wine from a man who is reminded of a quote by oysters.

It turns out, however, that Wesson is actually an OK guy who just happens to have a God-given ability to lay it on with a trowel and get along with the French. I talked to him briefly afterwards, and he didn't seem to take himself too seriously at all. I realize many people think I make things up, so let me assure you ahead of time that this is the actual, complete transcript of the interview:

ME: So. What do you think?

WESSON: I feel good. My arm felt good, my curve ball was popping. I felt I could help the ball team.

ME: What about the vinaigrette?

WESSON: It was definitely the turning point. One can look at vinaigrette from many angles. It's like electricity.

I swear that's what he said, and furthermore at the time it made a lot of sense.

BOB ELLIOTT AND RAY GOULDING

YOU AND YOUR SYMPTOMS

"By the time we discovered we were introverts, it was too late to do anything about it." So claim Bob Elliott and Ray Goulding, who began in radio in the late 1940s. Their commercials (remember Bert and Harry, the Piel brothers?) have won awards, they have had a hit Broadway show, have appeared in films and on television, and have played to standing-room-only crowds at Carnegie Hall. They've also written three books, and can still be heard on radio on "The Bob and Ray Public Radio Show."

BOB: More valuable health tips, as we present "You and Your Symptoms." Back with us to answer the questions you listeners send in is one of the nation's top medical authorities, Dr. L. L. Barnstall. I assume, sir, that the backlog of malpractice charges you were facing has been cleared away and that it's all right to call you "doctor" again.

BARNSTALL: Well, my professional status in this country is still pretty shaky. But I slipped ten bucks to the Katanga government in exile, and they issued me a license to do whatever I please with no questions asked.

BOB: Well, I'm sure that will instill our afflicted listeners' confidence, so let's take up this first letter from a woman in Minnesota. She writes: "I seem to be normal and healthy in every way, except for the fact that I have leaves growing out of my head in place of hair. I don't mind it too much in the spring and summer. But in autumn, I know I'll start to shed—and the job of raking up the house three or four times a day is a terrible nuisance. Can anything be done to alleviate my condition?"

BARNSTALL: Actually, this is more a problem for a tree surgeon than for whatever it is I happen to be. However, I would assume that the trouble starts when the frost causes the sap to drain out of the woman's head. So lighting smudge pots around her roots should prevent—

BOB: Excuse me, Doctor—but this woman is not entirely a tree. She just has leaves growing out of her head.

BARNSTALL: Oh, well, in that case, she probably isn't even susceptible to the chestnut blight and I'm sure there's no cause for alarm. The leaves should sprout again next spring and, with luck, her head may even blossom. What's next?

BOB: Well, I have one here—

BARNSTALL: Some people imagine the worst when they have the slightest symptom and go running to a doctor. They think doctors can work miracles.

BOB: Yes. Well, listening to your advice should cure them of that. Now I have a letter here from a man in Arizona. He writes: "I have often regretted the fact that I dropped out of medical school before I finished. Now I'm almost forty. Do you think I'm too old to go back and complete my studies?"

BARNSTALL: A man never becomes too old to prepare himself for the noble practice of medicine. The desire to become a doctor and alleviate the suffering of the afflicted knows no age limit. For who is to say when, in the course of our lives, the burning ambition to serve humanity may strike—and lead us to shout from the rooftops, "I shall—I must become a doctor"?

BOB: Gee, that was inspiring. Did one of your professors at medical school say that?

BARNSTALL: Maybe. I can't be sure. I dropped out before I finished.

BOB: I see. Well, then, suppose we move along to this next letter from a woman in Illinois. She writes: "Recently, I had a medical checkup in an effort to find out why I keep gaining weight. Afterward, my doctor told me that my hemoglobin was not overly dilapidory on the Richter scale—my cholesterol count was not endangering a cardiac malfunction—and that my metabolism rate merely indicated an abnormal caloric intake in proportion to my physical activity output in British thermal units. What do you think this means?"

BARNSTALL: I think it means she goes to a doctor who only speaks Spanish.

BOB: Okay. Well, that should relieve her mind. And I think we have time for just one more quickie here from a man in Utah. He writes: "Are you the same L. L. Barnstall who charged me for taking out my appendix in 1981? And if so, how do you explain the fact that recent X-rays showed I still have an appendix plus a sponge and a pair of scissors inside—but no digestive system?"

BARNSTALL: Well, any discussion with a layman concerning the human anatomy tends to—I mean, once in a while when you're in there rummaging around, you uhh—And besides, I think I just heard an ambulance siren, which probably means I'm urgently needed someplace. Good-bye.
        (*Hurried footsteps and door slam*)

BOB: And so the doctor takes his hurried leave on another errand of mercy. But be sure to join us next time when he'll be wandering back with more valuable health tips on "You and Your Symptoms."

ROY BLOUNT, JR.

TO LIVE IS
TO CHANGE

Roy Blount, Jr., a former newspaperman (Atlanta Journal) *and magazine editor* (Sports Illustrated), *has published essays, articles, fiction, and verse in* The Atlantic, The New Yorker, Vanity Fair, The New York Times, Life, Rolling Stone, *and other major publications. He is also the author of* Crackers, About Three Bricks Shy of a Load *(a title worthy of Lewis Grizzard), and* One Fell Soup.

At a great distance, William Barrett's memoir may look like one of those reactionary outbursts that so often occur when one's idealism has withered with age and one's knee has lost the power to jerk liberally.

After all, in the course of his text, the author manages to cancel the subscription of his youth to both Marxism and literary modernism. . . .

If his logic is correct, then we should be ready to die for anticommunism.

—Christopher Lehmann-Haupt

Shee-it. That ain't nothing. If *my* logic is correct—and you better not say it ain't and I hear about it, because me and Doyle Cathcart will come over there and beat the pure shit out of you. If my logic is correct, we should be ready to kill anybody that says anything smart-ass about General Westmoreland.

And you're listenin' to a man who used to get on Jean-Paul Sartre's ass for bein' a tool of the interests.

Shit yeah, I knew old Sartre. I remember the night before I

graduated the Sorbonne, he come over to my table in the Deux Magots and said he'd heard about me, did I want to help him write a leftist screed. "I doubt it'd *be* 'leftist,' " I snapped. I could reely snap in them days.

Cause I had been raised in a household where we strangled Spanish priests. That's right. Believed in assassinatin' anybody in America who'd ever been as high as cabinet-level. Saw Trotsky as an agent of the Big Railroads. Advocated the nationalization of mom-and-pop stores.

Yeah, I was born in Greenwich Village one night while my momma was trying to get the floor so she could demand less shilly-shallying at a Com'nist bomb-throwin' meetin'. They threw them round, cannonball-looking bombs with the fizzy fuses, like you used to see in the cartoons. My momma could throw one of them things twenty yards. Yeah. And my daddy, he knew Emma Goldman before Maureen Stapleton was *born*. In the summer they'd go to Provincetown and do modern art.

Nude theater. Hell, I was in my first nude theater when I was three months old. Crawled out on the stage while Edna St. Vincent Millay was just as nekkid as a jaybird bein' mounted by Eugene O'Neill in a cutaway swan suit, and my diaper slipped and the audience loved it. My folks, why they threw off their clothes so they could run out from the wings and grab me, but the audience made 'em leave me out there. Course O'Neill got the red-ass and stomped off. He wasn't no modernist, no more'n Sartre was a leftist.

By the time I was seventeen or so, I had composed an anti–Wall Street opera that lasted two and a half hours and had only one note in it, sung twice.

And acourse as the years rolled on I was right there at the barricades on everything, right on up through colored rights, Veetnam, Abstrac' Impressionism, and antinucular. I took all the right stands and said all the right things and wrote poems that I defy anybody to this *day* to explicate. I was writing stuff that made Ezra Pound's *Cantos* read like "Dan McGrew," and at the same time throwing sheep's blood at Nelson Rockefeller and doing more acid than Timothy Leary. I had my hair down to my ass and was sleeping with a gunrunning Guatemalan nun and an auto-parts sculptor from Chad and was writing long letters to *The Nation* in defense of Alger Hiss *because* he was guilty. My ex-wife was organizing hookers in Nuevo Laredo, my son was doing out-of-body travel in New Guinea, and my three daughters were down in Angola with a Cuban brigade.

And then one day I was listening to the weekly Forty-eight Hours of Rage broadcast on this underground Maoist radio station I pick up—I believe it was an Albanian reggae group singing a song against Adlai Stevenson—and eating some tofu I'd bought at a Whole Grain Weatherpeople rally and making some nonobjective silk-screens for the Debourgeoisization of Poland Committee, and somehow something jist, I don't know, I just sat down and said, "Fuck it."

You know. I mean, maybe Warren Beatty got a movie out of it, but where had it all gotten me? Where had it all gotten the world? And I turned on the TV and there was this preacher, Brother Luther Bodge, he was saying "Brother, if you have not found the light, you had better leave off your un-American ways. You had better move on down here to Sudge, Arkansas, where for the furtherance of this gospel I will sell you a lot in my Closer Walk Developments and soon as the Com'nist-inspired interest rates go down you can build yourself a nice house, and meanwhile you can vote against the forces of godless atheism and shout Hallelujah!"

And I did. And I started tawkin' like this. And shit, you know, it felt good. And me and Doyle Cathcart go out dynamitin' fish and puttin' up signs saying "Don't Nobody Better Think about Buildin' No Synagogues in This County" and readin' the Closer Walk Industries Simplified Holy Word ever' mornin' about four A.M. and then I come home to my lot here and think for about twelve or fifteen hours about how great a country this is, and about how much greater it's going to be after I go back up North for a couple of weeks and pitch scaldin' water on ever'body I used to know that ain't a Christian, which is *ever*'body I used to know and specially that nun. She was awful. She'd do *inny*thang.

I got to work on not saying *shit* so much. It feels so good sayin' it when you're a conservative. But I know it's a sin. And I got to stop bein' tempted to read old Ezra Pound. It's all right for the *content*, Brother Bodge says, the *content* is fine. There wasn't no foolin' Pound on social issues. But the *form* is Satan-inspired. You can tell that by comparin' it to Billy Graham's column in the paper.

Course Billy Graham ain't no Christian. No more'n this William Barrett memoir is truly reactionary. Course it's not something I'd buy anyway, being it ain't put out by Closer Walk. But it sounds to me like this William Barrett has got a ways to go yet before he's reely part of what's goin' on.

PATRICK F. McMANUS

JOURNAL OF
AN EXPEDITION

Patrick F. McManus, whose work often appears in Field and
Stream, *chronicles the lighter side of camping, hunting, and
fishing. In his comic sketches he ruminates on such characters
as Rancid Crabtree, who "bathed only on leap years," and a
boyhood friend named Retch Sweeney. McManus's books
include* They Shoot Canoes, Don't They?, A Fine and Pleasant
Misery, *and* Kid Camping from Aaiii! to Zip.

Rummaging through my files some time ago, I happened
across the journal I kept as leader of the expedition to
Tuttle Lake during the winter of '75. I was immediately struck
by the similarity the record of that momentous and heroic
struggle bore to the journals of earlier explorers of the North
American continent, and, lest it be lost to posterity, I immediately began editing the material for publication.

The other members of the expeditionary force consisted of
my next-door neighbor, Al Finley, and my lifelong friend,
Retch Sweeney. Neither man was particularly enthusiastic
when I first broached the idea of a mid-winter excursion to
Tuttle Lake.

"You must be crazy!" Finley said. "Why would we want to
do a stupid thing like that?"

"Well, certainly not for fame or fortune," I said. "We'd do
it for the simple reason that Tuttle Lake is there."

"Hunh?" Retch said. "Ain't it there in the summer?"

"Of course it's there in the summer," I told him irritably.

"What I mean is that it would be challenge for the sake of challenge."

Finley pointed out that there were two feet of snow on the ground.

"We'll use snowshoes," I told him. "We'll start early Saturday morning, snowshoe into Tuttle Lake, spend the night in my mountain tent, and snowshoe back out Sunday. It'll be a blast."

"Gee, I don't know," Finley said. "I've never been on snowshoes before. I better not go."

"That's a wise decision, Finley," Retch said. "A man your age shouldn't take any more chances than he has to."

"What kind of snowshoes should I buy?" Finley said.

Thus it was that the three of us found ourselves at trail's head, preparing for the assault on Tuttle Lake. The journal of the expedition begins at that point.

HISTORY OF THE TUTTLE LAKE EXPEDITION UNDER THE COMMAND OF PATRICK F. McMANUS

January 18, 1975—9:22 A.M. The weather being fair and pleasant, the men are in high spirits as they unload our provisions and baggage from the wagon for the trek into the mountains. The drivers of the wagon, a Mrs. Finley and a Mrs. Sweeney, offered to wager two of the men that they would "freeze off" various parts of their anatomy. I warned the men against gambling, particularly with wagon drivers, who are a singularly rough and untrustworthy lot. The throttle-skinners hurled a few parting jibes in our direction and drove away, leaving behind a billowing cloud of snow. This cloud apparently concealed from their view the man Retch Sweeney, who raced down the road after the departing wagon, shouting "Stop, Ethel, stop! I left the fifth of Old Thumbsucker under the front seat!" It was truly a heartrending spectacle.

9:45 A.M. I have assumed command of the expeditionary force. The men informed me that this is a false assumption, but I will not tolerate insubordination, particularly at such an early stage in the journey. I threatened both of them with suspension of rations from my hip flask. They immediately acquiesced to the old military principle that he who has remembered his hip flask gets to command.

11:00 A.M. The expedition has suffered an unexpected delay. I had directed two of the men to take turns carrying the Snappy-Up mountain tent, but it made them top-heavy and kept toppling them into the snow. We have now solved the difficulty by obtaining an old toboggan from a friendly native, who seemed delighted over the handful of trifles he requested for it. On future expeditions I must remember to bring more of those little green papers engraved with the portrait of President Jackson, for the natives seem fond of them.

All of our provisions and baggage are lashed to the toboggan, and I have directed the men to take turns pulling it. I myself remain burdened with the heavy weight of command. Rations from the hip flask cheered the men much and, for the time being, have defused their impulse to mutiny.

12:05 P.M. We have been on the trail for an hour. Our slow progress is a cause of some concern, since by now I had expected to be out of sight of our staging area. Part of the delay is due to Mr. Finley, who is voicing a complaint common to those who travel for the first time on snowshoes. He says he is experiencing shooting pains at the points where his legs hook on to the rest of him. To use his phrase, he feels like "the wishbone of a turkey on the day after Thanksgiving." I counseled him to keep tramping along and that eventually the pains would fade away. For the sake of his morale, I did not elaborate on my use of the term "eventually," by which I meant "in approximately three weeks."

1:10 P.M. We have stopped for lunch. Tempers are growing short. After kindling the propane camp stove, I had to settle a dispute between the men about who got to roast a wiener first. I narrowly was able to avert a brawl when Mr. Sweeney bumped a tree and dumped snow from a branch into Mr. Finley's Cup-a-Soup. Mr. Sweeney claims the mishap was unintentional, but his manner of bursting out in loud giggles gives me some cause for doubt. I have had to quick-draw the hip flask several times in order to preserve order.

I sent one of the men ahead to scout for a sign to Tuttle Lake. He returned shortly to the main party, very much excited, and reported a large number of fresh tracks. I went out with him to examine the tracks and to determine whether they were those of hostiles. Upon close study of the imprint of treads in the tracks, I concluded that a band of Sno-Putts had passed through earlier in the day. Upon our return to camp, the band of Sno-Putts appeared in the distance, and, sighting our party, came near and gunned their engines at us. After the exchange of a few friendly taunts, they went on their way.

For the last half-mile, Mr. Finley has been snowshoeing in a manner that suggests he is straddling an invisible barrel. We attempt to distract him from his discomfort with copious ridicule.

We are now about to begin the last leg of our journey—a two-mile ascent of Tuttle Mountain. The weather has turned raw and bitter.

5:05 P.M. After a lengthy and difficult climb, we have at last arrived at our destination—Tuttle Lake. During our ascent of the mountain, I found it prudent to order frequent rest stops, since I feared the excessive wheezing of the men might bring avalanches down upon us. Indeed, such was the extreme state of my own weariness that I at first did not grasp the obvious fact that we had arrived at Tuttle Lake. Mr. Finley was the first to make the discovery.

"This is Tuttle Lake," he gasped.

"I don't see no lake," Mr. Sweeney said.

"This is Tuttle Lake!" Mr. Finley shouted. "We make camp here!"

It took but a moment for me to perceive that Mr. Finley was correct in his assessment of the situation; the lake is frozen over and blanketed with a good three feet of snow. We are no doubt standing above its very surface. I am filled with wonderment, not only that we have finally triumphed in achieving the noble purpose of the expedition, but that Tuttle Lake should cling at an angle of forty-five degrees to the side of a mountain.

Snow is now falling with an intensity that beggars the imagination; either that, or we are caught in an avalanche. We are unable to see more than a yard before our faces. It is imperative that we get the Snappy-Up tent erected immediately.

7:15 P.M. The [obscenity deleted] Snappy-Up tent is not yet up. We are taking a rest break, whilst Mr. Sweeney, employing a cigarette lighter, attempts to thaw his handlebar mustache, which he fears might snap off if bumped. Mr. Finley went behind the tent to bury a snow anchor, whereupon he discovered a precipice. The drop was not great, or so we judged from the brief duration of his scream. The rest of the party were about to divide his share from the hip flask when they detected sounds of someone or something ascending the slope. We assumed it to be Mr. Finley, since few men and even fewer wild beasts possess the ability to curse in three languages. We celebrated his return with double rations from the hip flask.

9:30 P.M. We are now ensconced in our sleeping bags in the tent, after devouring a hearty stew, which I myself prepared. Darkness and the considerable violence of the snowstorm prevented me from reading the labels on the packages of dried food, which I emptied into the cooking pot. I then supplemented these basic victuals with a can of pork 'n' beans, several handfuls of spaghetti, four boiled eggs, six onions, half a head of cabbage, six wieners, a package of sliced salami, one wool mitten (recovered from the pot after dinner), and a sprig of parsley. The men were full of compliments about the tasty meal, although not until after I served dessert—each a cupful from the hip flask.

Strangely, I have been unable to find my package of pipe tobacco, which I had stashed in the provisions sack for safekeeping. It seems to have been replaced by a package of freeze-dried shrimp curry. Since smoking shrimp curry may be injurious to one's health, I have denied myself the pleasure of an after-dinner pipe. The disappearance of the tobacco is a matter of no little curiosity to me.

Upon preparing to enter his sleeping bag, which is of the style known as "mummy," Mr. Finley discovered that the snowshoeing had bowed his legs to such an exaggerated degree that he was unable to thrust them into the bag. The alternative of freezing to death or allowing Mr. Sweeney and me to straighten his legs was put to Mr. Finley. He pondered the alternative for some time and finally decided upon the latter course. I administered to him from the hip flask a portion commonly referred to as a "stiff belt," and, whilst Mr. Finley clamped his teeth on a rolled-up pair of spare socks, Mr. Sweeney and I bent his legs back into a rough approximation of their original attitude and inserted Mr. Finley into his bag, he now being capable only of drunken babbling. Now, to sleep.

January 19, 1975—1:30 A.M. Have just been startled awake by a ghastly growling seeming to originate from just outside the tent. After failing to frighten off the creature by the subterfuge of breathing rapidly, I regrouped my senses and immediately determined that the growling was gastronomical in nature and was emanating from the expeditionary force itself. I was suffering from a monumental case of indigestion, an affliction that comes upon me every time I succumb to eating parsley. My men, who seemingly possessed no greater immunity to that treacherous herb than I, moaned dreadfully in their sleep. In the knowledge that the growling is caused by something we've eaten rather than something we might be eaten by, I shall once again retreat into deep but fitful slumber.

6:15 A.M. The day dawned clear and cold. The men arose early, kindled the propane camp stove, and huddled around it for warmth. I have no notion of the temperature but have deduced from the fact that frost keeps forming on the flames that it is considerably below the freezing mark. The men complain bitterly over the loss to the cold of various parts of their anatomy, and I could not help but remind them of my advice pertaining to betting the wagon drivers against that possibility. They failed to express any gratitude, choosing instead to make threats on my life.

It is becoming increasingly clear to me that the hardships encountered on this expedition have taken a great toll on the men. They both say they have no appetite for breakfast and claim to have a strong taste of tobacco in their mouths, even though neither has been smoking. This sort of delusion is common among members of expeditions, and it is only with a great act of will that I force myself to the realization that the bits of pipe tobacco stuck in my teeth are only imaginary. When I try to encourage the men to down a few bites of frozen shrimp curry, they can only shudder and make strange gagging sounds that are scarcely audible over the chattering of their teeth. I realize now that time is of the essence, and that we must prepare for the return journey with the greatest expedience. The men realize this also, and without waiting for the command, rip the Snappy-Up tent from its icy moorings, wrap it around the baggage and leftover provisions, and heave the whole of it onto the toboggan.

I dispense to each man a generous ration from the hip flask. The retreat from Tuttle Lake begins.

7:35 A.M. We have descended the mountain much sooner than expected and, indeed, much faster than the main body of the party deemed either possible or agreeable. In the event that I fail to survive this expedition and so that the offending party may be suitably disciplined, I offer this account of the affair: Upon realizing that my hip flask was either empty or contained not more than a single shot which would not be wasted on him, Mr. Finley mutinied. He refused to take his turn at pulling the toboggan. He sat down in the snow alongside the craft and displayed a countenance that can only be described as pouting. After arguing with him briefly, Mr. Sweeney and I went off down the mountain without him. It was our mutual judgment that Mr. Finley would pursue and catch up with us, as soon as he came to his senses. We had progressed scarcely two hundred yards down from the campsite when we heard a fiendish shout ring out from above us. Upon turning, we could hardly believe what we saw, and it was a fraction of a second before we realized the full import of the mutinous madman's folly. He was perched atop the mound of baggage on the toboggan and hurtling down the slope toward us at a frightful speed. Before we could externalize the

oaths forming on our tongues, he had descended close enough
for us to make out quite clearly that he was grinning maniacally. "How do you steer one of these things?" he shouted
at us. Dispensing with any attempt at reply, the main party
broke into a spirited sprint that would have been considered
respectable for Olympic athletes even if it had not been exe-
cuted on snowshoes. All was for naught. The flying toboggan
caught us in mid-stride, flipped us in the air, and added us to
its already sizable load. We descended to the foot of the mountain in this unsightly fashion, clipping off saplings, blasting
through snowdrifts, and touching down only on the high
places. The ride, in retrospect, was quite exhilarating, but I
was unable to overcome my apprehension for what awaited
us at its termination. This apprehension turned out to be entirely justified. Indeed, some of the finer fragments of the
toboggan are still floating down out of the air like so much
confetti. Immediately upon regaining consciousness, Mr.
Sweeney and I took up clubs and pursued the unremorseful
villain across the icy wastes, but the spectacle of Mr. Finley
plunging frantically through the snow, even as he laughed
insanely, struck us as so pathetic that we were unable to
administer to him the punishment he so justly deserved.

12:30 P.M. The wagon drivers rendezvoused with us at the
appointed time, and we are now luxuriating in the warmth of
the wagon's heater. The mutineer Finley has been pardoned,
perhaps too soon, since he has taken to bragging monoto-
nously of his exploits on the expedition to Tuttle Lake.

"I wouldn't mind doing that again," he said. "How about
you fellows?"

"Perhaps," I replied, "but only for fame and fortune. I've
had enough of just-because-it's-there."

"I'll tell you one thing," Mr. Sweeney said to me. "The next
time I go on one of these winter expeditions, I'm going to get
me a hip flask just like yours. Where do you buy that two-
quart size, anyway?"

Before I entrust him with that information, I shall have to
assure myself he is fit for command.

THE KING
WHO HAD TO BE
QUEEN TOO

Jonathan Winters, a former Marine and disc jockey who has been acting weird on television since the 1950s, has also had prodigious careers in film and on the nightclub and concert stage. He has chronicled his decidedly offbeat observations in a best-seller called, appropriately enough, Winter's Tales: Stories and Observations for the Unusual.

Many, many years ago in tiny Nokando, high in the Himalayas near Tibet, lived a remarkable king and his subjects. Because almost a thousand years ago a terrible plague killed off all the women except one, all but one of his subjects were men. The only female was a very, very old withered and ugly woman, who, because she couldn't have children, was told to live in an abandoned cave outside the village.

King Nokando, in his middle age, was a handsome figure of a man. The tallest man in his kingdom, he was almost six feet. He could read and write, was exceptionally good in higher mathematics and fencing, a crack shot with a pistol or a rifle, a shoemaker, a very good chef who could make over fifty different dishes, and an excellent repairer of watches—but he was very lonely because he had no queen. Down through the years he would send for women through his many catalogs of *Ladies of the World.* But none of them arrived, either because they couldn't stand the freezing weather conditions and the

high altitude or because when they came within sight of Nokando they panicked and fled.

The king's male subjects lived on a strange diet of mountain
goat, mountain goat cheese, a kind of wild lettuce, strong soup
made from yak tail and, of course, large amounts of saltpeter
to keep their sexual desires in check. These men were relatively happy, since they always had lots of chores to do and
were busy with handicrafts they would sell to American tourists when they came once a year. But they too were concerned
about their king not having a consort. And so they held a big
assembly and decided that a small party should leave Nokando
in search of a queen.

In the meantime the king went through all his closets and
came across some marvelous women's robes, wigs and make-
up. Most of these had long ago belonged to the ugly old woman
who lived in the abandoned cave on the outskirts of the village.
Unbeknownst to his subjects, the king began to wear the wom-
en's clothes, right after breakfast and right after dinner at
night.

This behavior went on for years, certainly for as long as the
queen's search party was gone. The consort was ultimately
found in the province of Chow Mein: she was draped over a
crashed single-engine aircraft, hanging out of the cockpit. She
was barely alive. The men nursed her back to health; she was
beautiful, blue-eyed, blond, just twenty-seven, from Middle
America. She had been on her way around the world to write
a book when her plane went down.

The men told her they had a proposition. Since she was
without an airplane, her publishing house back in the States
had cut off her funds and the Pepsi Corporation, which had
sponsored her, didn't know of her whereabouts, she said she
would become the queen. "Go for it!" she said.

The party of men from Nokando set out with the lady. Oh,
wouldn't the king be happy at long last!

When the party arrived, the king married the blond pilot.
They had their honeymoon in Middle America and then returned to the kingdom of Nokando. The blond pilot lady was
now queen and all was well. Or so it seemed. It turned out

that just before the king's party of men and the blond aviatrix arrived in Nokando, the king visited a nuclear power plant in India because he wanted to improve his kingdom's lighting. When the king came home, he had his annual checkup. The Nokando doctors were shocked to find that the king had developed a little problem because of his visit to the power plant.

After a year or two of marriage the queen found out the king was firing blanks. So now the king of Nokando is in the cave on the edge of the village living with the old lady whose clothes he used to wear.

BIM BO SHOWS OFF BO-DACIOUS TA-TAS IN *BO LERO*

You might say that Texan Joe Bob Briggs pulls no punches. Anyone who would name one of his books A Guide to Western Civilization, *or* My Story *would have to be classified, at the very least, as strongly opinionated. Briggs, best known for his column on drive-in movies collected in* Joe Bob Goes to the Drive-in, *is also very funny.*

Sometimes you go to the drive-in and get so inspired you get those little goose bumps on the backside of your neck. Sometimes you go and get so inspired you get little goose bumps on the inside of your thigh. Sometimes you go and get chiggers on your feet. Sometimes you don't go. What I'm trying to say here is there's only a few times in life when you're watching the flick and in the middle of it something happens and, *bingo*, you see how a drive-in superstar is born. It happened with Mamie Van Doren in '58, the first year she wore a cashmere sweater four sizes too little. It happened with Peter Fonda in '69, when he did a shaggy-dog imitation and said, "I got to do my own thing in my own place and time." And, course, it happened to Jamie Lee Curtis in '78, the first year she got hosed down with watercolors and used for butcher-block practice.

This week is one of those magic moments. It happened. We knew it was possible, we knew she was coming along all these years, we knew it was only a matter of time before the bimbo ripped all her clothes off and ran around acting like a goose that's been wired up for brain research. We knew she could take a bath better than most actresses in the civilized non-Communist world. We knew she could toss her cookies on the big screen.

What we didn't know is she's also the Oral Roberts of the drive-in: She can raise male gazebos from the dead.

I'm talking Bo. Not Bobo. Not Bozo. Not Beauregard. The one and only Bo, the one that's spent half her life saying "Is it time to get nekkid again, John?" Bo Derek, Bimbo Bo. Bim Bo. A woman for the eighties.

Her new flick is *Bo Lero*, and I had to watch it four times before I could completely understand it. Like there's this one scene where she looks at George Kennedy and says, "I have to do something I've been dreaming about for years," and he gets an expression on his face like he just got his foot mashed in by a Caterpillar forklift, and then the flick goes into Super Slo-Mo, or Slo-Bo in this case, and she starts running through the grass and tossing her clothes all over creation and playing peek-a-boo with her buns and doing aerobicize with her garbonzas. But this is the kind of thing you have to wait for in the flick. They build up to it. It's maybe thirty, forty seconds into the movie before she starts jumping out of her jumpsuits.

Okay, here's the plot. Bo's a virgin and she can't find anybody that'll go to bed with her. Hey, we all know the problem. Bo, we're with you. So what does she do? She decides to go to the Sahara Desert. When she gets there, she starts wearing a chandelier on her head so she'll be attractive to the camel jockeys, but the only guy she can find is this wimp sheik who lays around smoking coconut juice out of a hippie pipe. He don't really want to go to bed with a Bim Bo wearing a chandelier either, so Bo has to try to get his attention, so she says, "I've come all this way to give you something you may not even want—my virginity."

The guy decides he'll check it out. So they go out in the desert and Bo watches a belly dancer shake her tummy like a piece of Jimmy Dean Pork Sausage and then Bo imitates her and we find out the gal's got muscles on every side. Then Bo asks the sheik how to do it, and the camel jockey pulls out a jar of honey and pours it all over her body and tries to lick it off, only he just ends up looking like a guy at the Kiwanis Convention that gets his head stuck in the fruit salad, and I'll tell you what, I don't know much about the sex habits of people of the Arab persuasion, but I think you can see right here why we can't get this Middle East business taken care of. Bo tells the turkey she wants to play around, and he pours *food* on her *stomach*. They don't even do that in Key West.

So Bo decides it's not happening in the Sahara, so she packs up her virginity and goes to Spain to try to force somebody to jump in the sack. Course, now it's twice as hard, cause everbody's heard she's into camels and honey. Anyhow, she goes to a bullfight and watches this guy fight a bull on a horse. The guy never gets down off his horse, and you'd probly think Bo could figure it out and say, hey, wait a minute, I think you need to get down on the ground and put a blanket in front of the bull or something like José Jimenez used to do, but they forget to do that and so Bo dresses up in another chandelier and goes to a goat dinner with the bullfighter and George Kennedy. I never did figure out why George Kennedy was following Bo around all the time, but I'd like to say right here this is Big George's greatest performance since *Chattanooga Choo Choo.*

Then Bo has to bribe this thirteen-year-old gypsy girl to take her to where the matador lives, but when they get there the guy's making the sign of the two-humped whale in a hot tub with a gypsy woman, and everybody is just a little p.o.ed. And then the thirteen-year-old nympho tells Bo the matador is *her* man too, and Bo says no way, José, but the little munchkin pops her top and says, "I am woman, ready, juicy too."

Then there's almost a bull attack and Bo puts Kleenex in her hair and gets high on Turkish farm products with another bimbo and then they go buy the matador's wine company and ride some horses on the beach and then the gypsy woman finds out Bo is hanging around and so she starts screaming, "You beech! You beech! You American beech!" until they bag her and toss her into the history books. Then, finally, the turkey agrees to go to bed with Bo, and so to make it sexy, Bo dresses up in a sheet and a spiked helmet and licks the guy's ear and says, "Will you do everything to me and show me everything I can do to you?"

And the guy says okay and pretty soon 27,000 violins start to play and the sound about busts out the windshield. You may think that's it. No more plot. He goes for the groceries and it's all over.

No way, José.

Next scene, the matador gets gored in the gazebos by a bull. Bo starts crying and says she wants to marry him anyhow. But the matador says no way he can do that, because there's not any Valvoline in the crankcase. So Bo runs into his room wearing some German overalls and points at him and says, "That *thing* is going to work, I guarantee you it is." And I don't know about you, but it was just so beautiful the way she said it, I get all choked up just remembering it now.

So Bo is gonna raise the dead gazebos. Course, there's a lot more plot, like this Scotsman guy that comes along and drops his skirt and jumps in bed with Bo's friend and says stuff like "Ay luvv yew, ah rilly dyuh." And then Bo figures out how to do it. First she makes like Lady Godiva, which you can understand if you're reading this in one of the non-Communist papers that didn't censor the *real* picture of Bo on horseback, and then the guy screams, "Make me whole again!" and then Bo shows up in the guy's bedroom and sticks her hair in the water fountain and shakes it on his stomach and throws a cape over his face and says, "Olé!" and then they do a tongue lock and, you maybe aren't gonna believe this, but they go to heaven. We're talking a movie Jerry Falwell should recommend to every member of his congregation. They get holy, and the guy gets the full use of his gazebos back, and we're talking the kind of experience that makes you want to go back to church and say, "No, Oral, make *me* whole again!"

We're talking Bo-dacious ta-tas. Bo does everthing. Twenty-eight breasts. Two snowcapped peaks. Slo-mo. Slow-Bo. Sex with food. Morocco Polio Weed. One guy in a dress. One wimp sheik. Bo kisses a horse. One thirteen-year-old nympho. Seven grocery-delivery scenes. Bo takes a bath. Bo takes a swim. Bo takes a sauna. Bo takes a ride on a horse. Bo takes a swan dive. Two belly dancers. Three bullfights by guys who won't get off their horses. Two motor vehicle chases. No kung fu. One quart blood. Drive-In Academy Award nominations for Bo, for George Kennedy, and for the bull. Four stars.

Joe Bob says check it out and see history made.

CYNTHIA HEIMEL

JEALOUSY: THE BIOLOGICAL IMPERATIVE

A former columnist for Playboy *and* The Village Voice, *Cynthia Heimel explores—with wit, sarcasm, and flashes of romanticism—the plight of the modern single woman. Her books include* Sex Tips for Girls *and* But Enough About You, *and she has also written a play for Off-Broadway called* A Girl's Guide to Chaos.

Worst thing in the world happened the other day. I was looking for a book and came across a secret cache of letters. Well, okay, *one* letter. The Kiwi was in England, thousands of miles away, and here was this letter I'd never seen before. Girlish handwriting. What to do?

I read the breezy little missive in a flash. Old girlfriend. Pining away for him. Lying in bed, eating salted nuts, drinking hibiscus tea, thinking about him.

Drinking hibiscus tea, thinking about him. The cow. The slut. The tramp. The tart. The troll.

I read the letter at approximately 1 A.M. By 2:30 it was clear I could never see him again—difficult since he lived with me, but not impossible. By 3:30 I realized I had no choice but to seek this woman out and ruin her life. By 5 A.M. they were both stone-cold dead, victims of a brutal bloodbath, and I was appearing at his funeral all in black, wearing an enigmatic smile behind my tasteful veil.

Ever have a fight transatlantically? Every well-chosen invective costs about $2.75. "If you're not home on the next flight you will not only never see me again but I will melt down your saxophones and dance on your guitars with hobnailed boots," I finally stated after $45 worth of strangled expletives and poisonous silences.

I was too enervated by my night of obsessive fury to round up the usual girlfriend network and spill the beans. My paranoia was baroque: I had, I figured, simply discovered the tip of the iceberg. Actually he was making it with every woman I had ever known or seen, maybe with men, maybe with dogs. When I tried to make breakfast I threw the toast across the room in a fit of frenzy. I took a Valium. Dissolved into tears. Finally called Cleo.

"I found this letter," I said.

"Come right over," she said.

A good girl, Cleo. She pointed out that there was a possibility, however slight, that I was overreacting.

"Give me a fucking break," I said. "How about the bit where she can't wait to feel his arms around her again?"

"*Again* is an extremely imprecise adverb," she advised. "And just remember, *she* wrote that letter, *he* didn't. She's obviously a silly bimbo and may well be harkening back to years ago. Believe me, this is a letter from a desperate hibiscus-tea drinker."

"She's going to be a lot more desperate after I've shoved a couple of knitting needles in her eyes."

Overreacting? *Moi?*

"Jesus Christ! *She* wrote the letter. *I* didn't. I can't control what she does." He was sitting in our living room, gray-skinned and shaking. Even the bags he had thrown into the doorway looked forlorn and frightened.

He denied everything.

I kept at him.

He kept denying.

At 6 A.M. he was crazed with jet lag and desperate for sleep.

"Just tell me the truth," I said. "It will be all right. I won't mind. I just want to know."

"Well, we did do it once. I'm really sorry, you were out of town for a month. It was lust, plain and simple. Sowing the wild seed. It meant nothing. It's a relief to tell you, really. I've felt so guilty."

Immediately I kicked him in the stomach. "Get out of this house right now. You scumbag. Don't come back or you're a dead man."

There are two, count 'em, morals to this story:

1. Don't leave incriminating letters lying around.
2. Don't look for trouble.

These two morals are intertwined. A person who leaves letters around the house is down on his hands and knees groveling for trouble. Being a firm believer in the there-are-no accidents school of life, I refuse to believe my lover accidentally left the particular bombshell where I might find it. I think things were going too smoothly. I think he wanted to stir things up, the passive-aggressive mouse.

But what kind of moronic impulse made me read it? I think things were going too smoothly. I think I wanted to stir things up—I'm a masochistic nit. We were colluding in this particular misery. It is of no use to anyone for me to know that he put a leg over this particular floozy. Except for torture value.

Here is a rule I have discovered too late: Do not feed paranoia. That means:

1. No sneaky reading of diaries.
2. No going through drawers.
3. No covert monitoring of answering machine messages.
4. No steaming open of suspect mail.

It is not only good manners to give one's lover his privacy, it is also in one's own self-interest. You know how your heart beats like a jackhammer in your chest when you do any of the above? It's the adrenaline pumping into your body because danger is lurking. Searching for infidelity is the most self-destructive practice in which one can indulge.

If you find something incriminating, you want to die. If you find nothing, you're totally flooded with self-revulsion for looking. Paranoia (read my lips) is nothing but self-punishment.

This is what I keep telling myself, over and over. It's not working.

He goes out for coffee, takes five minutes longer than expected, I'm suspicious. He comes home from band practice, takes a shower, I'm suspicious. He goes to work in the morning, I'm suspicious. He says he has a headache, I want him terminated.

"What can I do? I'm driving myself crazy," I said to Rita.

"You'll get over it in a couple of months," she said. "Sexual jealousy, contrary to what those nitwits in the sixties used to say—remember how they used to tell us we should all love each other and fuck everybody and not feel the teensiest bit possessive?—is a deep, primeval emotion. We all have it, sugar; it's built into our genes. It is a monster that lurks in our depths.

"Occasionally the monster surfaces, as when some imbecilic Kiwi leaves incriminating letters where paranoiac girls can find them. And when the monster is stirred, it takes a while for him to subside. But he'll go away again, providing there isn't another incident."

"If there is, the man is dogmeat."

"If there is, he is history. If you don't kill him, I will. Any man who obliquely informs his girlfriend regularly that he is fucking around is beneath contempt. Once is horrible. Twice is unforgivable."

"So you think I should forgive him?"

"What the hell, give it a shot."

"You know the worst part, Rita? Not the infidelity; the betrayal. As horrible as it is to envision his body intermingled with another's, while she pants and squeals and he presses his—"

"You're not at all well."

"As bad as all that is, it is worse knowing he lied to me, kept a secret from me."

"Enough already," she snapped. "This man is not just an extension of you. He has his own life, his own problems. Of course he didn't tell you outright! This is life, darlin', not the soap opera of your dreams."

"Ah, well."

"Let it go, hon. You gotta trust them, even when you're not sure they're trustworthy. Trust them or leave them. Nothing else will work. Trust me."

BILL BAROL

I STAYED UP
WITH JERRY

As a newsmagazine writer, Bill Barol stands out, with a distinctive, and occasionally hilarious, voice. A senior editor at Newsweek, *he is the author of the following, which originally appeared in that magazine.*

LAS VEGAS, Sept. 6, 5:50 P.M. PDT: The slogans of the Jerry Lewis Labor Day Telethon for Muscular Dystrophy are "Stay Up with Jerry and Watch the Stars Come Out" and "Miss a Little and You Miss a Lot." All right, then. This year I intend to sit through the telethon's entire 21½ hours, missing not one minute.

My plan, a kind of Vegas anthropology, is to consider the telethon solely as a show-business phenomenon. It's not my intention to make light of the cause, which is deadly serious, or the Muscular Dystrophy Association, which is beyond reproach. It's the show itself I'm interested in. Mix pathos and bathos, fold in the cloying clubbiness of old-time showbiz, add a few stars and a bunch of hacks and retreads, season with fatigue, and you have the kind of event that could only happen in Las Vegas.

It's ten minutes to air. The 25,000-square-foot Caesar's Palace Sports Pavilion is filling up; the last few guests, many of them in black tie, are being shown to their seats by white-uniformed midshipmen from the Merchant Marine Academy.

6 P.M.: Airtime. Jerry enters to a standing ovation. He introduces Casey Kasem and Julius LaRosa, and then Sammy

Davis, Jr., "who will always be here for whatever I need him to do, and tonight that's let me love him." Sammy: "This year, man, is gonna be the best. I love you." We're cooking now. Jerry brings out Ed McMahon, "the giant who has stood beside me, a marvelous force." Ed kisses Jerry. "You ready to go?" he asks. "Let's do it."

6:41 P.M.: "This gentleman is durable," Jerry says, "because he only does quality. And he only does quality because that's the way he thinks. And he's a super-talent. Mr. Paul Anka." Paul, who is looking more and more like Frank Sinatra as the years go by, sings a specialty version of "My Way": "*When Jerry phoned/I swear I groaned . . . /I'm working the Nugget/ But Jerry said/Alive or dead/So I'll do it his way . . .*" The "Applause" sign flashes on. Standing ovation. I feel like I've had a very fast, very vigorous massage.

7:15 P.M.: The first break. The national telethon will go off for fifteen minutes every hour and local stations will fill the time; in Las Vegas, a new audience is brought in.

7:51 P.M.: Jerry reintroduces "my main man, Sammy Davis, Jr." Sammy, dedicating his performance to a fellow performer stricken with MS: "I know some people think, it ain't gonna happen to the entertainers. It can't happen to them."

8:43 P.M.: Frank Sinatra, from Atlantic City, sings "What Now My Love" and "New York, New York." It's kind of sad to see. Nobody loves his old Frank Sinatra records more than I do, but tonight Sinatra is running on fumes and his mind is elsewhere—"I am about to be a brand new start of it in old New York," he sings. The Vegas crowd loves him anyway, giving him the biggest hand of the night when he's through.

9:30 P.M.: "Hiyo," Ed says.

10:03 P.M.: Sammy's back. He has changed from a tux into a short-waisted dark-gray suit. For those of you who like to keep track of this sort of thing, he is also wearing six big rings and something that looks like the astro-sign medallions the Swinging Czechoslovak Brothers used to wear on "Saturday Night Live."

10:30 P.M.: "Hiyo," Ed says. Two very nice young ladies have sneaked me in some milk and McDonald's Chocolaty

Chip cookies from the commissary, a strict violation of telethon rules. I stash them in my bag. The place is crawling with midshipmen.

10:45 P.M.: The Coasters, or three guys billing themselves as such. None of them, except maybe the one in the eleven-foot Afro toupee, looks old enough to be a Coaster. And none seems able to stay on key. This is depressing.

11:30 P.M.: Ed: "Hiyo." Jerry: "Our next guests have brought new dimensions to dance music as well as to rock," Jerry says, introducing Oingo Boingo. Oingo Boingo is terrible. The audience stares back at them in frank bafflement, wondering almost audibly why they couldn't have gotten Frank or Sammy or even the Coasters in their segment.

11:50 P.M: Jerry: "Here's a lady who really walks with style and who really sings with style, and we're very glad to have her walk and sing right here—Miss Susan Anton." "We're gonna do for you here in this midnight hour," Susan says dramatically, the band vamping behind her, *"the blues."* Well, sure. When I think of that great Afro-American art form, Susan Anton's the first person I think of.

12:30 A.M.: Jerry's back. He introduces Mr. T, and as the two chat Casey Kasem slips behind the cohost's podium. Problematic. Casey Kasem, as far as I know, has no signature saying comparable to Ed's "Hiyo." What's Casey Kasem going to do to get the crowd up at the start of the hour, count down the Top 40? I am beginning to understand the concept of lower back pain.

Now Mr. T climbs up into the audience. Jerry tells him to sit, because he's going to introduce "one of the brothers— Sammy Davis, Jr." Sammy is in midnight blue this trip. Jerry: "You got something for me? Lay it on me, man." Jerry and Sammy may be the only two people left in America who talk this way. It's "Begin the Beguine," then "Candy Man." When the songs end, Sammy and Mr. T meet at center stage. "If I can't sing like you," Mr. T says, "at least I can come out and shake the people's hand." "You are a classy man," Sammy tells him. "I mean that." Mr. T exits to a huge ovation, leaving me to try to figure out just what it is he does for a living. Whatever it is, he has apparently done it here tonight.

2:19 A.M.: The crew is setting up a bunch of multicolored sawhorses. I have this terrible fear there's a dog act coming up. Judging from the size of the sawhorses, though, which are a good three feet high, I'd say they'd have to be *big* dogs— Newfoundlands, say, or Black Labradors. Unlikely. As far as I know there are no performing Newfoundlands, even in Las Vegas.

2:24 A.M.: Worse than I thought. A bunch of clean-cut fresh-faced kids in multicolored satin warm-up jackets have started to gather around the multicolored barricades. Unless this is a high school drill team salute to "Les Misérables," which I doubt, I'd say they're some kind of professionally clean-cut fresh-faced singing and dancing troupe.

2:33 A.M.: The clean-cut fresh-faced kids are apparently something called The Young Americans, introduced by Jerry as "ambassadors of good will," which is never a good sign, and they are lip-syncing some sort of salute to the '50s. "Oh, yeah!" the Young Americans shout, and it's over. "Oh, *yeah!!*" Jerry shouts. "And they'll be back!"

2:46 A.M.: Jerry brings on Jerry Vale, describing him as "about the best at what he does," which praise sounds fainter every time I think of it, but never mind. You know what? *Jerry Vale has the most amazing hair.* It's the color of a platinum watch, and swept up high on one side like meringue. I cannot take my eyes off Jerry Vale's hair.

4:05 A.M.: "The young people are always there. You can always count on 'em."—Jerry.

5:29 A.M.: I think I lost my keys.

5:41 A.M.: Jerry thanks Fuji Photo Film in a zany Japanese dialect.

6:31 A.M.: Jerry: "Many people tell you the age of the romantic crooner is dead. Not as long as this man is in demand— Mr. Don Cherry!" I perk up for a second, thinking it's the jazz cornetist, although I can't imagine why Jerry would introduce him as a "romantic crooner." (Doesn't throw me, though. The advantage of being this tired is that you can laugh at cognitive dissonance. "Two contradictory ideas?" your weary mind says. "Hey, come on in, the water's fine!") But no. This Don Cherry is a lounge singer who belts out "You Always Hurt the One You Love."

8:58 A.M.: A tiny kid from "Star Search" sings "Over the Rainbow." I wish I could find something kind to say about this kid. I wish I could find my keys. Standing O #11.

9:24 A.M.: The people coming in now make me sick. I want to punch each and every one of them. I can tell, they think they're better than me just because they slept last night.

9:52 A.M.: Jerry introduces Bobby Berosini and his Orangutans. The orangutans grab Bobby's butt. He tries to slap them, but they slap him first. He shoots one with a toy gun and it falls down. Bobby's a little confused, apparently—"Something new for you here tonight," he says.

10:31 A.M.: Jerry brings out two jugglers. My mind is an utter, peaceful blank.

11:52 A.M.: The toteboard turns over to $22,301,614. "Yeah!" Jerry cries. "Go, and do! With the thing!"

11:53 A.M.: Casey mentions "La Bamba" and Jerry starts babbling in mock Spanish. Casey enunciates, as if he has learned each syllable phonetically: "Ha! Ha! Ha! Ha, ha, ha! To get serious for a moment . . ." A gasp goes up from the audience as Charo and her dancers enter. I don't believe I have ever seen anything like the outfit Charo is wearing. It is pink, with sequins and rainbow-colored ruffled sleeves. "The kick, the joy," Jerry intones, "of listening to the one and only, the incomparable Charo." Charo sings Madonna's "La Isla Bonita," and I'm too stunned by her sleeves to absorb the full import of this for a moment. When I regain my composure I realize that what I'm witnessing is a cross-cultural love thing, a true sharing, a caring and a giving, and I feel blessed. Then I black out, my head hitting the seat in front of me with a nasty *whack*.

12:31 P.M.: "How can you not go out cookin'," Jerry asks rhetorically, "when you present a guest like this next young lady—Miss Lola Falana!" To some sort of big-beat pseudo-gospel thing, Lola demands that "everybody put your hands together," and everybody does. In Vegas this phrase apparently carries the same persuasive power as a New Jersey cement contractor's suggestion that you might like to consider buying his product. Standing O #96.

1:55 P.M.: Time has no meaning. The tote goes over last year's total, to $34,103,874. Jerry weeps.

2:31 P.M.: Sammy Davis Fashion Update: a tux with loosened bow tie. "To be this big a cog in this machine," he says, "this Love Happening . . ." Now he's singing "What Kind of Fool Am I?" What a blockbuster. How I wish I could be here for it.

3:14 P.M.: Jerry sits alone at center stage. The toteboard reads $39,021,723. "It's been a long day," Jerry says quietly. "A good day. A good day for mankind. *My God*, what a good day for mankind." He's singing "You'll Never Walk Alone." The big, the final Standing Ovation, and he's gone. I study him as he walks off. Jerry Lewis looks much better than I do. As the fog swirls in around me I realize why this is: he hasn't spent the last 22 hours watching Jerry Lewis. I'm going to bed.

WILLIAM GEIST

TWINKIES AS FOOD

You may recognize William Geist from his witty reports on CBS's excellent "Sunday Morning" program with Charles Kuralt. He has been perhaps even more prominent as a columnist for the Chicago Tribune *and* The New York Times, *covering his favorite turf—the suburbs.*

You will remember from health class—if you weren't back there flipping ahead to the reproduction chapter—that there are five basic food groups: milk and milk products; meat and meat substitutes; vegetables and fruits; breads and cereals; and those foods developed in man's attempt to conquer outer space and develop better roofing materials.

The fifth group, referred to alternately as "fun," "snack," or "junk" foods, has emerged as the favorite of the American people. These foods are typically loaded with sugar, oil, and calories. They are of little nutritional value and the best of them rot your teeth.

I tend to like the salts and oils: Chee-tos, although the Agent Orange is difficult to get off your fingers; Pringles New Fangled Potato Chips, manufactured by Procter & Gamble, one of the leading manufacturers of washday detergents; and Doritos Nacho Cheese Tortilla Chips, because where else can your body get the nacho it needs?

My wife, on the other hand, is in the sweets camp. She craves double-stuffed Oreos, Hostess cupcakes, Twinkies, and even a nice dry brownie mix spooned right out of the box. She draws the line at eating those pink Sno-Balls, but does wear them on the toes of her bedroom slippers.

With sales of a billion annually, Twinkies is king of snack foods. Our own James Dewar of River Forest invented them fifty years ago. People don't even know that, which calls into question our entire educational system.

Twinkies are famous. Archie Bunker screams when Edith forgets to put them in his lunch box; there are Twinkie festivals and Twinkie-eating contests at colleges; a novel has just been written about a raid on a Twinkie factory; a Los Angeles man reportedly lived for seven years on a diet of Twinkies and Cutty Sark; and Suzanne Somers recently complained on television that she didn't like Monte Carlo because there weren't any Twinkies—even though she was accompanied there by Paul Anka.

Dewar sat in his living room in suburban Chicago on a recent day and spoke almost without emotion about The Creation. "We were selling Twinkie-shaped sponge cakes in 1930 for use as shortcake during the strawberry season," he said. "But the pans sat idle except for those six weeks. I had the idea to put in a cream filling—make that creamlike filling—and sell them year round. I got the name from a Twinkletoes Shoe billboard in St. Louis." It was also Mr. Dewar's idea to put the filling in the chocolate cupcakes, too. Incredible.

How long can the Royal Academy of Sciences, which has been announcing its Nobel Prizes this week, look the other way? They give awards to such people as James Cronin, the University of Chicago professor, for his work in "discovering violations of fundamental symmetry principles in the decay of neutral K-mesons." Fine. But we still can't get Egg Mc-Muffins after 11 A.M.

Of what possible value is all this research to our lives? What's going on in the scientific community? Wasn't it the science teacher in high school who tried to tell us that the earth is hurtling through space at sixty-six thousand miles per hour and spinning around one thousand miles per hour? If this were true, do you think your hair would stay combed five seconds? Why not give an award for something practical, something you could eat?

Dewar, known as "Mr. Twinkie" by those at the Continental Baking Company, is now retired. As he reflects on the historic moment in snack food history, he continually offers candy to visitors, never failing to take some himself. He suggests repairing to the kitchen for some ice cream.

At eighty-three years of age, Dewar looks like one of those 145-year-old Russian tribesmen who appear younger with each carton of yogurt—just as mentally and physically fit as could be. "I try to eat some Twinkies every day," he said. He had just eaten the last one in the house, as a matter of fact, and opened a refrigerator to see what else he had to offer. Inside were a dozen Cokes, apple strudel, a canister of fudge, a box of Fannie Maes, and nothing more. The freezer contained ice cream bars, some gourmet vanilla ice cream, a bag of jelly beans, and that was it. We had our way with both compartments.

He showed me photographs of his four children, fifteen grandchildren, and twelve great-grandchildren. "They all love Twinkies," he said. "Damned right. One of my boys played professional football, but I'm the hero of the family for inventing Twinkies."

He poured himself a cup of coffee, ladled in three teaspoonfuls of sugar, then set out some brownies and chocolate peanut butter bars. "Yes, Twinkies have been very, very good to me," he said, as I drifted off into insulin shock.

Not only does the inventor of Twinkies live out here, but the little yellow torpedoes are manufactured in nearby Schiller Park. Russ Wilke, assistant superintendent of the International Telephone & Telegraph, Continental Baking Company, Hostess Cake Division Plant, gave me a tour.

He has not lost his enthusiasm for snacks in all his years with the company and was the perfect guide for this Willy Wonka tour. At every turn he said, "Isn't this fascinating?" And it was: double waterfalls of chocolate cascading onto 368 Ho Hos each minute; gargantuan taps gushing forth creamed filling; eighty-two-foot-long ovens baking Suzy-Qs; cooling towers that spun around thousands of cupcakes; and thousand-pound vats of Twinkie mix.

Peering into a huge vat of six hundred pounds of chocolate

icing, I told Russ that my wife would just jump in if she were along. Without smiling, Russ replied, "You get used to it after a while."

Several years ago, a local columnist could write that Twinkies were the one thing he could think of that nobody had ever said anything bad about. Times have changed.

A so-called public interest science and nutrition researcher recently attacked Twinkies and other snack foods. He said they are bad. Clearly they aren't. They are good. Nearly one billion Twinkies will be consumed this year, and Mr. Dewar will thereby be responsible for bringing a greater sum of un-alloyed happiness to mankind than all the fundamental symmetry principle violations in China.

Nutritionists have said they are hazardous to your health and some claim that they even contribute to criminal behavior. Dr. Lendon Smith, the famous pediatrician, said in a telephone interview that Hostess should be taken to court for advertising Twinkies as "wholesome."

He conceded that people will probably go right on eating them because they evoke pleasant childhood memories, or because we have been brainwashed by advertising or have been taught to think of sweets as rewards or are addicted to sugar, or just because someone said we aren't supposed to eat them.

Smith contends that such junk foods contribute significantly to colds, coughs, allergies, hyperactivity, depression, and noncompliance with parents and teachers in the children he sees in his practice.

He expressed surprise at Mr. Dewar's health. Dewar laughed at that—laughed in the face of modern medical science!—and showed me a column written by Rex Reed saying that after Ann-Margret's nearly fatal fall in Lake Tahoe, she built herself up on a diet of Twinkies.

"Even Dr. Smith would have to admit," Mr. Dewar said with a wink, "they did a nice job."

STEPHANIE BRUSH

CAN YOU BE FRIENDS WITH YOUR BRAIN?

Dubbed "America's hottest young humorist," a phrase which makes me cringe slightly (it's kind of like being called "America's hottest young poet"), Stephanie Brush may nevertheless deserve that term, and all the other accolades she's received. Her first book, Men: an Owner's Manual, *was a best-seller, and her second,* Life: a Warning, *is even funnier, indicating a growth in talent that will be a joy to watch.*

What do human beings, station wagons, and plutonium all have in common?

Under the right conditions, they are all capable of something *very* special in life known as a "breakdown."

"Breakdowns" don't happen to just *anyone*, although many of us brag nearly every day that we are "about" to have one—but then we fail to follow through because some kind of last-minute "emergency" comes up. (Failing to Follow Through with a Breakdown is an accepted form of false advertising in the wacky world of interpersonal communication.)

Throughout the millennia those of us "disposed to breakdown" (known as the "breakdown-friendly") have developed a unique approach to our daily problems, known as "repression." The "repressed" approach has led to people making some *very* interesting decisions behind the wheels of cars at 75 mph; but it has also made sex (not *intrinsically* a very interesting activity) one of the most universally fascinating subjects on earth.

An incipient breakdown can attack you just as easily sleeping or waking. Sometimes you can sit up in bed in the morning feeling perfectly fine, and then discover that you have bitten the leg off your end table, or awakened half the neighbors screaming, "MITZI MUST DIE!"

STRANGER-THAN-TRUTH BEDFELLOWS

Perhaps you'd like to play "guest shrink" for a minute, and work on the significance of the following all-too-common anxiety dreams:

You are having dinner in a restaurant with Dr. Henry ("the maneuver") Heimlich. You get a large bit of steak lodged in your throat and begin gagging and choking violently. Dr. Heimlich says, "Waiter, check, please."

You are on your usual commute over the Liberty Bridge into Pittsburgh, only the bridge has been replaced by a thin strand of hemp rope, and all the commuters are dressed like Indiana Jones and crossing the rope bridge hand-over-hand. You are wearing bedroom slippers.

You are climbing Mount Lassen with your eleventh-grade physics teacher and Broadway producer David Merrick. And when you look at the mountain, you realize that it is actually a giant stack of high school senior themes on "The Most Unforgettable Person I Have Ever Met." Mr. Merrick tells you that he would like you to turn these documents into a musical comedy. By Wednesday.

You are being stood up in front of a firing squad, and everyone you have ever met is seated in bleachers as an audience. Your mother is selling popcorn.

All these dreams fill you with a sense of futility and inadequacy. In fact, this is an area where *professional therapy* can serve as "an anchor" in your life. Therapy can replace the nagging suspicion that you are inadequate with a sense of absolute certainty that you are.

A LIFE ON THE COUCH

It is ironic that no one ever *expects* to be in therapy for more than a few months. Therapy is sort of like going to a mechanic and saying you have a little rattle in the engine, and he says, "Fine, you can have the car next week." And you come back in a week and he has completely taken the car apart and all the pieces are lying on the floor of the garage.

"What good is my car in a million pieces?" you say to the mechanic, and he nods wisely and says, "Ah, but at least everything is out where you can *see it.*"

A lot of people fear the "power" of the therapist, who can seemingly say some kind of "magic word," and your mind just suddenly flips open, like one of those improved new toothpaste dispensers.

But actually, there is nothing intrinsically harmful about "free association."

Say your sister "Bette Black" has always been your *bête noire,* so you spend a lot of time dreaming about black sheep causing a big fight in the backseat of a '64 Impala. After about five years of analysis, your therapist might point out that sheep rarely ride in the backseat of Chevrolet autos, and that your association is probably "symbolic" of something. You might say something along the lines of "Son-of-a-gun." Or even "Aha."

This is why therapy is a good idea if you intend to stay in it for about seventy-eight years, and you have an endless capacity for saying things like "I think I'm getting close to something, but I don't know what it is."

You will never find out what "it" is, but you will get closer and closer to "it" as therapy progresses.

YOUR BRAIN, MADE SIMPLE

In general, professional therapists do not like it very much if you go around reading psychology textbooks and interpreting the information you read all by yourself. Therapists are afraid that this practice will put "ideas in your head," and they feel that your head is a very bad place for ideas ever to be.

But since you are the only landlord specifically empowered to administrate the space between your ears, perhaps you should have a better idea of the tenants living up there.

The brain actually consists of three jolly components: the id, the ego, and the "Superego."

The Superego is the part of the brain that polices your activities, telling you you shouldn't slice the arms off kittens and sass your parents and steal from vending machines. (The id says, "What do you think you've got thin wrists for? Steal from vending machines! Make sure you get a Chunky bar!" The ego usually gets caught in the crossfire during exchanges like this and has to sit around a lot waiting things out; usually getting hungry.)

It is the Superego which endows us with the power to "feel guilty" about things. It is ironic that the U.S. Constitution grants us the right to life, liberty, and the pursuit of Quite a Lot of Fun. And yet our Pilgrim forefathers eschewed gratuitous amounts of fun (especially when there were rows to be hoed and turkeys to be plucked).

We are in a quandary because the Principles of Country & Western Music demand that we pursue fun in its many dimensions, particularly pickin' and grinnin' and other activities.

And we feel understandably torn between Fun and Non-Fun.

It is our Superego that usually stands in the Doorway to Fun and says, "I'm sorry. I don't see your name on the list here . . ."

TRICKS OF THE BRAIN

Carl Jung went a little further in picking apart the brain in his ground-breaking work on "the human unconscious." Your "unconscious," you see, is always with you—the part of your brain you don't have access to and frequently don't want to know about. ("*That* brain! I've never seen it before in my life!") Think of it sort of as a movie version of your real life, only with much better dialogue. The showtimes only occur when you are asleep.

Members of primitive societies were able to transfer their "evil" unconscious thoughts into all sorts of inanimate or subhuman things, like trees, shrubbery, chickens, and hyenas. In modern society, only younger brothers fulfill this function. (As in *"Louis did it."*) If you were a Masai warrior, you could just say "A *chicken* did it," and not even get spanked. In cases like this, primitive people often had a better deal.

Freud believed greatly in the secret power of the unconscious. In his great book *Die Accidenten Existen Nicht*, he stated that there was no such thing as "common household accidents." "Little bitty accidents are always a message C.O.D. from the unconscious," Freud said, "so heads up and give a listen." When you "bite your tongue," are you not feeling remorse over some harsh words you spoke to a friend? When you "stumble" on the rug, are you not "tripping up" a desire to throttle a parent or child? When you hold a revolver against your temple and squeeze off six shots in rapid succession (as reported by a patient of Freud's who was rejected by the military because of ear trouble), are you not "blowing your brains out" in the hope of "dying immediately" and thus ending your misery?

UNDERSTANDING MODERN TERMS

Many of the findings of Freud and Jung have been debunked by "new-wave" mental-health professionals, who feel much more comfortable using terminology from a number of modern disciplines, such as nuclear physics, childrens' literature, cooking, and horticulture.

Probably the most important part of your modern personal-growth regimen is knowing whether or not you are "centered." And what kind of "center," you may ask, do you need?

It is helpful to think of it this way. There are two kinds of people: Avocado people and Twinkie people.

Twinkie people have a soft, cream-filled center. (Also, if you look closely, they have been getting smaller in recent years, which may be significant, and then again may not.)

Avocado people are smooth and rich on the outside and have a hard, firm inner core. An avocado is *centered*. Think of an

avocado without its center and all you have is guacamole.
How do you know if *you* have a "center"?

• Do you listen constantly to the opinions of other people?
Do you keep a notebook of the opinions of other people, just
in case you get asked your opinion and you know in advance
you aren't going to have one?
• Do you watch commercial endorsements by actors who play
doctors on TV (and when the actor says, "I'm not a doctor,
but an actor who plays a doctor on TV," do you say to yourself, "Well, what the hoo-ha? I'm going to buy that product
anyway. He sure *looks* like a doctor.")?
• Do you buy sex manuals authored by people whose book-
jacket photos clearly indicate they've never had sex in their
lives?

If any of this applies to you, do not despair.
Being "centered" is only a word so far, not an actual *thing*.
If it ever becomes a "thing," then you should worry.

GETTING NORMAL
Many people opt to leave therapy when they reach the age of
adulthood (usually around thirty-eight), citing such reasons as
"finding new resources of self-esteem," "learning to accept
my true identity," and "running completely out of money."
At this point, the therapist counsels the patient on whether
he or she is making the "right decision."

WELL, ARE YOU?
They say that one of the main points of therapy is to *get rid
of your rage*. But a lot of people don't realize that their rage
is much more interesting than they are.
If Frank Kafka had gone into therapy, for example, he would
have become an accordionist and played at weddings. If W. A.
Mozart had gone into therapy, he would have "symbolically
separated" from his father, Leopold. If Mad King Ludwig of

Bavaria had gone into therapy, he would have become Out-patient King Ludwig, and none of his castles would have been listed in *Europe on $20 a Day*.

Probably you can't help wondering what people did in the 5,000-odd years of human evolution before therapy was invented. What did people do when they had personality disorders, for example, in ancient Egypt?

Let's say there was a certain middle-class Joe in downtown Luxor who had a lot of problems: he was worshiping a particular cat who didn't return his affections, and then he lost his job down at the Papyrus Outlet, and then the River Nile flooded all over his new Prayer Carpets, and he was losing sleep imagining the pyramids were moving fifteen cubits west each day, and his mother was demanding and Tut-tutting him all the time, and he didn't know where to turn, because all the available oracles were booked up for the month. It wasn't as if there were some overeducated Egyptian with a goatee and a rented office who could charge him fifty pieces of gold an hour to free-associate. He had to figure out the answers *himself*.

Therapists cannot convincingly argue that their skills are the glue which is keeping Civilization as We Know It (in the absence of a truly effective United Nations) from falling apart at the seams.

At best, they can only argue that if everyone in therapy suddenly dropped out tomorrow—and everyone's extra $75-a-week suddenly went into mass circulation—then international trade would be unbalanced to such a degree that the New York Stock Exchange would have to close down for a week, giving the Soviet Union a chance to move in on every Western Alliance nation.

It is a thought that every one of us should conscientiously work to repress.

THE MARATHON RUN OF LONESOME ERNIE, THE ARKANSAS TRAVELLER

Jean Shepherd, whose career has spanned radio, TV, film, and theater, is perhaps best-known for his nostalgic and hilarious fictional reminiscences. He is the author of In God We Trust, All Others Pay Cash *(marvelously adapted for the screen as* A Christmas Story*),* Wanda Hickey's Night of Golden Memories, *and* A Fistful of Fig Newtons.

The troop train had been under way for about three hours when the saga of Ernie began. You don't use a word like "saga" lightly, if you have any sense, but what happened to me and Gasser and Ernie is sure as hell a saga. At least, certainly, what happened to Ernie.

Without warning, Company K, our little band of near-sighted, solder-burned Radar "experts," had been rousted out of the sack at three o'clock in the morning, two full hours before reveille, given a quick short-arm, issued new carbines and combat field equipment, and had been told to fall out into the company street when Sergeant Kowalski blew his goddamn whistle. Stunned, we milled about under the yellow light bulbs of our icy barracks. Some laughed hysterically; others wept silently. A few hunched over their footlockers, using stubby pencils to make last-minute finishing touches to their wills.

Me, I just slumped half-asleep on the bunk, full field pack on my back, tin hat squashing my head down to my shoulder blades, and waited for the worst.

"Well, gentlemen, as my father always said, it's wise to get a good early start on a trip. That way you avoid traffic and . . ."

"Zynzmeister, will you fuck the hell off!" Gasser yelled from his upper bunk where he was busily stuffing his legendary store of candy bars, especially Milky Ways and Powerhouses, into his gas mask.

"Gasser," Zynzmeister said in his cool way, "a good brisk spin in the open air will do wonders for you. Take you out of your rut. New sights, new scenes, new people, new . . ."

"Zynzmeister, will you please, just this once, blow it out your goddamn manure chute." Gasser went back to stuffing candy bars.

"Ah, it is always thus. Coarse language is eternally the last refuge of the barren and infertile mind." Zynzmeister, our resident George Bernard Shaw, hefted his barracks bags with casual elegance amid the barracks uproar.

Corporal Elkins, our company driver and disappointed ex-air cadet, peered at me from under his tin hat.

"I told you that staff sergeant I met at Headquarters Company was not bullshitting. All you guys laughed, god dammit. Now look who's laughing."

"Elkins, I do not recall laughing at any rumors around here recently," I answered, "except the one that Edwards came up with that Kowalski has only one ball."

"Yeah, lemme tell you, we're liable to all get our asses shot off."

Several heads encased in tin helmets raised up at this. Elkins had come out with what we all secretly were thinking.

"The first goddamn guys they go for are the poor fuckin' Radar slobs." Elkins spit nervously into a butt can.

"Ironically, that is true, Elkins. In spite of the fact that our SCR 585 rarely works and when it does continually gives us false and misleading information. For that reason, gentlemen,

I believe that Company K is merely a decoy to draw out enemy fire, much in the manner that a wooden duck decoy, while looking like a duck, is a clever device used to . . ."

Whistles blew in the frigid dark streets of the company, cutting off Zynzmeister in mid smart-ass crack. Clinking and clanking with damn near a hundred pounds of lethal equipment apiece, we jostled sullenly out the door of our barracks forever.

First Sergeant Kowalski, wearing his Signal Corps mackinaw, tin hat, gas mask, and, in spite of the pitch-dark night, his green air corps sunglasses, stalked back and forth restlessly in the company street.

"All right, you mens, get your asses in gear. Let's move it."

He carried, of course, his damn clipboard. He was trailed by Corporal Scroggins, a red-faced lout from Hazard, Kentucky, who had been imported from the Infantry in order to help Kowalski impose a little military discipline on our effete rabble of Signal Corps intelligentsia. Lieutenant Cherry, our company commander, sat quietly in his jeep in front of the Orderly Room. Off to the west, in the direction of the Motor Pool, the low angry rumble of an approaching truck convoy meant to each one of us only one thing. Scroggins blew his whistle. We lined up automatically in our usual four ragged lines: Gasser to my right, Edwards to my left, Zynzmeister behind me.

"At ease."

Kowalski himself sounded a bit subdued. We fell silent except for the faint clank and creak of equipment.

"You guys probably have noticed the fact you been issued new carbines. And also you been issued new field gear. And also it is three ayem, which is two hours before reveille. Now, many of you are probably askin' what is this all about? Am I correct?"

All around me in the blackness there was a restless rattle of carbines and a faint shuffling of feet. Kowalski was always a great one for the rhetorical question. He also had a notable talent for belaboring the obvious.

"Lieutenant Cherry will now give you the dope on what's gonna happen. You mens listen good. I don't wanna have no dumbhead comin' up to me after this formation and askin' no stupid questions. I got enough on my hands now without answerin' no stupid questions."

Kowalski paused for a long significant moment in order to let his broadside sink in.

"Atten-HUT!"

All around me were the familiar sounds of the company coming to what it liked to call "Attention," which meant a slight shifting of the feet, a look of fierce concentration in the eye, and a faint pulling in of the stomach muscles.

"At ease."

We relaxed. "At ease," in the Army does not mean what it means in civilian life. It means primarily "Shut up and listen." Lieutenant Cherry casually eased himself out of the company jeep and languidly took his position in front of Kowalski, who stared stonily ahead of him.

"Gen'lmen." Lieutenant Cherry's voice had soft, rich southern overtones. His steel-rimmed glasses picked up a glint of light from the mess hall.

"Company K is about to embark on a great adventure."

His voice trailed off as he stared upward into the night sky. The sinister rumble of the approaching convoy grew louder and louder. The lieutenant calmly looked up and down the ranks of Company K. A hand rested on each hip, his legs spread wide out. I felt the faint whistle of the ice-cold winter wind under the brim of my helmet.

"We are shipping."

Gasser, in the gloom next to me, quietly cleared his throat. The lieutenant went on:

"This is not a maneuver, nor is it an exercise. We have received orders to be transported at oh-four-hundred as of this date to an undisclosed point, from which point we will be further transported by aircraft to an undisclosed destination. I have no information other than the following details."

Kowalski handed the lieutenant his clipboard. Edwards, to my left, muttered "balls." The lieutenant glanced at a fluttering sheet of paper on the clipboard.

"In a few minutes we will move out by truck convoy to the train siding at Area Two."

Area Two was about fifteen miles away in a remote, mysterious part of the camp that was enclosed by high wire fences. No one ever came back from Area Two. He continued:

"At that point we will assign each of you a shipment number. At my command you will file into the troop train which will be waiting for us. We will do this with a minimum of lost motion. As of this moment, Company K is on full alert, which means you will not move an inch out of the company area and will remain on this spot until the convoy arrives."

Somewhere, I heard the muttered voice of Elkins: "Oh, God Almighty, I knew it!"

"This troop train will be sealed, since we are part of a highly secure troop movement. There will be no intermingling with other units, which will be assigned to their own cars on the train. On the train itself, you will be allowed to choose your seats, but after that you will remain in that seat as much as possible. A few of you may be assigned work details while on the train. If you are, I will notify you. Sergeant Kowalski has notified me that all your GI insurance forms are in order, that your medical records are up to date, and that for once you all successfully passed this morning's short-arm. I am pleased. I add my personal 'good luck' to the entire company."

He handed his clipboard back to the sergeant just as the first rumbling troop carrier lumbered into the company street.

From behind me in the darkness I heard the voice of an unknown terror-stricken Radar man mutter: "Christ, for one'st I wish I had the clap."

There was an answering ripple of tense tittering. Company K at long last stood silent and ready for come-what-may.

BRRRRROOOOOMMM . . . BRRRROOOOOOOMMM . . . BRRRRRRROOOOOOOM.

A pair of baleful, glaring headlights rounded the corner at the end of the company street, where the road ran between the Day Room and our fragrant mess hall, scene of so many painful events and unforgettable meals. In the blackness, the first truck in the convoy lurched to a halt, its engine burbling angrily. Another roared around the corner and formed up behind the first. One after another they came. Whistles blew. Scroggins and Kowalski yelled orders. Squad after squad peeled off at a dog-trot and piled into the black, menacing vehicles. The usual Company K give-and-take of Quit shovin', you son of a bitch, Up yours, TS Mack, and Blow it out your ass was, in this grim predawn moment, notably absent.

My squad—Gasser, Zynzmeister, Elkins, and the rest—trotted woodenly to the rear of the third truck in line. We huddled side by side in the darkness on the hard wooden seats. I peered out the rear of the truck as the troop carrier slowly began to move with that malevolent suppressed thunder of all military trucks, with their special mufflers and oversized transmissions. The smell of GI's on the move seeped through the cold black air; sweat, gun grease, cartridge webbing, gas mask rubber, and, of course, fear. We rumbled past Barracks 903-T, now standing silent and empty, its yellow light bulbs gleaming sullenly on lonely butt cans. On our left, the doors of the silent Supply Room yawned blackly. Even the Supply Room hangers-on had been loaded into trucks like the rest of us.

"And so our happy band of warriors takes leave of their old familiar haunts and . . ."

"Will you stuff a sock in it, Zynzmeister!"

Someone lit a cigarette. Gasser unpeeled a Baby Ruth bar.

"Y'know, I never thought I'd miss this dump, but already I . . ."

Elkins interrupted me instinctively, as he had for the past two years:

"Boy, when I think that you guys all laughed at me."

"Gentlemen, let us all satisfy Elkins for once by according him a round of laughter. All together now, men. Let's hear those guffaws."

The squad guffawed hollowly in unison in the rumbling, noisy darkness.

"Okay, you guys, you just wait."

Someone hummed tunelessly Elkins' beloved Air Force song:

"Off we go, into the wild blue . . ."

"Screw you."

"Clever, Elkins. The perfect riposte." Zynzmeister needled Elkins. The two were great friends, and their friendship consisted of Zynzmeister using Elkins the way a basketball uses a bounding board.

The convoy droned on through what remained of the night, past the rifle range, the Motor Pool, the BOQ, and the Number One Service Club. The squad now rode in silence. It was be9ginning to sink in that we really were leaving and that we'd probably never see this place again.

Finally, the convoy crept through the gates of the high tough chicken-wire fence that surrounded Area Two. A red and white sign gleamed in the headlights:

RESTRICTED AREA. NO PERSONNEL BEYOND

THIS POINT WITHOUT SPECIAL PROVOST MARSHAL CLEARANCE.

Two MP's stood with rifles in the port position as Company K growled by to its uncertain fate. We passed a few dark buildings and a couple of dimly lighted offices. The convoy finally lurched to a halt. Whistles blew, and we poured out onto the gravel road.

For the first time we saw It—a long black string of railroad cars that stretched off into the night fore and aft. A dozen floodlights lit up the scene like a stage set. A grasshopper would have had trouble getting out of the area without attracting seven MP's. Any thoughts of sneaking away into the night disappeared instantly. Under the glare, our uniforms looked unnaturally green and the scratches on our helmets showed up like scars on a fish belly. Our faces, normally tanned, looked milky and tinged with bluish beards. I glanced at Edwards. He looked about twelve under his pile of field equipment. Even Zynzmeister was silent.

We assembled into our usual company formation. Being Radar, ours was a small company, little more than a swollen platoon. Lined up next to the train sidings under the floods, we looked curiously small and sad.

Lieutenant Cherry, flanked by two alien officers, a major

and a captain, both bearing large yellow envelopes and thick folders, gave us our instructions in his molasses-and-grits voice:

"At ease, men. This is Major Willoughby, our troop train commander."

Major Willoughby, a sagging billowing man with the face of a pregnant basset, smiled briefly from amid his jowls. His piss-cutter hat, square on his head, was pulled down low so that his two pendulous ears swung out to either side like fleshy barn doors. On his rumpled sleeve was sewn, carelessly, the patch of the Transportation Corps. It was a patch few of us had ever seen. He had the look of an old-time railroad man whose life revolved around timetables, green eye shields, cigar butts, and traveling salesmen.

"This is Captain Carruthers, the Deputy Commander." Carruthers was thin, dapper, and had a worried look on his pinched white face.

"Captain Carruthers is responsible for the safe arrival of every man on this train. He has assigned each one of you an individual number and he will personally check each of you off and on at the embarkation point and the point of debarkation. I cannot stress enough the importance of remaining in your seats as much as possible while en route."

Someone coughed behind me in that phony way you cough when the medical officer is giving you a short-arm. I knew what he was thinking. Apparently, so did Cherry.

"There is a latrine at the end of every car. You will ask your squad leader's permission to use it, in order to avoid crowding and confusion. We will leave our car only for meals, and then in the order of your transit numbers. At my command we will file into the car by squads. Each of you will give your name, rank, and serial number and will be handed a card bearing your transit number. Do not lose this. You will then immediately board the train and select a seat. You will do this with a minimum of bitching and seat changing."

He paused. From way off in the distance came a blast of the locomotive's horn: short, impatient. Lieutenant Cherry glanced at his watch. It was precisely 0400. Kowalski, at Lieutenant Cherry's nod, bellowed:

"Atten-HUT! First Squad in column, right face. Move out."

First Squad, ahead of us, clanked forward in single file toward the open door of our car. For the first time I noticed that the car appeared to be painted a dull green color and on its side was its name: *The Georgia Peach*. My squad moved forward. Up ahead of me, on either side of the metal train steps, were the major and the captain, checking off names and handing out cards. One by one, Company K disappeared into *The Georgia Peach*. I half-expected someone to scream at the last instant:

"NO, NO! I CAN'T GO. I FORGOT MY CLOTHES AT THE DRY CLEANERS!" or to unsling his carbine and scream:

"YOU'LL NEVER TAKE ME ALIVE. COME AND GET ME, YOU RATFINK ARMY BASTARDS!"

But no. Like sheep following their leader, one by one, we silently went over the cliff. Major Willoughby stared into my face with moist brown pouch-lined eyes. I barked out my name, rank, and serial number. For a long moment he gazed at his clipboard. I had one wild moment of hope.

He can't find my name! My name ain't there! Whoopee!

"Ah yes, here we are." Major Willoughby's voice sounded like the rumble of steam in a friendly old overheated boiler. When you're around locomotives long enough you begin to sound like one. He shuffled through a stack of cards and finally handed me mine. It was small, blue, and to the point. My name, rank, and serial number were typed at the top above the decisive black numbers. They stood out bold and aggressive: 316. The major rumbled:

"Have a good trip, son."

I mounted the step and entered the car. Already it seemed that half the seats were taken. I moved down the aisle and found an empty. I unhooked my heavy field pack and hung it on the rack made of piping which was above the seat, hanging my helmet and carbine next to the pack. I took off my gas mask and flung it up on the rack. Finally, at least a half-ton lighter, I slipped into the seat next to the window. It was hard, and seemed to be covered in material made from old hairbrushes, scratchy and unyielding. Amid the hullabaloo as the rest of Company K found its seats all around me, I examined the car.

Lit by dim overhead lights, it had been stripped of anything resembling civilian comfort. The windows were sealed with black, tightly stretched canvas. Ahead of me, Zynzmeister addressed the throng:

"You will notice the deluxe accommodations which are a featured part of our holiday tours. Our guide will describe the scenic wonders as we roll . . ."

Gasser, who had sat down next to me, laughed his irritating braying laugh.

"Hey, Zynzmeister," he yelled, "hey, Zynzmeister."

Zynzmeister was busily stowing his gear above his seat. With casual elegance he turned.

"Already I am being paged. Ah, I am pleased that you have decided to come with us, Gasser, on our mystery tour."

"What's your number, Zynzmeister?" Gasser yelled from beside me.

"Ah . . . I believe I have been designated number three eighty-four." Zynzmeister waved his card in the air.

"Boy, don't tell me," Gasser yelled above the din, "they gave you just an ordinary number, like the rest of us slobs?"

Zynzmeister smiled benignly. "Of course not, Gasser. Three eighty-four is an old Zynzmeister family number. It is the street number of our family mansion on Chicago's posh North Lake Shore Drive. It is also, coincidentally, the berth number that the Zynzmeisters were issued on the *Mayflower*, so naturally . . ."

He was drowned out by a roar of Company K-style badinage, which ran heavily to Bullshit, What a lot of crap, and Some guys are so full of it that their eyes are turning brown. Zynzmeister waved to his fans and eased himself into his seat.

After that, things happened very quickly. Lieutenant Cherry strode up the center aisle with his clipboard, glancing at each seat as he went. His face was expressionless, almost as though nothing unusual was happening, that in fact he spent his life embarking into the unknown. Kowalski struggled with Goldberg's bloated, overweight barracks bags. Goldberg, in spite of the fact that we all carried, theoretically, the same equipment, had managed as he always did to make his barracks bag fatter and bulkier than anyone else's. He was the only one in the company who had gained weight in our mess hall. He had found a home in the Army.

"What the hell you got in here, Goldberg? It feels like you got eight bowling balls in here."

Gasser leaned over and whispered in my ear, "I'll bet he's got his wife in that B bag."

Goldberg, a newlywed, and one of the few Company K members who was married, had managed to take his wife Sylvia wherever we were shipped. It was rumored that she even managed to go over the Obstacle Course with him one day.

There was a shudder and a couple of heavy thumps and the troop train began to move. We heard the sound of distant train whistles as we picked up speed. I have since seen countless movies on late TV that purport to show a troop train. None were remotely like the real thing; no guitars, no crap games, no scared GIs writing a last letter to their loved ones, no exchanging of photos of "sweethearts" and wives. Our car rolled along with just a minor mutter of restrained conversation. Gasser dozed off next to me, and I read a Raymond Chandler which I had picked up at the PX. Edwards leaned over the seat in front of me and said:

"I hear we're being shipped to Georgia. Fort Benning."

"Come on. They don't give you new carbines to go to Fort Benning. And whoever heard of a Radar company going there anyway?"

Edwards shook his head. "Well, that's what I heard."

"Yeah?" I continued. "Well, keep me informed on the next one you hear."

Kowalski stalked up and down the car, checking equipment and answering questions here and there. Occasionally someone got up and asked permission of the corporal to go to the toilet. We squeaked and rumbled on. Not a sliver of light from the outside world, where it now must be broad daylight, entered *The Georgia Peach*. We could just as well be taking a train through hell, which some of us suspected we were. I stuck the copy of *Farewell, My Lovely* into the crack between the seat and the wall next to me. Gasser's head lolled against my shoulder. I opened up my shirt to let in a little air. It was hot as hell in *The Georgia Peach*.

I had just begun to drop off into the great dark sea of sleep when someone shook me roughly. I glanced up in a daze, at first not quite remembering where I was. I was confused for a moment because the barracks seemed to be swaying. It was Lieutenant Cherry smiling down at me. I sat up to attention instantly, since in the past the lieutenant had rarely addressed me personally, and then never by name, calling me "Soldier" and "You there." Gasser was also sitting bolt upright next to me. The lieutenant addressed us both.

"You two guys have drawn KP. Every company on the train provides three men for KP. You guys and Ernie drew the tickets. You'll be on duty twenty-four hours—four on, four off—any questions?"

Gasser and I in unison muttered: "Nosir."

Good Christ Almighty! I thought, KP on a goddamn troop train! Everybody else will be laying around on their butts, sleeping and goofing off, and me and Gasser and Ernie will be on the goddamn Pots and Pans. God dammit to hell!

"By the way," Cherry went on, "I will guarantee you will not pull KP again for a minimum of sixty days. Okay? Put on your fatigues, leave all your gear here, and take off. The chow car is eight cars ahead. Now get moving."

Lieutenant Cherry moved on down the car to give Ernie his bad news.

Ernie was a tall, thin Iowan with a pale, tired-looking face. I only knew him slightly, since he was an antenna specialist and I was a Keyer man, along with Gasser and the rest of my platoon. Antenna men always had sad faces, since they spent a lot of their time clinging to a mast a couple of hundred feet in the air, where occasionally they would meet their sudden end. We had lost two in one day when some fool—we never discovered who—had hit a switch and rotated the disk while they were aloft tuning it. The damn thing flung them out into space like a kid's slingshot hurling ball bearings. Ernie just missed being one of them. He was about ten feet below them on the mast when it happened.

The only other squad that carried the weight of doom on their shoulders were the Power Supply men. Twenty-five thousand volts at up to two amps is damn near enough juice to ionize the whole city of Hackensack. One day when a couple of safety interlocks failed to function, one of the Power Supply men went up in a puff of light purple smoke, leaving behind only the remains of a charred dog tag and half of a seared canteen.

Keyer men were considered the dilettantes of Company K. We were also the company's intellectual elite, since the keyer was by far the most complex component to maintain, and its inherent instability lent credence to our image as Bohemian, unpredictable artists. Our keyer unit, which was wired with secret dynamite charges for immediate detonation in case of enemy capture, was the heart of our radar.

Silently, Gasser began to pull on his fatigues. I did likewise, making sure that I was putting on my crap fatigues. Every experienced soldier always keeps one pair of clean, reasonably decent fatigues for casual wear around the company area. The other pair is used for crap details such as Latrine Orderly or KP. This suit is often impregnated with everything from chicken guts to sheep dung, which is used to fertilize the lawn around the Officers' Club. This suit is mean, rancid, and gamy beyond civilian understanding.

At last Gasser and I stood up in our fragrant work uniforms. Ernie came up from the far end of the car. Wordlessly, the three of us moved down the center aisle, little realizing at the time that we had begun a saga that was eventually to be a legend throughout the entire Signal Corps.

Gasser led the way. I followed; Ernie trailed behind. As we moved up the aisle, three or four of our peers emitted faint chicken-clucking sounds, the universal GI signal that says roughly: The Army has done it again. Another indignity has been heaped upon the defenseless enlisted man's head. I find this amusing, since it has not happened to me, at least this time. My clucking denotes both sympathy and faint scorn since you were dumb enough to get caught in the Army Crap Detail net. Cluck cluck cluck.

The chicken has to be one of nature's most maligned creatures, being a universal symbol of cowardice as well as petty harassment and general measliness. My heart goes out to the chicken. What has the chicken done to deserve this reputation? Is the chicken more cowardly than, say, the mole or the gopher? It is one of those unanswerable questions. Even the chicken's daily provender is looked upon with scorn and derision. "Chicken feed" aptly describes most of our salaries. I have never heard anyone term his paycheck "goat meal" or "squirrel food," always "chicken feed."

These murky thoughts drifted through my GI brain as we went up the aisle toward the chow car. We went through car after car filled with alien soldiers wearing mysterious patches. Gasser muttered over his shoulder:

"Christ, did you get a load of those Paratroopers back there? What in the hell are we heading for?"

The same thought had occurred to me when we went through one car filled with wiry, mean-looking GI's wearing gleaming jump boots and the kind of expressions that you see at three o'clock in the morning on the faces of the birds in poolrooms and all-night diners. They all wore crazy patches that looked like a smear of blood with a mailed fist clenching a length of chain emerging right at you. Behind me, Ernie added his two bits:

"I swear that must have been a company of Mafia hit men. Did you see that captain?"

Their CO, sprawled at the head of the car, looked like a carnivorous orangutan dressed in skintight fatigues with a trench knife at his waist.

"I'm sure as hell glad they're on our side," I chirped, stepping over a pile of gas masks.

"Don't be too sure, buddy," Gasser answered without looking back. One thing that really got to me was that this captain wore a single set of captain's bars on his fatigue collar. They were painted a dull, lethal black. You just don't see outfits like that in the late late movies.

Eventually we arrived at the chow car. Actually, it was two chow cars; one for cooking, the other for serving. The feeding facilities on a troop train are not exactly in the civilian elegant dining car tradition. Since there were two or three thousand soldiers aboard, they were fed like hogs at the trough. It was all very functional. The serving car had a long stainless-steel table that ran the entire length of the car itself. At intervals there were holes a couple of feet in diameter cut in the gleaming steel, and huge thirty-two-gallon garbage cans filled with GI food were lowered into the holes. Only the tops showed. Mashed potatoes in one, creamed chipped beef in another, soggy string beans, and at the far end "Dessert," garbage cans filled with cherry Jell-O or runny fruit salad. The soldiers to be fed moved in an endless line through the car, carrying their mess kits. Sweating KPs on the other side of the steel table ladled out the glop. It was a messy job, messy and hot and hypnotic. In the next car the cooks and a team of KPs toiled away, brewing up oatmeal, meatloaves, and stewed squash in a bath of searing heat that would have done a sauna proud. Since there were so many on the train, the feeding went on almost without a break. When one part of the endless line had returned to its car after breakfast, another part of the line was ready for lunch. The instant Gasser and Ernie and I arrived, the mess sergeant, a sweaty tech wearing a white apron and a crew cut, put us to work.

"You guys from that Signal Corps bunch, right?"

Gasser grunted.

"Okay, grab them aprons. And you"—he nodded to me—"you're on gravy. And you, get down there on them peas. And you, you're on Harvard beets."

I was gravy, Ernie was peas, and Gasser was Harvard beets. Seconds later I began ladling. Now, on a swaying troop train there is a real trick to ladling gravy into lurching mess kits filled with ice cream and salmon loaf and chopped cucumbers. The job leaves a lot of room for artistic interpretations. Hour after hour faceless yardbirds jostled past amid the din of complaints and muffled cursings. There were sudden wild bursts of laughter. Through it all, the mess sergeant kept yelling mechanically:

"Keep it movin'. God dammit, keep it movin'. God dammit, kept it movin'. Hey you, this ain't no Schrafft's or nothin'. If you don't like what you get, dump it in the can at the end of the car, but don't hold up the damn line. God dammit."

I have often since wondered what became of that poor, driven mess sergeant. No ribbons, no applause, only an endless belt of hungry, wooden faces year after year. He must have had one of the most realistic views of mankind of anyone around. Like some keeper in the cosmic zoo of humanity where it is always Feeding Time, which is not at all the same as Dining Time or Lunch Time. He presided over his steaming feeding trough with a wild look of dogged persistence in his eye and a leather voice prodding the herd on.

"Keep movin', God dammit, keep movin'. Come on, you guys, let's have more mashed potatoes out here. Change them cans quick. Hey, quit spillin' that coffee all over the damn floor. Get a goddamn mop, fer Chrissake, stupid. Let's go, let's go. Keep movin'."

Time became all jumbled as I hunched over my vast tub of dark brown, steaming gravy. My wrist ached from ladling, ladling, ladling. After a couple of hours in the heat, the sergeant told us to strip down to our shorts and GI shoes. It was a little relief, but not much. Steam rose in swirling clouds from the boiling hot food; sweat dropped from my dog tags and into the gravy. Who cared? A little sweat never hurt anyone. I toiled on. Gasser wielded his beet ladle with dash and élan. Ernie was switched from peas to string beans. Other KPs from time to time emerged in pairs from the cooking car, struggling on the slippery floor, carrying giant cans of soup or gravy or scrambled eggs. As one tub was emptied, another was immediately lowered into the slot.

I quickly discovered that the gravy ladle was highly controversial, since gravy has to be handled with skill, not to mention restraint. Too much wrist on the ladle and some poor joker's whole meal was swimming in brown glue; ice cream, fruit salad, and all. I grew hard and unyielding, impervious to the steady torrent of abuse that was heaped upon me. I ladled gravy mechanically, with no prejudice or favoritism. After all, when you're feeding half the U.S. Army on a thundering troop train there is no place for faint heart or even mere civility.

"No gravy, please. Hey you, NO GRAVY!" meant absolutely nothing to me as I ladled on hour after hour.

At long intervals the line would peter out to a faint trickle and the exhausted sergeant would holler out:

"O.K., you guys. Take a ten-minute break. You're doin' a great job, yessir, a great job. If you want any apples or ice cream or anything, just grab 'em but don't leave the car."

An endless supply of food is the quickest way to kill an appetite. One day there will be some hotshot doctor who will write a diet book based on that fact. Put any fatty in a room with tons of ice cream, mashed potatoes, and chocolate cake, with butterscotch malted coming out of the faucets, and within five hours the fatty will not be able to stand the sight of food.

I squatted down on a packing case behind the counter, my legs stiff from all the standing, my ladle hand sore and tired, my forearms and elbows itching from dried gravy. Ever since that hellish twenty-four hours of KP I have never again touched gravy in any form. Gasser sat with his head hanging low around his knees, blood-red beet juice dripping from his hairy chest. He looked like a major casualty that had taken an 88 shell right in the gut. Ernie leaned back against the side of the swaying car, his legs outstretched, straddling his string-bean tub, his eyes closed. The ten minutes flashed by in milliseconds.

"Here they come again, you guys. Keep it movin', come on, quit stragglin'. God dammit, this ain't no Schrafft's."

I tried ladling with my left hand for a while to ease my aching wrist and elbow. I was rapidly developing a severe case of Gravy Ladle Tendonitis, which occasionally still troubles me. Unfortunately, with my left hand I was gravying more shoes than potatoes and had to switch back. I tried the over-hand motion; sidearm. The complaints rose and fell like the beating of an angry surf on an unyielding rocky shore.

From time to time through the surrealistic blur of the endless line I would spot a familiar face as Company K went by. They were no longer my friends, just more links in a chain that went round and round.

As the three of us toiled on along with other KPs from other units, the outside world ceased to exist. Was it day, was it night? Was it winter, was it summer? What year was it? Do they still have years? What country were we in? Were we in any country? Had we died and were we now toiling in purgatory, struggling hopelessly for redemption? Who am I? What is my name?

I ladled on and on. During one of our breaks, Gasser, chewing on a piece of celery, ambled over, trailing beet juice, to where the sergeant was moodily checking a tub of purple Kool-Aid, known to the troops as the Purple Death.

"Hey, Sarge, when do we get our four hours off?" The sergeant glanced up from the tub of inky fluid in which floated two tiny chunks of ice about the size of golf balls. He was stirring it with a huge, long-handled wooden paddle.

"Huh? What'd you say?" He wiped the sweat from his brow with his left hand and flicked it into the Kool-Aid.

"When do we get our four hours off?"

"What four hours off?" The sergeant barked a dry, hard, yapping laugh. "Jeez, what the hell are they sending me now? I ain't had four hours off since last November."

Gasser chewed angrily on his celery. "Our lieutenant informed us that we would have four hours on and four hours off and that . . ."

The sergeant shook his head slowly in the incredible wonder that anyone could believe such a transparent fairy tale. Gasser got the message. So did we.

Ernie, slumped next to me, was slowly drinking a canteen cup of cold milk.

"Boy, I'll say one thing about this job. You sure get thirsty. Boy, do you get thirsty."

"Yeah. It's all this sweating," I said, running my hand over my chest like a squeegee, pushing a wave of sweat ahead of it. My dog tags dripped steadily. Ernie nodded.

"Boy, I never sweated so much in my life."

The humidity in the car from all the steam, the moving bodies, and the fact that the ventilation system had gone out during the second year of Lincoln's administration, made the chow car about as comfortable as the inside of a catcher's mitt during the second half of a doubleheader in July.

"Well," I yawned, stretching my aching back, "it's a great way to lose weight."

"What weight?" Ernie said as he gulped his milk. Ernie was the only guy I have ever known standing six feet six and wearing size fifteen shoes who wore a shirt with a thirteen and a half collar and had a twenty-seven-inch waist. Ernie was so skinny that if he stood sideways in the wind, he made a high, whistling sound. He looked like the guy in those ads in the back pages of *Boy's Life* captioned: Are you a 98 lb. weakling? The guy that gets the sand kicked in his face. One time on a twenty-mile march, Goldberg hollered out:

"Hey, Ernie, will you please march over on the other side of the platoon? I keep hearin' your bones rattle and I get out of step."

The platoon laughed at that, and so did Ernie, who was a good guy, although very quiet. Few of us at the time would have guessed at the fate that lay ahead of him.

He raised his long, white, boy face—he looked a little like a nineteen-year-old Uncle Sam with no beard—and repeated:

"Boy, I'm so damn thirsty I could drink some of your crummy gravy."

"Don't worry, Ernie," I said, "we only got about fifteen hours to go and we'll be home free."

I tried to pump as much sarcasm into my voice as I could manage without getting into trouble with the sergeant, who was listening to our exchange of pleasantries. The clank of many feet approaching cut short whatever Ernie was going to say. We went back into the trenches.

From time to time during the long hours I was switched to Jell-O, which I found was even trickier, if possible, than gravy.

For one thing, it bounces around on the ladle and occasionally takes on a life of its own. GI Jell-O ranges in consistency from golf ball rubbery to a kind of oozy reddish gruel, and you never know what kind you're going to get on any given ladle scoop. I learned to play the windage, rolling my Jell-O scoop from side to side in the manner of a Cessna 150 approaching a narrow grass runway in high, gusty crosswinds.

Your GI mess kit folds open like a clam and has a treacherous metal handle which can operate, or nonoperate, at its own will. Half of the clam shell is a shallow oval-shaped compartment. The other side, of equal size and also oval, has raised divisions which theoretically separate the Jell-O from the mashed potatoes or the beets from the ice cream. Like most theories, the actuality was very different. For one thing, the metal of the mess kit transmits heat better than platinum wire carries electric current. A dollop of steaming mashed rutabagas in one compartment instantly turns the mess kit into an efficient hotplate. Ice cream ladled into another compartment instantly melts and is heated to the consistency of lukewarm pea soup, which is often what it tastes like after the peas have slopped over into the ice cream and the fish gravy has oozed over from the big dish. So naturally, all such old-fashioned concepts as specific tastes and conventional meal sequences are totally irrelevant when you're dining tastefully out of a red-hot mess kit. For one thing, you usually eat your dessert first in the futile hope of getting at just a little unmelted ice cream before it's too late.

Over the years I became quite fond of some specific mixtures. For example, vanilla ice cream goes surprisingly well when mixed with mashed salmon loaf. The ice cream makes a kind of sweetish coolish salmon salad out of it, a little like drugstore tuna salad. If the ice cream is chocolate, however, or maybe tutti-frutti, you've got problems.

Goldberg, the leading Company K chow hound, had a simple solution. He'd just take his big metal GI spoon and immediately mix everything in his mess kit together, forming a heavy brownish-pinkish paste in which floated chunks of, say, fried liver or maybe a pork chop or two, and just spoon it down between gulps of Kool-Aid or GI coffee or whatever we had to drink. It was all gone in maybe thirty or forty seconds. Goldberg would let out a shuddering belch and get back on the chow line for another go-round.

There were others, perhaps more fastidious, who would eat only one thing per serving, going through the line first for turnips, which they would devour, then getting back in the line for the steamed cauliflower, then finally, after three or four trips through the line, topping it off with the Jell-O or the canned pineapple.

Then there were those, and Gasser was a leading member of this group, who lived entirely on Butterfinger bars. It's hard to say which group was right. I'll say one thing. A stretch in any one of the Armed Forces is a sure cure for what my aunt Clara always called "picky" eaters. It's not that GI food wasn't good. It was, in fact, better than most guys regularly got at home. It just had a tendency to get all mixed up and run together, so that in the end being picky was even more stupid in the Army than it is in real life.

The Army is also a sure cure for what is called "light sleepers." After the first ninety days among the dogfaces you can sleep standing up, sitting down, going to the john, firing a rifle, making love, or swimming underwater with a pack on your back. In all my four years I never once ran into an insomniac. Insomnia is a civilian luxury, like credit cards and neurotic mistresses.

It must have been about the tenth or fifteenth hour that I became conscious, dimly through the hullabaloo and the scorching heat, that somebody in my immediate vicinity was snoring fitfully. Every time I glanced around it stopped. Who the hell was it? Again the snoring commenced. After fifteen or twenty minutes of this irritating phlegmy sound, I realized that it was me. It has been said that the human mind is capable of only one act at any given instant, but I can't see how this can be since on numerous occasions I have found myself soundly asleep and still doing other things.

As I ladled on, flipping Jell-O over my left shoulder occasionally, for luck, I thought of these things. An extended stretch of KP is good for your philosophical side. The mind wanders aimlessly to and fro like a blind earthworm burrowing in total darkness amid buried tree roots and dead snails. There is a certain basic soul-satisfaction in low down, mindless menial labor. The body completely takes over. A mess kit swims into view; your arm flips Jell-O at it without thought or understanding. The pores are open. Your entire physical being is now functioning without a controlling mind, like the heart and the liver, which go about their work without conscious control.

Down the long line of KPs ladles rose and fell, feet in heavy GI boots clanked by. Gravy, mashed potatoes, turnips, beets, scrambled eggs, all became one. Once a voice snapped me out of my restful reverie.

"How'r y'all makin' it?"

I glanced up from the brown sea of gravy, or Jell-O, or whatever I was scooping at the time.

"Uh . . . what? You talking to me?"

It was Lieutenant Cherry.

"Uh . . . yeah, I guess so. Sir."

"Just thought I'd drop by. See how you guys were makin' out."

The steam clouded up the lieutenant's glasses. Even his gleaming silver bars were misty. He moved down past Gasser, who waved at him with his ladle, and we toiled on.

During the next break, one of the other KPs, a short Mexican Pfc from an Engineering company joined our little group. His name was Gomez and he had the smell of Regular Army about him, crafty and laconic.

"Hey, Gomez," Gasser said between mouthfuls of powdered scrambled eggs, "what do you guys do in your outfit?"

"We're Engineers."

Gomez was one of those guys whom you have to prod continually to get anything at all out of.

"Yeah, but what do you *do*?" Gasser kept on prodding.

"What the hell do you think we do? What do you think the Engineers do?"

Gasser thought about this solemnly for a moment. Finally Ernie chipped in with his two cents:

"I almost got assigned to the Engineers out of Basic. But I got the Signal Corps instead."

Gomez, sensing a slur, shot back: "Well, y'can't win 'em all. Some guys are lucky; other guys are just dumb."

We rocked back and forth on our haunches in the steady rumbling silence for a while, until Gasser, swabbing out his mess kit with a chunk of bread, continued our listless investigation of the life and times of Pfc Gomez, Engineer Corps, USA.

"Gomez, I don't like to pry but I am very curious about what your unit does. Now take me and my sweaty friends here. We are in Radar. By that I mean we are in a unit that gets no promotions, no stripes whatsoever. We just get a lot of shocks, and fool around with soldering irons and crap like that. And . . ."

Gasser knew what he was doing. Radar men were universally looked upon by the great mass of real soldiers about the same way that the Detroit Lions evaluated George Plimpton.

"Shee-it," Gomez said, "don't tell me about Radar. I got a cousin in it, a goddamn fairy. He has to squat to piss."

Ernie cleared his throat and counterattacked: "Listen, Gomez, we had nine guys in the hospital last month alone, all with the clap."

Gomez picked his teeth casually with a kitchen match. "Probably give it to each other," he muttered.

God, I thought, would I like to turn Zynzmeister loose on this bird.

"Okay, you guys, let's get movin'. Here they come." The sergeant banged a spoon loudly on the stainless steel as once again the devouring swarm of human locusts engulfed us, eating everything in their path, leaving behind desolation and bread crusts.

By now all of us had broken through that mysterious invisible pane of glass that separates dog fatigue from what is called "the second wind." A curious elation, a lightheaded sense of infinite boundless strength filled me. I whistled "Three Blind Mice" over and over as I maniacally ladled my beloved gravy. Me, the Gravy King.

"Three blind mice, see how they run . . .
Three blind mice, see . . ."

For the first time in my life I really looked at gravy. In the Hemingway sense, gravy was true and real. My gravy was the most beautiful gravy ever seen on this planet, brown as the rich delta land of the Mississippi basin; life-bringer, source of primal energy. How lovely was my gravy. It made such sensual, swirling patterns as it dripped down over the snowy mashed potatoes and engulfed the golden pound cake with its rich tide of life force. I wondered why no one had ever seen this glory before. Was I on the verge of an original discovery involving gravy as the universal healer, a healer which could bind mankind together once they had discovered that the one thing that they had in common was my lovely, lovely gravy? Maybe I should wander the earth, bearing the glad tidings. *Salvation through gravy. Gravy is love. God created gravy, hence gravy is the Word of God. More gravy, more gravy is what we all need!*

Yes, it is such thoughts as these that surface when the mind sags with fatigue and reason flees.

"Hey, you on the gravy."

It was the mess sergeant yelling from the other end of the car.

"Yes?" I heard myself replying. "I am the Gravy King."

"Not any more you're not, Mack. You and your buddies are going into the other car to take over Pots and Pans. Now get movin', let's keep it movin'."

With sorrow in my heart I laid down my trusty gravy ladle and the three of us, trailing sweat, struggled into the next car. It was like leaving purgatory and entering hell. Murky, writhing figures, moaning piteously, stirred great vats of bubbling food. Others squatted in the muck, peeling great mounds of reeking onions. The heat was so enormous that I could actually hear it, a low pulsating hum. A buck sergeant wearing skintight fatigues cut off just below the hips herded the three of us through the uproar to the far end of the car. Three guys armed with hoses spewing scalding water and cakes of taffy-brown GI soap capable of dissolving fingernails at thirty paces and long-handled GI brushes struggled to clean what looked like four or five hundred GI pots. The buck hollered at the three:

"You guys are relieved. Get back to the other car, on the double. You're gonna relieve these guys on the serving line."

The three pot-scrubbers, all with the look in their eyes of damned souls out for a dip in the River Styx, dropped their brushes and swabs and without a sound rushed out of hell, unexpectedly pardoned.

"Oh, Mother of God," Gasser mumbled as two sweating GIs appeared carrying more dirty pots, which they hurled on top of the pile.

Thus began a period of my existence which has haunted me to this day. From time to time, when driving late at night, my car radio will inadvertently pick up Fundamentalist preachers who thunder warnings of mankind's approaching doom and hold out promises of indescribable hells. I clutch the wheel in sudden fear, because I have been there.

The oatmeal pots are the worst. GI oatmeal is cooked in huge vats which become lined with thick burnt-concrete en-crustations of immovable oatmeal matter. Oatmeal is even worse than powdered egg scabs, which are matched only by the vats used to concoct mutton stew.

Through the long hours Ernie, Gasser, and myself struggled against the tide of endless pots. The GI soap had shriveled my hands into tiny crab-claws, and my body was now beyond sweat. Even Gasser had fallen silent. Ernie, poor Ernie, had entered the last and crucial phase of his approaching ordeal.

Curious thing about the truly deadening menial tasks: great stretches of time pass almost instantly. When you approach the animal state you also begin to lose the one characteristic that sets us apart from the rest of the earth's creatures, the blessed (or cursed) sense of Time. Anthropologists tell us that truly primitive man had no sense, to speak of, of the passing moments. The more civilized one becomes, the more conscious and fearful of the passage of time. Maybe that's why the simple peasants live to enormous ages of a hundred and thirty years or more, while astronauts and nuclear physicists die in their forties. To the three of us, amid the scalding water and searing soap, there was no Time.

It is for this reason that I cannot honestly say how long our trial lasted. For all I know, it might have been a century or two. Maybe ten minutes. But I guess it to be more on the order of forty years. It ended suddenly and totally without warning. The buck brought in three more victims, and we were sprung.

Like our predecessors, like hunted rats, we scurried out, back to the serving car, which now seemed incredibly cool and civilized. The car stood empty for the first time. Only the mess sergeant, alone, lounged casually against his stainless-steel rack, smoking a Camel. All that remained of the torrent of food was a simple aluminum colander piled high with apples. The sergeant blew a thin stream of Camel smoke through his nostrils as he smiled in benevolence upon us.

"You guys did good, real good. You kept 'em movin'. How 'bout an apple?"

I grabbed an apple with my crab-claw and bit into its heavenly crisp coolness, its glorious moistness, its . . .

It was at that moment that I became a lifelong apple worshiper. I have often thought since of becoming the founder of the First Church of the Revealed Apple.

We milled a bit, chomping on the McIntoshes.

"You guys can go back to your company any time you want now. If you'd like to hang around here and cool off, be my guests. And remember, you ain't gonna pull KP for at least sixty days. How does that grab ya?"

The three of us, dressed only in our brown GI shorts, heavy GI shoes, and salt-encrusted dog tags, were flooded, each of us, with a sense of release. We had done a rotten, miserable, mountainous, incredibly rugged job and battled on until it was actually finished. "Hey, one of you guys help me with this goddamn door. The bastard sticks."

The sergeant was struggling with a vast sliding panel that

formed part of the wall of the car. Gasser grabbed the handle and the two of them slid the door back. A torrent of fresh air poured into the car, flushing out the old cauliflower smells and the aroma of countless mess kits and gamy socks.

"Would you look at that!" Gasser cheered. "The world is still there."

Ernie hitched up his sweaty underwear shorts higher on his bony hips and the three of us surged to the door to watch the countryside roll by. The air was crisp and cool, yet tinged with a faint balminess. Hazy purple hills rolled on the horizon. Short scrub pines raced past the open door. The four of us, including the sergeant, were the only people on this sealed train—with the exception of the engineer and maybe his fireman—who were looking out at the beautiful world. The sergeant chain-lit another Camel.

"Any of you guys want a cigarette?" He waved his pack in the air. None of us smoked.

"Look, I ain't supposed to open this door except to air out the car, so if anyone asks you, that's what I was doin'."

I bit into my third apple and gazed up at the fleecy white clouds and the deep blue sky. The train was riding on a high raised track. The rough gravel walls of the embankment slanted steeply down to the fields below. A two-lane concrete road paralleled the track as it ran through farm fields and patches of pines. We were moving at a fair clip.

"Hey, Sergeant," Ernie asked, "where the hell are we? What state is this?"

We had been on the road for what seemed an eternity. The sergeant peered out at the landscape.

"Well"—he paused and took a deep drag—"if you was to ask me, I'd guess that we was someplace in Arkansas. Now that's just an educated guess."

"Arkansas!" Gasser said, and edged toward the door to get a closer look. "That's the last place I'd a'guessed."

The three of us watched a battered old pickup truck loaded with bushel baskets roll along for a while below us. The pale face of a girl peered up at us. A man in faded overalls and a railroad engineer's cap sat next to her, driving and puffing on a short fat cigar. We rode side by side for many seconds. She gazed at us; we gazed back. I waved. She glanced quickly at the mean-looking driver and then back at us. She waved timidly, as though she were afraid he might see her.

"Gee, that's a real Arkansas girl." Ernie sat down on the floor of the car with his legs hanging over the edge in the breeze.

"That's the first Arkansas person I have ever seen." Gasser and I sat beside him. Now all three of us had our legs hanging out over the racing roadbed. The girl in the truck glanced uneasily at the driver. She looked maybe thirteen or fourteen.

"Hey, do you think they are real hillbillies?" Gasser asked with great wonder and curiosity in his voice. He was from the West Coast, where hillbillies were something seen only in Ma and Pa Kettle films.

She continued to stare up at us. The old truck trailed blue smoke as it roared along. The three of us, who had not seen a female human being for many months, found her incredibly magnetic. Her long black hair trailed in the wind and billowed around her pale sharp features.

"You think that guy drivin' the Dodge is her father?" Gasser asked rhetorically. The sergeant, a man of the world, one who had seen all of life stream past the open doors of his mess car, said in his flat voice:

"Ten to one that's her husband."

"Ah, come on, you're kidding." Ernie found it hard to believe.

"Listen, you guys, in these hills it ain't nothin' for a fifty-year-old man to marry a twelve-year-old chick. What they say is, around here, 'If she's big enough she's old enough.' A virgin in these parts is any girl that can outrun her brothers." He flipped the butt end of his Camel neatly over our heads and out into the wind.

Silently the three of us watched the truck as it suddenly turned left into a gravel road lined with scraggly pines. It disappeared behind us in a cloud of dust. Ernie craned his neck out further into the slipstream to catch a last glimpse of the disappearing Dodge.

"Y'know, she was kind of cute," he said to no one in particular.

"Yep. She sure was, son." The sergeant was in a thoughtful expansive mood. "They all are in these hills. Eatin' all that fatback and grits must do som-pin to 'em. Lemme tell you one thing, and you listen. Don't you ever say nothin' like that 'she's cute' business around any of the men in these hills."

Gasser looked up from his rapt contemplation of the speeding gravel.

"What do you mean?"

"Every one of these shitkickers carries a double-barrel twelve-gauge Sears Roebuck shotgun in his pickup, for just that purpose alone. I'll bet that bastard would have blasted you quicker'n a skunk. He wouldn't think twice about it. Any sheriff around here'd probably give him a medal for doin' it."

"Hey, you guys, we're slowing up." I had noticed that gradually the train had been losing speed. The embankment was even higher here than it had been farther back. The concrete road looked miles below us. I looked forward. Ahead, the long sealed train curved gently to the left like a great metal snake. Big green hills, vast vacant fields, and a few scraggly shacks trickled away to the horizon. There was some sort of trestle with lights and tanks a half-mile or so ahead of the train.

The sergeant looked over my shoulder to see what was going on. "We're probably stoppin' to take on another crew, or some water or som-pin."

Gradually, the train eased to a stop. For the first time in hours we did not sway. There was no rumble of trucks on the roadbed. We all sat in silence. The three of us sitting on the door sill, our legs hanging out over the gravel, enjoyed the bucolic scene. Birds twittered; a distant frog croaked. In the bright blue sky high above, a couple of chicken buzzards slowly circled.

At that precise instant events were set in motion that none of us would ever forget. It was Gasser who lit the fuse. Leaning forward so that his head extended far out into the soft, winy Arkansas air, he said:

"Do you guys see what I see?"

Ernie and I craned forward and looked in the direction Gasser had indicated. Down below us, far below us, was a dilapidated beaten-up old shack by the side of the concrete road. It looked like one of those countless roadside hovels that you see throughout the land on the back roads of America which appear to be made entirely of rusting Coca-Cola signs. It was deep in weeds and oil drums, but above it, swinging from a sagging iron crossbar, was a sign that bore one magic word:

BEER

There are few words that mean more under certain circumstances. All the thirst, the hungering insatiable throat-parching thirst earned during our sweaty backbreaking twenty-four hours of KP engulfed the three of us like a tidal wave of desire. Gasser, his tongue hanging out, dramatically gasped:

"Beer! Oh, God Almighty, what I wouldn't give for just one ice-cold, foamy, lip-smacking beer!"

Through the window of the shack we could see, dimly, a couple of red-necked natives happily hoisting away.

"Listen, you guys, I'm goin' forward to the can. You can leave for your company any time you care to. I'll see you guys around."

The sergeant disappeared from our lives forever. We were alone. Authority had gone to the can. The devil took over. I leaped to my feet.

"Listen, I got a couple of bucks in my fatigue jacket hanging right over there back of the table. I am prepared to buy if one of you is prepared to go and get it."

I scurried over to my fatigues and quickly brought back the two bucks. Already I could taste that heavenly elixir: ice cold and brimming with life. Beer! Real, non-GI, genuine beer!

Ernie looked at Gasser; Gasser looked at Ernie. We were one in our insane desire for a brew.

"Okay, you guys," I hissed, "guess how many fingers I'm holding up."

Gasser barked: "Two."

Ernie, his voice trembling with emotion, said: "Uh . . . one."

He had sealed his fate. It was the last word we ever heard him utter.

"You're it, baby," I cheered, and handed him the two bucks. "Get as much as you can for this," I added.

Ernie grabbed the money and leaped lightly over the edge and down the steep gravel slope, his feet churning. He half-slid, half-ran down the long incline. We could hear the disappearing sounds of tiny gravel avalanches as he headed toward the shack. Ernie, like the two of us, was wearing only his sweat-stained brown GI underwear shorts, his GI shoes, and dog tags.

"Oh, man, I can taste that Schlitz already!" Gasser thumped on the floor in excitement with his right fist. "Yay, beer!" he cheered.

Below us, Ernie had entered the shack. We caught glimpses of his naked back through the window as the transaction was underway. Heads bobbed. Ernie glanced up at us and smiled broadly.

Seconds ticked by and then, without warning, the faint voices of shouting trainmen drifted back to us from far forward. At first I did not grasp their significance.

It has been wisely said many times that all of us are given clear warnings of disaster, but few of us bother to read the signs. Gasser peered toward the rear of the train.

"Jesus," he mumbled, "I never realized how long this bastard was."

The train stretched behind us almost to infinity, all the windows sealed against prying eyes, lurking enemies.

Time hung suspended amid the faint chirpings of crickets and the distant cawing of crows. Ernie's head reappeared briefly in the window. He held up a large paper sack in triumph. And then it happened.

eeeeeeeeeeeeeeeeeeeeeeee . . .

Like the distant wail of an avenging banshee, our sealed troop train shuddered a long menacing evil creak as it slowly began to move. I grabbed Gasser's arm.

"Gasser! We're moving!"

Gasser wordlessly leaned out to see if Ernie was on his way.

The gravel inched slowly past our hanging feet. We were barely moving. Gasser soundlessly waved his arms, hoping that Ernie would get the message. We couldn't yell because at least fifty officers would have heard and known that we had done the one thing beyond all law, namely illegally leaving a top-security sealed troop movement. That's firing squad stuff.

Suddenly Ernie appeared at the side of the shack. He looked smaller, shorter, as he struggled through the weeds, carrying his precious sack of beer. At first he didn't seem to notice that the train was moving. Gasser and I both waved frantically. Already the train was gathering momentum.

"Oh, my God," Gasser gasped. "Oh, my God! Ernie!"

Ernie broke into a frantic run. Through the quiet air we could hear the distant clank of beer bottles and the thud-thud-thud of his GI shoes. He angled upward along the steep incline, slipping and sliding as he ran.

"Ah, he's got it made," Gasser said with relief as Ernie drew nearer and nearer.

At first it really did look like there was no problem. Ernie pounded toward us, his right arm cradling the bag of beer like a halfback lugging a football. The train moved faster and faster, but Ernie was closing the gap. Then he hit a patch of loose shale. He slid down the side of the bank, his legs churning.

Gasser, clinging to the back edge of the car, extended his hand far out into the breeze.

"Ernie! Grab my hand! ERNIE!"

Ernie's eyes rolled wildly as he struggled on. His left hand reached high, his fingers within inches of Gasser's grasping mitt.

The engine of our train let go a long, moaning blast. I sometimes hear this in my sleep, ringing hollow and lost, like a death knell.

I grabbed Gasser's knees to hold him in the car. "I'll hold your legs, Gasser," I grunted. "Grab him!"

Gasser leaned even farther out over the racing gravel. I braced my feet on the floor, fear clutching my gut like an octopus. Gasser kept saying over and over again: "Oh, Jesus Christ, oh, Jesus Christ, Christ Almighty . . ."

Peering between Gasser's straining legs I saw Ernie's contorted exhausted face, his legs pounding weaker and weaker.

clink-clink-clink-clink-clink-clink . . .

The sound of his dog tags jingled with each painful stride.

. . . clink-clink-clink.

And then all three of us knew it. He was not going to make it.

Ernie was gone. But he pounded on, dropping farther and farther behind. He had become a tiny distant stick-man, naked and alone. He still clung to the beer.

The mess car was now swaying and rocking along at almost full speed. We both gazed outward at Ernie's tiny figure, still hopelessly striding along down on the sad two-lane country road. The sun was going down over the distant hills. The sky had purpled.

As the faint clink-clink-clink-clink of Ernie's dog tags receded forever into limbo, both Gasser and I knew without exchanging a word that we had been part of a historic moment. At the time, naturally, we didn't realize that the Legend of Ernie would grow and grow until every enlisted man in the Signal Corps knew his name and would tell the story of the GI who was lost from the sealed troop train. Some, naturally, don't believe he ever existed. After all, as a people we Americans prefer to believe that all heroic figure were frauds and shams. But I was there. I knew Ernie.

The train rounded a great bend. We entered the gloom of a high Arkansas valley. Gasser got to his feet. I followed. Without a word we donned our fatigues and headed back to Company K, men bearing a fear and a grief that few know in their lifetime.

As we inched our way through car after car, amid seas of alien troops, we held our own counsel. Back in *The Georgia Peach*, Company K lay sprawled, travel-stained by the long trip. Listless eyes gazed at us as we went back to our seats. I eased myself down into the scratchy mohair. Gasser glanced up and down the car before taking his seat. He whispered:

"Play it cool. Don't tell 'em a goddamn thing."

We sat, and for a moment we both feigned sleep. Lieutenant Cherry loomed over us.

"The mess sergeant tells me you guys did a real fine job, and I want you to know I'm proud of you, y'hear?"

He patted Gasser's shoulder and moved on back toward the rear of the car where Ernie had once sat. Seconds later he returned.

"Hey, you guys, where's Ernie?"

"Uh . . ." I beamed up at the lieutenant, wearing my Innocent face, the one that had gotten me out of endless hassles in the past. "Uh . . . gee, Lieutenant . . . hehheh . . . I don't know. I guess he . . ."

Gasser chimed in, his voice sounding as phony as a latex fourteen-dollar bill:

"He must be in the latrine. Yeah, he must be in the latrine, Lieutenant, sir."

"Fellows, the latrines have been locked up for over an hour for cleaning."

The lieutenant, sensing trouble the way all good officers can, leaned forward and peered deeply into both of our souls, his silver bars gleaming with all the weight of the U.S. Congress behind them.

"Where. Is. Ernie?"

He waited, a long, pregnant wait. I knew it was no use. I felt Gasser sag in the seat next to me.

"Lieutenant," I said. "Lieutenant, we lost Ernie."

Lieutenant Cherry's face aged ten years; his skin the parchment white of an old man. His glasses glinted in the yellow light of *The Georgia Peach.*

"You lost Ernie?"

Dumbly, we both stared up at him, terror-stricken. He repeated his plaint, his primal query:

"You lost ERNIE?"

Gasser, his voice sobbing a little like the air coming out of a deflating birthday balloon, squeaked:

"You see, Lieutenant, he . . . this . . . ah . . . that is, we . . . there was this stop and . . . we all wanted a beer, and there was this place, and . . ."

His voice cracked, his sentences were broken and incoherent.

Suddenly Lieutenant Cherry leaned lower. His voice came in a hush:

"Listen, you two," he whispered tensely, "don't you ever say a word to anyone about this. Do you realize I'll have to sign a Statement of Charges if this gets out? It's bad enough if you wreck a jeep, but to lose a Pfc from a sealed troop train!"

He paused, his eyes gleaming through his GI glasses.

"Don't you mention a word of this. I'll fix it somehow through Headquarters."

He disappeared, his shoulders hunched with care. We never heard another word of Ernie in Company K. No one ever mentioned his name again.

There are times when I awake at 3 A.M. from a fitful sleep hearing the clink-clink-clink of poor Ernie's dog tags. Ernie, lost forever in Arkansas, wearing only his GI underwear, forever AWOL, a fugitive from a sealed troop train. Is he out there yet, a haggard wraith living on berries and dead frogs? A fearful outcast? Does he know the war is over? That all wars are past?

The clink-clink-clink of Ernie's dog tags says nothing.

BOB UECKER AND MICKEY HERSKOWITZ

THE ALL-UKE TEAM

Bob Uecker has made a career out of claiming to be a lousy major league baseball player—and, well, he was. But what he lacked in pure talent as a catcher for the Braves, Cardinals, and Phillies he's more than made up for as a successful broadcaster and television personality. With nationally syndicated sports columnist Mickey Herskowitz, Uecker has recorded "Outrageous but True" baseball stories in his book Catcher in the Wry.

I am more fortunate than most former big-leaguers, because I have no feelings of frustration, of promise unfulfilled. I think I got everything out of my talent I could.

To begin with, I lacked speed. I had to compensate with a few tricks. One was to knock my hat off as I ran down the first-base line, to make it appear that I was really moving.

I hated to lead off an inning, especially in a park that had Astroturf. I would hit a bouncing ball to third base and they'd whip the ball to second and then to first. It really made you look bad when they practiced their double plays with nobody on base.

The one ability I did have, and tried never to lose, was the ability to laugh at myself, or at the foibles of a game little kids play for free. After a long day, moving on to another town, the fellows usually needed some comic relief.

Once, with the Braves, we were coming in for a landing. The time when many players tighten up is when the plane touches down, and there is this great whoosh before the brakes grab. I picked up the intercom mike in the back of the plane and announced, "This is your captain speaking. Please remain seated and keep your safety belts fastened until the plane HAS HIT THE SIDE OF THE TERMINAL BUILDING and come to a complete stop."

It was fun watching the blood leave their faces for a few seconds.

That was my way of bringing the guys together, of reminding them that man can't live by box score alone. I meant it one night, sort of, when I said on the *Tonight Show:* "Winning and losing is nothing. Going out and prowling the streets after the game is what I liked. You'd get half in the bag and wake up the next morning with a bird in your room—that's what baseball is all about."

In that spirit, I have been persuaded to select my own All-Star team, an all-character team, composed of players whose contribution to the game went beyond winning or losing. To be eligible, their careers had to cross mine, meaning they had to have played at least one game in the National League in the years between 1961 and 1968. I gave special consideration to those whose service had a distinctive and human quality, and also to those I thought might be seriously offended by being left out. Herewith,

THE BOB UECKER ALL-STAR TEAM

FIRST BASE—Marv Throneberry, Mets. The competition was hotter here than at any other position, with the likes of Dick Stuart, Norm Larker, and Gordy Coleman all in the running. A special honorable mention should go to Joe Pepitone, for his lasting contribution to the game. Pepitone is believed to be the first player to bring a hair blower into the locker room. Throneberry wins for a career that led not to the Hall of Fame, but to a Lite Beer commercial. He once was called out for failing to touch second base on a triple. When he complained, the umpires pointed out that he had missed first base, too.

SECOND BASE—*Rod Kanehl*, Mets. Led the league for three straight years in getting hit by pitches, and defined team spirit as being willing "to take one on the ass for the team." Once, as a pinch runner, he scored from second on a passed ball to give the Mets a 7–6 lead over the Phillies. Casey Stengel was so elated he told Hot Rod to stay in the game. When Kanehl asked which position, Casey said, "I don't care. Play any place you want to." Kanehl grabbed his glove and ran onto the field. He told Felix Mantilla to move from third to second, moved Elio Chacon from second to short, and put himself in at third. "That's the kind of ballplayers we want," Stengel said later. "Tell him to do something, and he does it."

SHORTSTOP—*Ruben Amaro*, Phillies. One of the slickest glove men ever to play the game, but I have included him for two reasons. Ruben hit even fewer homers (two) in his career than I did, and he is the only man I ever heard of who was drafted by both the American and Mexican armies. He deserves it.

THIRD BASE—*Doug Rader*, Astros. He was playing for Houston, in San Diego, the night that Padres owner Ray Kroc got on the p.a. system and apologized to the crowd for how lousy his team was. Rader rushed to the defense of the Padres, adding that Kroc "must have thought he was talking to a bunch of short-order cooks." The next week, Rader received angry letters from short-order cooks all over the country. The Padres turned the whole affair into a ticket promotion, letting in free anyone wearing a long white hat when the Astros returned to town. It all worked out swell in the off season, when Houston traded Rader to—you guessed it—San Diego.

OUTFIELD—*Roberto Clemente*, Pirates. One of the really complete players of his era, Roberto was also one of the great hypochondriacs. He suffered from insomnia, and claimed that sleeping pills kept him awake. The year he won his second batting title, he said he had gotten malaria from a mosquito, typhoid fever from a pig, and food poisoning from a fish—all man's natural enemies. "I feel better when I am sick," he once said. Roberto was one beautiful wreck.

Frank Thomas, Pirates, Reds, Cubs, Mets, Phillies, Astros, Braves, etc. He played for eleven teams, three in one season. Known as the Big Donkey, partly because his bat had a kick in it (when it connected), and partly because he suffered from hoof-in-mouth disease. It seemed that every few months Thomas would be traded, always leaving with the same declaration: "It's nice to know that somebody wants you."

Frank Howard, Dodgers. It was a thrill to watch him play the outfield. Jim Murray wrote that at six-eight, Howard was the only player in baseball who clanked when he walked. Early in his career, you never knew if he would drive in more runs than he let in. He had one of the biggest swings in the game, and once took a mighty cut just as Maury Wills slid across the plate, trying to steal home. A gentle giant, Howard was more shaken than Wills. "Please, Maurice," he begged, "don't ever do that again."

PITCHERS—Ken MacKenzie, Mets, left-hander. The first Yale graduate I know of to pitch in the big leagues after World War II. Casey Stengel once brought him in from the bullpen to face the San Francisco Giants with the bases full. The next three hitters were Orlando Cepeda, Willie Mays, and Willie McCovey. Stengel handed him the ball and said, "Pretend they are the Harvards." Another time, MacKenzie was sulking on the bench. "Do you realize," he said, "that I am the lowest-paid member of the Yale Class of '59?" Stengel reminded him, "Yes, but with the highest earned run average."

Honorable mention, *Masanori Murakami*, Giants, left-hander. There has to be a category for the only Japanese ever to pitch in the National League. Described as "sneaky fast," he compiled a 5-1 record in two seasons of relief, then returned to Japan, homesick for his native land. He spoke almost no English, but had a sense of humor. Or at least, the writers who covered the Giants did. Asked to name his favorite American songs, Murakami replied, "Horro, Dorry," and "Up a Razy Liver."

Turk Farrell, Phillies, Dodgers, Astros, right-hander. Early in his career, as a member of the Phillies' famed Dalton Gang, he set a record for barro fights. A hard thrower, with a big follow-through, Turk later set a record for most times getting hit by batted balls on various parts of the body. A line drive by Henry Aaron once glanced off his forehead, but Farrell stayed in the game. He carried a gun in spring training one year in Arizona, and shot snakes as he walked from his hotel to the ball park. A Falstaffian figure, he beat his old club, the Phillies, in a game that went fourteen innings and ended shortly before 1:00 A.M., and boasted in the clubhouse: "Nobody beats Farrell after midnight."

Honorable mention, *Gaylord Perry*, many teams, right-hander. When he came to the big leagues, one scouting report said he was only a "marginal prospect" to stay in the majors. Twenty-two years later, he was gunning for his three hundredth win. Once, after Nellie Fox had singled in the winning run against him, Perry broke Nellie's bat at home plate. He confessed some of his other sins in a book called *Me and the Spitter*, but swore he had reformed and no longer threw the illegal pitch because he wanted to set a good example for the kids.

You may have noticed that my All-Star team has no catcher. There were several candidates for this honor. Some had talent, but their humor was just warped enough to keep them in contention, such as Tim McCarver and Joe Torre. Others were not handicapped by their talent, such as John Bateman and Choo Choo Coleman.

In the end, I decided to leave the position vacant because I have been taught that it is in poor taste to give an award to yourself.

P. J. O'ROURKE

HOW TO DRIVE FAST ON DRUGS WHILE GETTING YOUR WING-WANG SQUEEZED AND NOT SPILL YOUR DRINK

P. J. O'Rourke edited the National Lampoon *during the late 1970s and wrote some of its wildest material. He has since gone on to write for* Playboy, Vanity Fair, *and* Esquire, *and has recently been serving a stint as "investigative humorist" for* Rolling Stone. *His stuff may seem wild, even "sick," but, as in the best humor, there is an undercurrent of seriousness that undercuts the ample belly laughs.*

When it comes to taking chances, some people like to play poker or shoot dice; other people prefer to parachute-jump, go rhino hunting, or climb ice floes, while still others engage in crime or marriage. But I like to get drunk and drive like a fool. Name me, if you can, a better feeling than the one you get when you're half a bottle of Chivas in the bag with a gram of coke up your nose and a teenage lovely pulling off her tube top in the next seat over while you're going a hundred miles an hour down a suburban side street. You'd have to

watch the entire Mexican air force crash-land in a liquid petroleum gas storage facility to match this kind of thrill. If you
ever have much more fun than that, you'll die of pure sensory
overload, I'm here to tell you.

But wait. Let's pause and analyze *why* this particular matrix
of activities is perceived as so highly enjoyable. I mean, aside
from the teenage lovely pulling off her tube top in the next
seat over. Ignoring that for a moment, let's look at the psy-
chological factors conducive to placing positive emotional values on the sensory end product of experientially produced
excitation of the central nervous system and smacking into a
lamppost. Is that any way to have fun? How would your
mother feel if she knew you were doing this? She'd cry. She
really would. And that's how you know it's fun. Anything
that makes your mother cry is fun. Sigmund Freud wrote all
about this. It's a well-known fact.

Of course, it's a shame to waste young lives behaving this
way—speeding around all tanked up with your feet hooked
in the steering wheel while your date crawls around on the
floor mats opening zippers with her teeth and pounding on
the accelerator with an empty liquor bottle. But it wouldn't
be taking a chance if you weren't risking *something*. And even
if it is a shame to waste young lives behaving this way, it is
definitely cooler than risking *old* lives behaving this way. I
mean, so what if some fifty-eight-year-old butt-head gets a
load on and starts playing Death Race 2000 in the rush-hour
traffic jam? What kind of chance is he taking? He's just waiting
around to see what kind of cancer he gets anyway. But if young,
talented *you*, with all of life's possibilities at your fingertips,
you and the future Cheryl Tiegs there, so fresh, so beautiful—
if the two of *you* stake your handsome heads on a single roll
of the dice in life's game of stop-the-semi—now *that's* taking
chances! Which is why old people rarely risk their lives. It's
not because they're chicken—they just have too much dignity
to play for small stakes.

Now a lot of people say to me, "Hey, P.J., you like to drive
fast. Why not join a responsible organization, such as the
Sports Car Club of America, and enjoy participation in sports

car racing? That way you could drive as fast as you wish while still engaging in a well-regulated spectator sport that is becoming more popular each year." No thanks. In the first place, if you ask me, those guys are a bunch of tweedy old barf mats who like to talk about things like what necktie they wore to Alberto Ascari's funeral. And in the second place, they won't let me drive drunk. They expect me to go out there and smash into things and roll over on the roof and catch fire and burn to death when I'm sober. They must think I'm crazy. That stuff scares me. I have to get completely shit-faced to even think about driving fast. How can you have a lot of exciting thrills when you're so terrified that you wet yourself all the time? That's not fun. It's just *not fun* to have exciting thrills when you're scared. Take the heroes of the *Iliad*, for instance—they really had some exciting thrills, and were they scared? No. They were drunk. Every chance they could get. And so am I, and I'm not going out there and have a horrible car wreck until somebody brings me a cocktail.

Also, it's important to be drunk because being drunk keeps your body all loose, and that way, if you have an accident or anything, you'll sort of roll with the punches and not get banged up so bad. For example, there was this guy I heard about who was really drunk and was driving through the Adirondacks. He got sideswiped by a bus and went head-on into another car, which knocked him off a bridge, and he plummeted 150 feet into a ravine. I mean, it killed him and everything, but if he hadn't been so drunk and loose, his body probably would have been banged up a lot worse—and you can imagine how much more upset his wife would have been when she went down to the morgue to identify him.

Even more important than being drunk, however, is having the right car. You have to get a car that handles really well. This is extremely important, and there's a lot of debate on this subject—about what kind of car handles best. Some say a front-engined car; some say a rear-engined car. I say a *rented* car. Nothing handles better than a rented car. You can go faster, turn corners sharper, and put the transmission into reverse while going forward at a higher rate of speed in a rented car than in any other kind. You can also park without looking, and can use the trunk as an ice chest. Another thing about a rented car is that it's an all-terrain vehicle. Mud, snow, water, woods—you can take a rented car anywhere. True, you can't always get it back—but that's not your problem, is it?

Yet there's more to a really good-handling car than just making sure it doesn't belong to you. It has to be big. It's really hard for a girl to get her clothes off inside a small car, and this is one of the most important features of car handling. Also, what kind of drugs does it have in it? Most people like to drive on speed or cocaine with plenty of whiskey mixed in. This gives you the confidence you want and need for plowing through red lights and passing trucks on the right. But don't neglect downs and 'ludes and codeine cough syrup either. It's hard to beat the heavy depressants for high-speed spin-outs, backing into trees, and a general feeling of not giving two fucks about man and his universe.

Overall, though, it's the bigness of the car that counts the most. Because when something bad happens in a really big car—accidentally speeding through the middle of a gang of unruly young people who have been taunting you in a drive-in restaurant, for instance—it happens very far away—way out at the end of your fenders. It's like a civil war in Africa; you know, it doesn't really concern you too much. On the other hand, when something happens in a little bitty car it happens right in your face. You get all involved in it and have to give everything a lot of thought. Driving around in a little bitty car is like being one of those sensitive girls who writes poetry. Life is just too much to bear. You end up staying at home in your bedroom and thinking up sonnets that don't get published till you die, which will be real soon if you keep driving around in little bitty cars like that.

Let's inspect some of the basic maneuvers of drunken driving while you've got crazy girls who are on drugs with you. Look for these signs when picking up crazy girls: pierced ears with five or six earrings in them, unusual shoes, white lipstick, extreme thinness, hair that's less than an inch long, or clothing made of chrome and leather. Stay away from girls who cry a lot or who look like they get pregnant easily or have careers. They may want to do weird stuff in cars, but only in the backseat, and it's really hard to steer from back there. Besides, they'll want to get engaged right away afterwards. But the other kind of girls—there's no telling what they'll do. I used to know this girl who weighed about eighty pounds and dressed in skirts that didn't even cover her underwear, when she wore any. I had this beat-up old Mercedes, and we were off someplace about fifty miles from nowhere on Christmas Eve in a horrible sleetstorm. The road was really a mess, all curves and big ditches, and I was blotto, and the car kept slipping off the pavement and sliding sideways. And just when I'd hit a big patch of glare ice and was frantically spinning the wheel trying to stay out of the oncoming traffic, she said, "I shaved my crotch today—wanna feel?"

That's really true. And then about half an hour later the head gasket blew up, and we had to spend I don't know how long in this dirtball motel, although the girl walked all the way to the liquor store through about a mile of slush and got all kinds of wine and did weird stuff with the bottlenecks later. So it was sort of okay, except that the garage where I left the Mercedes burned down and I used the insurance money to buy a motorcycle.

Now, girls who like motorcycles really will do *anything.* I mean, really, *anything you can think of.* But it's just not the same. For one thing, it's hard to drink while you're riding a motorcycle—there's no place to set your glass. And cocaine's out of the question. And personally, I find that grass makes me too sensitive. You smoke some grass and the first thing you know you're pulling over to the side of the road and taking a break to dig the gentle beauty of the sky's vast panorama, the slow, luxurious interplay of sun and clouds, the lulling trill of breezes midst leafy tree branches—and what kind of fun is that? Besides, it's tough to "get it on" with a chick (I mean in the biblical sense) and still make all the fast curves unless you let her take the handlebars with her pants off and come on doggy-style or something, which is harder than it sounds; and pantless girls on motorcycles attract the highway patrol, so usually you don't end up doing anything until you're both off the bike, and by then you may be in the hospital. Like I was after this old lady pulled out in front of me in an Oldsmobile, and the girl I was with still wanted to do anything you can think of, but there was a doctor there and he was squirting Phisohex all over me and combing little bits of gravel out of my face with a wire brush, and I just couldn't get into it. So take it from me and don't get a motorcycle. Get a big car.

Usually, most fast-driving maneuvers that don't require crazy girls call for use of the steering wheel, so be sure your car is equipped with power steering. Without power steering, turning the wheel is a lot like work, and if you wanted work you'd get a job. All steering should be done with the index finger. Then, when you're done doing all the steering that you want to do, just pull your finger out of there and the wheel will come right back to wherever it wants to. It's that simple. Be sure to do an extra lot of steering when going into a driveway or turning sharp corners. And here's another important tip: Always roll the window down before throwing bottles out, and don't try to throw them through the windshield unless the car is parked.

Okay, now say you've been on a six-day drunk and you've just made a bet that you can back up all the way to Cleveland, plus you've got a buddy who's getting a blow job on the trunk lid. Well, let's face it—if that's the way you're going to act, sooner or later you'll have an accident. This much is true. But that doesn't mean that you should sit back and just let accidents happen to you. No, you have to go out and cause them yourself. That way you're in control of the situation.

You know, it's a shame, but a lot of people have the wrong idea about accidents. For one thing, they don't hurt nearly as much as you'd think. That's because you're in shock and can't feel pain, or if you aren't in shock, you're dead, and that doesn't hurt at all so far as we know. Another thing is that they make great stories. I've got this friend—a prominent man in the automotive industry—who flipped his MG TF back in the fifties and slid on his head for a couple hundred yards, and had to spend a year with no eyelids and a steel pin through his cheekbones while his face was being rebuilt. Sure, it wasn't much fun at the time, but you should hear him tell about it now. What a fabulous tale, especially during dinner. Besides, it's not all smashing glass and spurting blood, you understand. Why, a good sideswipe can be an almost religious experience. The sheet metal doesn't break or crunch or anything—it flexes and gives way as the two vehicles come together with a rushing liquid pulse as if two giant sharks of steel were mating in the perpetual night of the sea primordial. I mean, if you're on enough drugs. Also, sometimes you see a lot of really pretty lights in your head.

One sure way to cause an accident is with your basic "moonshiner's" or "bootlegger's" turn. Whiz down the road at about sixty or seventy, throw the gearshift into neutral, cut the wheel to the left, and hit the emergency brake with one good wallop while holding the brake release out with your left hand. This'll send you spinning around in a perfect 180-degree turn right into a culvert or a fast-moving tractor-trailer rig. (The bootlegger's turn can be done on dry pavement, but it works best on top of loose gravel or small children.) Or, when you've moved around backwards, you can then spill the wheel to the right and keep on going until you've come around a full 360 degrees and are headed back the same way you were going; though it probably would have been easier to have just kept going that way in the first place and not have done anything at all, unless you were with somebody you really wanted to impress—your probation officer, for instance.

An old friend of mine named Joe Schenkman happens to have just written me a letter about another thing you can do to wreck a car. Joe's on a little vacation up in Vermont (and will be until he finds out what the statute of limitations on attempted vehicular homicide is). He was writing to tell me about a fellow he met up there, saying:

. . . This guy has rolled (deliberately) over thirty cars (and not just by his own account—the townfolks back him up on this story), inheriting only a broken nose (three times) and a slightly black-and-blue shoulder for all this. What you do, see, is you go into a moonshiner's turn, but you get on the brakes and stay on them. Depending on how fast you're going, you roll proportionately; four or five rolls is decent. Going into the spin, you have one hand on the seat and the other firmly on the roof so you're sprung in tight. As you feel the roof give on the first roll, you slip your seat hand under the dash (of the passenger side, as you're thrown hard over in that direction to begin with) and pull yourself under it. And here you simply sit it out, springing yourself tight with your whole body, waiting for the thunder to die. Naturally, it helps to be drunk, and if you have a split second's doubt or hesitation through any of this, you die.

This Schenkman himself is no slouch of a driver, I may say. Unfortunately, his strong suit is driving in New York City, an area that has a great number of unusual special conditions, which we just don't have the time or the space to get into right here (except to note that the good part is how it's real easy to scare old ladies in new Cadillacs and the bad part is that Negroes actually *do* carry knives, not to mention Puerto Ricans; and everybody else you hit turns out to be a lawyer or married to somebody in the Mob). However, Joe is originally from the South, and it was down there that he discovered huffing glue and sniffing industrial solvents and such. These give you a really spectacular hallucinatory type of a high where you think, for instance, that you're driving through an overpass guardrail and landing on a freight-train flatcar and being hauled to Shreveport and loaded into a container ship headed for Liberia with a crew full of homosexual Lebanese, only to come to and find out that it's true. Joe is a commercial artist who enjoys jazz music and horse racing. His favorite color is blue.

There's been a lot of discussion about what kind of music to listen to while staring doom square in the eye and not blinking unless you get some grit under your contacts. Watch out for the fellow who tunes his FM to the classical station. He thinks a little Rimsky-Korsakov makes things more dramatic—like in a foreign movie. That's pussy style. This kind of guy's idea of a fast drive is a seventy-five-mile-an-hour cruise up to the summer cottage after one brandy and soda. The true skidmark artist prefers something cheery and upbeat—"Night on Disco Mountain" or "Boogie Oogie Oogie" or whatever it is that the teenage lovely wants to shake her buns to. Remember her? So what do *you* care what's on the fucking tape deck? The high, hot whine of the engine, the throaty pitch of the exhaust, the wind in your beer can, the gentle slurping noises from her little bud-red lips—that's all the music your ears need, although side two of the first Velvet Underground album is nice if you absolutely insist. And no short jaunts either. For the maniacal high-speed driver, endurance is everything. Especially if you've used that ever-popular pickup line "Wanna go to Mexico?" Especially if you've used it somewhere like Boston. Besides, teenage girls can go a long, long time without sleep, and believe me, so can the police and their parents. So just keep your foot in it. There's no reason not to. There's no reason not to keep going forever, really. I had this friend who drove a whole shitload of people up from Oaxaca to Cincinnati one time, nonstop. I mean, he stopped for gas but he wouldn't even let anybody get out then. He made them all piss out the windows, and he says that it was worth the entire drive just to *see* a girl try to piss out the window of a moving car.

Get a fat girl friend so you'll have plenty of amphetamines and you'll never have to stop at all. The only problem you'll run into is that after you've been driving for two or three days you start to see things in the road—great big scaly things twenty feet high with nine legs. But there are very few great big scaly things with nine legs in America anymore, so you can just drive right through them because they probably aren't really there, and if they *are* really there you'll be doing the country a favor by running them over.

Yes, but where does it all end? Where does a crazy life like this lead? To death, you say. Look at all the people who've died in car wrecks: Albert Camus, Jayne Mansfield, Jackson Pollock, Tom Paine. Well, Tom Paine didn't *really* die in a car wreck, but he probably would have if he'd lived a little later. He was that kind of guy. Anyway, death is always the first thing that leaps into everybody's mind—sudden violent death at an early age. If only it were that simple. God, we could all go out in a blaze of flaming aluminum alloys formulated specially for the Porsche factory race effort like James Dean did! No ulcers, no hemorrhoids, no bulging waistlines, soft dicks, or false teeth . . . *bash!! kaboom!! Watch this space for paperback reprint rights, auction, and movie option sale!* But that's not the way it goes. No. What actually happens is you fall for that teenage lovely in the next seat over, fall for her like a ton of condoms, and before you know it you're married and have teenage lovelies of your own—getting felt up in a Pontiac Trans Am this very minute, no doubt—plus a six-figure mortgage, a liver the size of the Bronx, and a Country Squire that's never seen the sweet side of sixty.

It's hard to face the truth, but I suppose you yourself realize that if you'd had just a little more courage, just a little more strength of character, you could have been dead by now. No such luck.

TOM BODETT

MOOD PIECE

Alaskan Tom Bodett is known to many as the reasonable, unhurried, humorous voice for Motel 6 and as a commentator on National Public Radio's "All Things Considered." He has put together two collections of his work, As Far as You Can Go Without a Passport *and* Small Comforts.

I had kind of a mood on lately. It lasted nearly a week before I snapped out of it. I was absolutely miserable and so was everyone around me. Bad moods are strange things. They seem to compound themselves and look for dark events to add to the gloom. Mysteriously, they can even cause them to happen. Some religions call this karma, others a loss of grace, but whatever it is, it stinks.

The bad mood scenario goes typically like this.

You wake up late, bound out of bed, and jam your foot under the closet door. This dislodges the big toenail from its setting, which hurts worse than if you'd taken the whole leg off at the knee. Recovering through rapid breathing, you throw on some clothes and fire up the coffeepot. While urging the brew cycle to its conclusion you sift through a stack of yesterday's mail and find a piece you'd overlooked, an official envelope from the City. It's one of those "Hold firmly here, grasp and snap" deals that never work. You put your fingers at the indicated points and give it a stiff pull, neatly tearing the entire packet in two. It turns out to have been your personal property tax statement, and the rip went precisely through the amount due, rendering it unreadable.

Your temples start to throb, so you pour a fresh cup of coffee and turn on the radio to try and settle down. A little music usually soothes, but instead of music you're met with a barrage of incomprehensible jazz being forced through a saxophone at a pressure of ninety pounds per square inch. It's about as soothing as listening to an aircraft engine seize up in a small room, so you snap off the radio with a finality that sends the volume knob rolling under the stove. You figure it's time to stop screwing around and go to work.

There is just the tiniest ball of rust bouncing around in your fuel filter. It's remained there harmlessly for months, biding its time for a morning such as this. Halfway to town, which is exactly as far as you can get from both home and a qualified mechanic at the same time, this little ball of rust decides to head north and lodge itself inside the opening of the main fuel jet. This shuts the engine off quicker than if you'd used the key, leaving you with absolutely no clue as to what went wrong.

After forty-five minutes of dinking around with a stripped-out crescent wrench, you throw up your hands and decide to thumb a ride to town for help. As you slam the hood shut on your shirttail, you think you hear the unmistakable snicker of a rust ball buried deep within the bowels of a disabled wonder of modern engineering.

Your gray mood has turned a deep charcoal, and walking into an auto repair shop is never a good way to cheer up. There's always some grim mechanic who's the hottest thing since the magnetic screwdriver and thinks you're the worst thing that could ever happen to an internal combustion engine, rust notwithstanding. No matter what the problem turns out to be, it's always something you did wrong, and he'll inconvenience his entire day to get you back on the road out of the goodness of his heart and a nominal fee plus tax.

As far as bad moods go, this one is getting downright dangerous, so you head back home to start over. Pulling into the driveway you accidentally flatten the sleeping cat that you never liked anyway, and feel just awful about it. When your wife sees the mood you're in, she thinks you did it on purpose, and you wonder why you didn't do it a long time ago if you're going to get blamed for it anyway. It starts to look like this string of bad luck is just never going to quit.

I saw a logger I once worked with get so mad about something he tore his clothes off, sat down in them, and cried. He looked so silly that everybody laughed, which made him so much madder he started throwing dirt and rocks at us. We laughed even harder at that and were doubled over with cramps and tears by the time he caught on and started laughing himself. We laughed ourselves out, he put his clothes back on, and we went back to work. After that, anytime a guy got really upset about something, he'd pretend to be tearing his clothes off, and everybody'd laugh. That would be the end of it.

I lost my ability to blow it off somewhere along the line, and have to make myself remember those logging days when ill-fortune settles in for one of its marathon visits. They say all humor is rooted in tragedy and it's our capacity to laugh that sustains us. Humans are the only critters who have this ability, and it's a good thing we do. It wouldn't look very good for the tourists if we all had to rip our clothes to pieces every time the truck broke down.

FEAR AND LOATHING AT THE WATERGATE: MR. NIXON HAS CASHED HIS CHECK

Professional wildman and inventor of "gonzo" journalism, Hunter S. Thompson has faced each assignment in his career like a primal carnivore, not resting until he has gnawed the truth from the marrow of its bones. Thompson's latest collection, Generation of Swine, *is deservedly a best-seller. His earlier political work, especially his coverage of the Watergate affair for* Rolling Stone, *must be ranked as some of the best (and funniest) journalism, gonzo or otherwise, this country has produced.*

PART I

THE WORM TURNS IN SWAMPTOWN . . . VIOLENT TALK AT THE NATIONAL AFFAIRS DESK . . . A NARROW ESCAPE FOR TEX COLSON . . . HEAVY DUTY IN THE BUNKER . . . NO ROOM FOR GONZO? "HELL, THEY ALREADY HAVE THIS STORY NAILED UP AND BLEEDING FROM EVERY EXTREMITY."

Reflecting on the meaning of the last presidential election, I have decided at this point in time that Mr. Nixon's landslide victory and my overwhelming defeat will probably prove to be of greater value to the nation than would the victory my supporters and I worked so hard to achieve. I think history may demonstrate that it was not

only important that Mr. Nixon win and that I lose, but that the margin should be of stunning proportions. . . . The shattering Nixon landslide, and the even more shattering exposure of the corruption that surrounded him, have done more than I could have done in victory to awaken the nation. . . . This is not a comfortable conclusion for a self-confident—some would say self-righteous—politician to reach. . . .
    —George McGovern in the *Washington Post:* August 12, 1973

Indeed. But we want to keep in mind that "comfortable" is a very relative word around Washington these days—with the vicious tentacles of "Watergate" ready to wrap themselves around almost anybody, at any moment—and when McGovern composed those eminently reasonable words in the study of his stylish home on the woodsy edge of Washington, he had no idea how close he'd just come to being made extremely "uncomfortable."

I have just finished making out a report addressed to somebody named Charles R. Roach, a claims examiner at the Mid-Atlantic Regional Headquarters of Avis Rent-a-Car in Arlington, Virginia. It has to do with a minor accident that occurred on Connecticut Avenue, in downtown Washington, shortly after George and his wife had bade farewell to the last staggering guests at the party he'd given on a hot summer night in July commemorating the first anniversary of his seizure of the presidential nomination in Miami.

The atmosphere of the party itself had been amazingly loose and pleasant. Two hundred people had been invited—twice that many showed up—to celebrate what history will record, with at least a few asterisks, as one of the most disastrous presidential campaigns in American history. Midway in the evening I was standing on the patio, talking to Carl Wagner and Holly Mankiewicz, when the phone began ringing and whoever answered it came back with the news that President Nixon had just been admitted to the nearby Bethesda Naval Hospital with what was officially announced as "viral pneumonia."

Nobody believed it, of course. High-powered journalists like Jack Germond and Jules Witcover immediately seized the phones to find out what was *really* wrong with Nixon . . . but the rest of us, no longer locked into deadlines or the fast-rising terrors of some tomorrow's election day, merely shrugged at the news and kept on drinking. There was nothing unusual, we felt, about Nixon caving into some real or even psycho-somatic illness. And if the truth was worse than the news . . . well . . . there would be nothing unusual about that either.

One of the smallest and noisiest contingents among the 200 invited guests was the handful of big-time journalists who'd spent most of last autumn dogging McGovern's every lame footstep along the campaign trail, while two third-string police reporters from the *Washington Post* were quietly putting to-gether the biggest political story of 1972 or any other year— a story that had already exploded, by the time of McGovern's "anniversary" party, into a scandal that has even now burned a big hole for itself in every American history textbook written from 1973 till infinity.

One of the most extraordinary aspects of the Watergate story has been the way the press has handled it: What began in the summer of 1972 as one of the great media-bungles of the cen-tury has developed, by now, into what is probably the most thoroughly and most professionally covered story in the his-tory of American journalism.

When I boomed into Washington last month to meet Steadman and set up the National Affairs Desk once again, I expected—or in retrospect I *think* I expected—to find the high-rolling *news-meisters* of the capital press corps jabbering blindly among themselves, once again, in some stylish sec-tor of reality far-removed from the Main Nerve of "the story" . . . like climbing aboard Ed Muskie's *Sunshine Special* in the Florida primary and finding every media star in the nation sipping Bloody Marys and convinced they were riding the rails to Miami with "the candidate" . . . or sitting down to lunch at the Sioux Falls Holiday Inn on election day with a half-dozen of the heaviest press wizards and coming away convinced that McGovern couldn't possibly lose by more than ten points.

My experience on the campaign trail in 1972 had not filled me with a real sense of awe, vis-à-vis the wisdom of the national press corps . . . so I was seriously jolted, when I arrived in Washington, to find that the bastards had this Watergate story nailed up and bleeding from every extremity—from "Watergate" and all its twisted details, to ITT, the Vesco case, Nixon's lies about the financing for his San Clemente beach-mansion, and even the long-dormant "Agnew Scandal."

There was not a hell of a lot of room for a Gonzo journalist to operate in that high-tuned atmosphere. For the first time in memory, the Washington press corps was working very close to the peak of its awesome but normally dormant potential. The *Washington Post* has a half-dozen of the best reporters in America working every tangent of the Watergate story like wild-eyed junkies set adrift, with no warning to find their next connection. *The New York Times*, badly blitzed on the story at first, called in hotrods from its bureaus all over the country to overcome the *Post*'s early lead. Both *Time*'s and *Newsweek*'s Washington bureaus began scrambling feverishly to find new angles, new connections, new leaks and leads in this story that was unraveling so fast that *nobody could* stay on top of it. . . . And especially not the three (or four) TV networks, whose whole machinery was geared to visual/action stories, rather than skillfully planted tips from faceless lawyers who called on private phones and then refused to say anything at all in front of the cameras.

The only standard-brand visual "action" in the Watergate story had happened at the very beginning—when the burglars were caught in the act by a squad of plainclothes cops with drawn guns—and that happened so fast that there was not even a still photographer on hand, much less a TV camera.

The network news moguls are not hungry for stories involving weeks of dreary investigation and minimum camera possibilities—particularly at a time when almost every ranking TV correspondent in the country was assigned to one aspect or another of a presidential campaign that was still boiling feverishly when the Watergate break-in occurred on June 17. The Miami conventions and the Eagleton fiasco kept the Watergate story backstage all that summer. Both the networks and the press had their "first teams" out on the campaign trail until long after the initial indictments—Liddy, Hunt, McCord et al.—on September 15. And by election day in November, the Watergate story seemed like old news.

It was rarely if ever mentioned among the press people following the campaign. A burglary at the Democratic National Headquarters seemed relatively minor, compared to the action in Miami. It was a "local" (Washington) story, and the "local staff" was handling it . . . but I *had* no local staff, so I made the obvious choice.

Except on two occasions, and the first of these still haunts me. On the night of June 17, I spent most of the evening in the Watergate Hotel: From about eight o'clock until ten I was swimming laps in the indoor pool, and from 10:30 until a bit after 1:00 AM I was drinking tequila in the Watergate bar with Tom Quinn, a sports columnist for the now-defunct *Washington Daily News.*

Meanwhile, upstairs in room 214, Hunt and Liddy were already monitoring the break-in, by walkie-talkie, with ex-FBI agent Alfred Baldwin in his well-equipped spy-nest across Virginia Avenue in room 419 of the Howard Johnson Motor Lodge. Jim McCord had already taped the locks on two doors just underneath the bar in the Watergate garage, and it was probably just about the time that Quinn and I called for our last round of tequila that McCord and his team of Cubans moved into action—and got busted less than an hour later.

All this was happening less than 100 yards from where we were sitting in the bar, sucking limes and salt with our Sauza Gold and muttering darkly about the fate of Duane Thomas and the pigs who run the National Football League.

Neither Bob Woodward nor Carl Bernstein from the *Post* were invited to McGovern's party that night—which was fitting, because the guest list was limited to those who had lived through the day-to-day nightmare of the '72 campaign. . . . People like Frank Mankiewicz, Miles Rubin, Rick Sterns, Gary Hart, and even Newsweek correspondent Dick Stout, whose final dispatch on the doomed McGovern campaign very nearly got him thrown out of the *Dakota Queen II* at 30,000 feet over Lincoln, Nebraska, on the day before the election.

This was the crowd that had gathered that night in July to celebrate his last victory before the Great Disaster—the slide that began with Eagleton and ended, incredibly, with "Watergate." The events of the past six months had so badly jangled the nerves of the invited guests—the staffers and journalists who had been with McGovern from New Hampshire all the way to Sioux Falls on election day—that nobody really wanted to go to the party, for fear that it might be a funeral and a serious bummer.

By the end of the evening, when the two dozen bitter-enders had forced McGovern to break out his own private stock—ignoring the departure of the caterers and the dousing of the patio lights—the bulk of the conversation was focused on which one or ones of the Secret Service men assigned to protect McGovern had been reporting daily to Jeb Magruder at CREEP, and which one of the ten or twelve journalists with access to the innards of George's strategy had been on CREEP's payroll at $1,500 a month. This journalist—still publicly unknown and undenounced—was referred to in White House memos as "Chapman's Friend," a mysterious designation that puzzled the whole Washington press corps until one of the President's beleaguered ex-aides explained privately that "Chapman" is a name Nixon used, from time to time, in the good old days when he was able to travel around obscure Holiday Inns under phony names. . . .

R. Chapman, Pepsi-Cola salesman, New York City . . . with a handful of friends carrying walkie-talkies and wearing white leather shoulder holsters. . . . But what the hell? Just send a case of Pepsi up to the suite, my man, and don't ask questions: your reward will come later—call the White House and ask for Howard Hunt or Jim McCord; they'll take care of you.

Right. Or maybe Tex Colson, who is slowly and surely emerging as the guiding light behind Nixon's whole arsenal of illegal, immoral, and unethical "black advance" or "dirty tricks" department. It was Colson who once remarked that he would "walk over his grandmother for Richard Nixon" ... and it was Colson who hired head "plumber" Egil "Bud" Krogh, who in 1969 told Daniel X. Friedman, chairman of the psychiatry department at the University of Chicago: "Anyone who opposes us, we'll destroy. As a matter of fact, anyone who doesn't support us, we'll destroy."

Colson, the only one of Nixon's top command to so far evade Watergate's legal noose, is the man who once told White House cop Jack Caulfield to put a firebomb in the offices of the staid/liberal Brookings Institution, in order to either steal or destroy some documents he considered incriminating. Colson now says he was "only joking" about the firebomb plan, but Caulfield took it so seriously that he went to the White House counsel John Dean and said he refused to work with Colson any longer, because he was "crazy."

Crazy? Tex Colson?

Never in Hell. "He's the meanest man in American politics," says Nixon's speechwriter Pat Buchanan, smiling lazily over the edge of a beer can beside the pool outside his Watergate apartment. Buchanan is one of the few people in the Nixon administration with a sense of humor. He is so far to the right that he dismisses Tex Colson as a "Massachusetts liberal." But for some reason, Buchanan is also one of the few people—perhaps the only one—on Nixon's staff, who has friends at the other end of the political spectrum. At one point during the campaign I mentioned Buchanan at McGovern Headquarters, for some reason, and Rick Sterns, perhaps the most hardline left-bent ideologue on McGovern's staff, sort of chuckled and said, "Oh, yeah, we're pretty good friends. Pat's the only one of those bastards over there with any principles." When I mentioned this to another McGovern staffer, he snapped: "Yeah, maybe so ... like Josef Goebbels had principles."

My own relationship with Buchanan goes back to the New Hampshire primary in 1968 when Nixon was still on the dim fringes of his political comeback. We spent about eight hours one night in a Boston hotel room, finishing off a half gallon of Old Crow and arguing savagely about politics: As I recall, I kept asking him why a person who seemed to have good sense would be hanging about with Nixon. It was clear even then that Buchanan considered me stone crazy, and my dismissal of Nixon as a hopeless bum with no chance of winning anything seemed to amuse him more than anything else.

About eight months later, after one of the strangest and most brutal years in American history, Richard Nixon was President and Pat Buchanan was one of his top two speechwriters along with Ray Price, the house moderate. I didn't see Pat again until the McGovern Campaign in '72 when Ron Ziegler refused to have me on the Nixon Press Plane and Buchanan intervened to get me past the White House Guard and into what turned out to be a dull and useless seat on the plane with the rest of the White House press corps. It was also Buchanan who interviewed Garry Wills, introducing him into the Nixon Campaign of 1968—an act of principle that resulted in an extremely unfriendly book called *Nixon Agonistes*.

So it seemed entirely logical, I thought—going back to Washington in the midst of this stinking Watergate summer—to call Buchanan and see if he felt like having thirteen or fourteen drinks on some afternoon when he wasn't at the White House working feverishly in what he calls "the bunker." Price and Buchanan write almost everything Nixon says and they are busier than usual these days, primarily figuring out what *not* to say. I spent most of one Saturday afternoon with Pat lounging around a tin umbrella table beside the Watergate pool and talking lazily about politics in general. When I called him at the White House the day before, the first thing he said was "Yeah, I just finished your book."

"Oh Jesus," I replied, thinking this naturally meant the end of any relationship we'd ever have. But he laughed. "Yeah, it's one of the funniest things I've ever read."

One of the first things I asked him that afternoon was something that had been simmering in my head for at least a year or so and that was how he could feel comfortable with strange friends like me and Rick Sterns, and particularly how he could possibly feel comfortable sitting out in the open—in plain sight of the whole Watergate crowd—with a known monster whose affection for Richard Nixon was a matter of fairly brutal common knowledge—or how he felt comfortable playing poker once or twice a week sometimes with Rick Sterns, whose political views are almost as diametrically opposed to Buchanan's as mine are. He shrugged it off with a grin, opening another beer. "Oh, well, we ideologues seem to get along better than the others. I don't agree with Rick on anything at all that I can think of, but I like him and I respect his honesty."

A strange notion, the far left and far right finding some kind of odd common ground beside the Watergate pool and particularly when one of them is a top Nixon speechwriter, spending most of his time trying to keep the Boss from sinking like a stone in foul water, yet now and then laughingly referring to the White House as The Bunker.

After the sixth or seventh beer, I told him about our abortive plot several nights earlier to seize Colson out of his house and drag him down Pennsylvania Avenue tied behind a huge gold Oldsmobile Cutlass. He laughed and said something to the effect that "Colson's so tough, he might like it." And then, talking further about Colson, he said, "But you know he's not really a Conservative."

And that's what seems to separate the two GOP camps, like it separates Barry Goldwater from Richard Nixon. Very much like the difference between the Humphrey Democrats and the McGovern Democrats. The ideological wing versus the pragmatists, and by Buchanan's standards it's doubtful that he even considers Richard Nixon a Conservative.

My strange and violent reference to Colson seemed to amuse him more than anything else. "I want to be very clear on one thing," I assured him. "If you're thinking about having me busted for conspiracy on this, remember that I've already deliberately dragged you into it." He laughed again and then mentioned something about the "one overt act" necessary for a conspiracy charge, and I quickly said that I had no idea where

Tex Colson even lived and didn't really want to know, so that even if we'd wanted to drag the vicious bastard down Pennsylvania Avenue at sixty miles per hour behind a gold Oldsmobile Cutlass we had no idea, that night, where to find him, and about halfway into the plot we crashed into a black and gold Cadillac on Connecticut Avenue and drew a huge mob of angry blacks who ended all thought of taking vengeance on Colson. It was all I could do to get out of that scene without getting beaten like a gong for the small crease our rented Cutlass had put in the fender of the Cadillac.

Which brings us back to that accident report I just wrote and sent off to Mr. Roach at Avis Mid-Atlantic Headquarters in Arlington. The accident occurred about 3:30 in the morning when either Warren Beatty or Pat Caddell opened the door of a gold Oldsmobile Cutlass I'd rented at Dulles airport earlier that day, and banged the door against the fender of a massive black and gold Cadillac roadster parked in front of a late-night restaurant on Connecticut Avenue called Anna Maria's. It seemed like a small thing at the time, but in retrospect it might have spared us all—including McGovern— an extremely nasty episode.

Because somewhere in the late hours of that evening, when the drink had taken hold and people were jabbering loosely about anything that came into their heads, somebody mentioned that "the worst and most vicious" of Nixon's backstairs White House hit men—Charles "Tex" Colson—was probably the only one of the dozen or more Nixon/CRP functionaries thus far sucked into "the Watergate scandal" who was not likely to do any time, or even be indicted.

It was a long, free-falling conversation, with people wandering in and out, over a time-span of an hour or so—journalists, pols, spectators—and the focus of it, as I recall, was a question that I was trying to get some bets on: How many of the primary Watergate figures would actually serve time in prison?

The reactions ranged from my own guess that only Magruder and Dean would live long enough to serve time in prison, to

Mankiewicz's flat assertion that "everybody except Colson" would be indicted, convicted, sentenced, and actually hauled off to prison.

(Everybody involved in this conversation will no doubt deny any connection with it—or even hearing about it, for that matter—but what the hell? It did, in fact, take place over the course of some two or three days, in several locations, but the seed of speculation took root in the final early-morning hours of McGovern's party . . . although I don't remember that George himself was involved or even within earshot at any time. He has finally come around to the point where his friends don't mind calling him "George" in the friendly privacy of his own home, but that is not quite the same thing as getting him involved in a felony-conspiracy/attempted murder charge that some wild-eyed, Nixon-appointed geek in the Justice Department might try to crank up on the basis of a series of boozy conversations among journalists, politicians, and other half-drunk cynics. Anybody who has spent any time around late-night motel bars with the press corps on a presidential campaign knows better than to take their talk seriously . . . but after reading reviews of my book on the '72 campaign, it occurs to me that some people will believe almost *anything* that fits their preconceived notions.)

And so much for all that.

August 2 Patio Bar beside the Washington Hilton Swimming Pool

Steadman and his wife had just arrived from England. Sandy had flown in the day before from Colorado and I had come up from Miami after a long vacation in the decompression chamber. It was a Tuesday or Wednesday afternoon, I think, and the Watergate Hearings were in progress but we'd decided to take the first day off and get ourselves under control. One of the first things I had to do was make out a long overdue accident report for that night, two weeks earlier, when the door of my rented car smacked into the Cadillac at four in the morning. The Avis people were threatening to cut off my coverage for "non-cooperation" so I'd brought the insanely complicated accident report down to the patio table by the pool, thinking to fill it out with the help of eight or nine Carlsbergs.

Steadman was already sketching distractedly, swilling beers at a feverish rate and muttering darkly to himself about the terrible conditions in the hotel and how earlier that morning while passing through the coffee shop, a huge ceiling lamp had fallen from the ceiling and nearly killed him.

It was "teddible teddible," he said, "the damn thing came so close that it knocked my briefcase full of drawings out of my hand. Six inches closer and it would have caved in my head!"

I nodded sympathetically, thinking it was just another one of those ugly twists of luck that always seem to affect Ralph in this country, and I kept on grappling with the accident report.

Steadman was still babbling. "God, it's hot . . . Ah, this teddible thirst . . . what's that you've got there?"

"The goddamn accident report. I've got to make it out."

"Accident report?"

"Yeah, I had a small wreck the last time I was here about two weeks ago. . . ."

"All right, all right. . . . Yes, two more Carlsbergs."

". . . And the car blew up the next night and I had to abandon it in Rock Creek Park at four in the morning. I think they're still billing me for it."

"Who?"

"The Avis people."

"My God, that's teddible."

"I only had it two nights. The first night I had this wreck, and the next night it blew up."

"What were you doing in this wretched city at four in the morning?"

"Well, actually we were thinking about going out to Tex Colson's house and jerking him out of bed, tying him behind the car with a big rope, and dragging him down Pennsylvania Avenue . . . then cutting him loose in front of the White House Guard Gate."

"You're kidding. . . . You don't really mean that. You wouldn't do a thing like that, would you?"

"Of course not. That would be a conspiracy to commit either murder or aggravated assault, plus kidnapping . . . and you know me, Ralph; that's not my style at all."

"That's what I mean. You were drunk perhaps, eh?"

"Ah, we were drunk, yes. We'd been to a party at McGovern's."

"McGovern's? Drinking? Who was with you?"

"Drinking heavily, yes. It was Warren Beatty and Pat Caddell, McGovern's poll wizard, and myself and for some reason it occurred to me that the thing to do that hour of the morning was to go out and get Colson."

"My God, that's crazy! You must have been stoned and drunk—especially by four in the morning."

"Well, we left McGovern's at about 2:30 and we were supposed to meet Crouse at this restaurant downtown. . . . McGovern lives somewhere in the Northwest part of town and it had taken me two hours to find the damn house and I figured it would take me another two hours to get out again unless I could follow somebody. Crouse was about a block ahead of me when we left. I could see his taillights but there was another car between me and Crouse and I was afraid I'd lose him in that maze of narrow little streets, almost like country lanes.

" 'We can't let Crouse get away,' I said. So I slammed it into passing gear and passed the car right in front of me in order to get behind Crouse, and all of a sudden here was a car coming the other direction on this street about fifteen feet wide—just barely enough room for two cars to pass and certainly not enough room for thrce cars to pass, one of them going about seventy miles an hour with a drunk at the wheel.

"I thought, hmmmm, well . . . I can either slow down or stomp on it and squeeze in there, so I stomped on it and forced the oncoming car up over the curb and onto the grass in order to avoid me as I came hurtling back into my own lane, and just as I flashed past him I happened to look over and saw that it was a police car. Well, I thought, this is not the time to stop and apologize; I could see him in my rear view mirror, stopping and beginning to turn around. . . . So instead of following Crouse, I took the first left I could, turned the lights off and drove like a bastard—assuming the cop would probably chase Crouse and run him down and arrest him, but as it happened he didn't get either of us."

"What a rotten thing to do."

"Well, it was him or me, Ralph . . . as a matter of fact I worried about it when we didn't see Tim at the restaurant later on. But we were late because we did some high-speed driving exercises in the Southeast area of Washington—flashing along those big empty streets going into corners at eighty miles an hour and doing 180s . . . it was a sort of thunder road driving trip, screwing it on with that big Cutlass."

"Enormous car?"

"A real monster, extremely overpowered . . ."

"How big is it? The size of a bus?"

"No, normal size for a big car, but extremely powerful—much more, say, than a Mustang or something like that. We did about an hour's worth of crazed driving on these deserted streets, and it was during this time that I mentioned that we should probably go out and have a word with Mr. Colson—because during a conversation earlier in the evening, the consensus among the reporters at McGovern's party was that Colson was probably the only one of Nixon's first-rank henchmen who would probably not even be indicted."

"Why's that?"

"He had managed to keep himself clean, somehow—up to that point anyway. Now, he's been dragged into the ITT hassle again, so it looks like he might go down with all the others.

"But at that point, we thought, well, Colson really is the most evil of those bastards, and if he gets off there is really no justice in the world. So we thought we'd go out to his house—luckily none of us knew where he lived—and beat on his door, mumbling something like: 'God's mercy on me! My wife's been raped! My foot's been cut off!' Anything to lure him downstairs . . . and the minute he opened the door, seize him and drag him out to the car and tie him by the ankles and drag him down to the White House."

"He could identify you . . ."

"Well, he wouldn't have time to know exactly who it was— but we thought about it for a while, still driving around, and figured a beastly thing like that might be the only thing that could get Nixon off the hook, because he could go on television the next afternoon, demanding to make a nationwide emergency statement, saying: 'Look what these thugs have done to poor Mr. Colson! This is exactly what we were talking about! This is why we had to be so violent in our ways, because these thugs will stop at nothing! They dragged Mr. Colson the length of Pennsylvania Avenue at four in the morning, then cut him loose like a piece of meat!' He would call for more savage and stringent security measures against 'the kind of animals who would do a thing like this.' So we put the plot out of our heads."

"Well, it would have been a bit risky . . . wouldn't have done the Democratic Party any good at all, would it?"

"Well, it might have created a bit of an image problem— and it would have given Nixon the one out he desperately needs now, a way to justify the whole Watergate trip by raving about 'this brutal act.' . . . That's an old Hell's Angels gig, dragging people down the street. Hell's Angels. Pachucos, drunken cowboys.

"But I thought more about it later, when I finally got back to the hotel after that stinking accident I'm still trying to explain . . . and it occurred to me that those bastards are really mean enough to do that to Colson, themselves—if they only had the wits to think about it. They could go out and drag him down the street in a car with old McGovern stickers on the bumpers or put on false beards and wave a wine bottle out the window as they passed the White House and cut him loose. He'd roll to a stop in front of the Guard House and the Guard would clearly see the McGovern sticker on the car screeching off around the corner and that's all Nixon would need. If we gave them the idea, they'd probably go out and get Colson tonight."

"He'd be babbling, I'd think—"

"He'd be hysterical, in very bad shape. And of course he'd claim that McGovern thugs had done it to him—if he were still able to talk. I really believe Nixon would do a thing like that if he thought it would get him out of the hole. . . . So I thought about it a little more, and it occurred to me what we should do was have these masks made up—you know those rubber masks that fit over the whole head."

"Ah, yes, very convincing. . . ."

"Yeah, one of them would have to be the face of Haldeman, one the face of Ehrlichman, and one the face of Tony Ulasewicz."

"Yes, the meanest men on the Nixon Staff."

"Well, Colson's the meanest man in politics, according to Pat Buchanan. Ulasewicz is the hit man, a hired thug. I thought if we put these masks on and wore big overcoats or something to disguise ourselves and went out to his house and kind of shouted: 'Tex, Tex! It's me, Tony. Come on down. We've got a big problem.' And the minute he opens the door, these people with the Haldeman and Ehrlichman masks would jump out from either side and seize him by each arm—so that he sees who has him, but only for two or three seconds, before the person wearing the Ulasewicz mask slaps a huge burlap sack over his head, knots it around his knees, and then the three of them carry him out to the car and lash him to the rear bumper and drag him down the street—and just as we passed the White House Guard Station, slash the rope so that Colson would come to a tumbling bloody stop right in front of the Guard . . . and after two or three days in the Emergency Ward, when he was finally able to talk, after coming out of shock, he would swear that the people who got him were Haldeman, Ehrlichman, and Ulasewicz—and he would *know* they were mean enough to do it, because that's the way *he* thinks. He's mean enough to do it himself. You'd have to pick a night when they were all in Washington, and Colson would swear that they did it to him, no matter what they said. He would *know* it, because he had *seen* them."

"Brilliant, brilliant. Yes, he'd be absolutely convinced—having seen the men and the faces."

"Right. But of course you couldn't talk—just seize him and go. What would you think if you looked out and saw three people you recognized, and suddenly they jerked you up and tied you behind a car and dragged you forty blocks? Hell, you *saw* them. You'd testify, swear under oath . . . which would cause Nixon probably to go completely crazy. He wouldn't know *what* to believe! How could he be sure that Haldeman, Ehrlichman, and Ulasewicz hadn't done it? Nobody would know, not even by using lie detectors. . . . But that's a pretty heavy act to get into—dragging people around the street behind rented Avis cars, and we never quite got back to it, anyway, but if we hadn't had that accident we might have given it a little more thought although I still have no idea where Colson lives and I still don't want to know. But you have to admit it was a nice idea."

"That's a lovely thing, yes."

"You know Colson had that sign on the wall in his office saying ONCE YOU HAVE THEM BY THE BALLS, THEIR HEARTS AND MINDS WILL FOLLOW."

"Right."

"He's an ex-Marine captain. So it would be a definite dose of his own medicine."

"Do you really think he deserves that kind of treatment?"

"Well, he was going to set off a firebomb in the Brookings Institution, just to recover some papers. . . . Colson is not one of your friendlier, happier type of persons. He's an evil bastard, and dragging him down the street would certainly strike a note of terror in that crowd; they could use some humility."

"Poetic justice, no?"

"Well, it's a little rough . . . it might not be necessary to drag him forty blocks. Maybe just four. You could put him in the trunk for the first thirty-six blocks, then haul him out and drag him the last four; that would certainly scare the piss out of him, bumping along the street, feeling all his skin being ripped off. . . ."

"He'd be a bloody mess. They might think he was just some drunk and let him lie there all night."

"Don't worry about that. They have a Guard Station in front of the White House that's open twenty-four hours a day. The Guards would recognize Colson . . . and by that time of course his wife would have called the cops and reported that a bunch of thugs had kidnapped him."

"Wouldn't it be a little kinder if you drove about four more blocks and stopped at a phone box to ring the hospital and say, 'Would you mind going around to the front of the White House? There's a naked man lying outside in the street, bleeding to death. . . .' "

". . . and we think it's Mr. Colson."

"It would be quite a story for the newspapers, wouldn't it?"

"Yeah, I think it's safe to say we'd see some headlines on that one."

PART II

FLASHBACKS AND TIME WARPS . . . SCRAMBLED NOTES AND RUDE COMMENTS FROM THE HIGH COUNTRY . . . DEAN VS. HALDEMAN IN THE HEARING ROOM . . . A QUESTION OF PERJURY . . . EHRLICHMAN SANDBAGS AN OLD BUDDY . . . ARE THE SHARKS DESERTING THE SUCKFISH?

EDITOR'S NOTE:

Due to circumstances beyond our control, the following section was lashed together at the last moment from a six-pound bundle of documents, notebooks, memos, recordings, and secretly taped phone conversations with Dr. Thompson during a month of erratic behavior in Washington, New York, Colorado, and Miami. His "long-range-plan," he says, is to "refine" these nerve-wracking methods, somehow, and eventually "create an entirely new form of journalism." In the meantime, we have suspended his monthly retainer and canceled his credit card. During one four-day period in Washington he destroyed two cars, cracked a wall in the Washington Hilton, purchased two French horns at $1,100 each, and ran through a plate-glass door in a Turkish restaurant.

Compounding the problem was the presence in Washington, for the first time, of our artist Ralph Steadman—an extremely heavy drinker with little or no regard for either protocol or normal social amenities. On Steadman's first visit to the Watergate Hearing Room he was ejected by the Capitol Police after spilling beer on a TV monitor and knocking Sam Ervin off his feet while attempting to seize a microphone to make a statement about "the rottenness of American politics." It was only the timely intervention of *New York Post* correspondent John Lang that kept Steadman from being permanently barred from the Hearing Room.

In any case, the bulk of what follows appears exactly as Dr. Thompson wrote it in his notebooks. Given the realities of our constant deadline pressure, there was no other way to get this section into print.

THE NOTEBOOKS

"Jesus, this Watergate thing is unbelievable. It's terrible, like finding out your wife is running around but you don't want to hear about it."

> —Remark of a fat man from Nashville
> sharing a taxi with Ralph Steadman

Tuesday morning 6/26/73: 8:13 A.M. in the Rockies. . . .

Bright sun on the grass outside my windows behind this junk TV set and long white snowfields, still unmelted, on the peaks across this valley. Every two or three minutes the doleful screech of a half-wild peacock rattles the windows. The bastard is strutting around on the roof, shattering the morning calm with his senseless cries.

His noise is a bad burden on Sandy's nerves. "Goddamnit!" she mutters. "We *have* to get him a hen!"

"Fuck him; we *got* him a hen—and she ran off and got

herself killed by coyotes. What the crazy bastard needs now is a bullet through the vocal cords. He's beginning to sound like Herman Talmadge."

"Talmadge?"

"Watch what's happening, goddamnit! Here's another true Son of the South. First it was Thompson . . . now Talmadge . . . and then we'll get that half-wit pimp from Florida."

"Gurney?"

I nodded, staring fixedly at the big blueish eye of the permanently malfunctioned "color TV" set that I hauled back from Washington last summer, when I finally escaped from the place. . . . But now I was using it almost feverishly, day after day, to watch what was *happening* in Washington.

The Watergate Hearings—my daily fix, on TV. Thousands of people from all over the country are writing the networks to demand that this goddamn tedious nightmare be jerked off the air so they can get back to their favorite soap operas: "As the World Turns," "The Edge of Night," "The Price Is Right" and "What Next for Weird Betty?" They are bored by the spectacle of the Watergate hearings. The plot is confusing, they say; the characters are dull, and the dialogue is repulsive.

The President of the United States would never act that way—at least not during baseball season. Like Nixon's new White House chief of staff, Melvin Laird, said shortly before his appointment: "If the President turns out to be guilty, I don't want to hear about it."

This is the other end of the attitude-spectrum from the comment I heard, last week, from a man in Denver: "I've been waiting a long time for this," he said. "Maybe not as long as Jerry Voorhis or Helen Gahagan Douglas . . . and I never really thought it would happen, to tell you the truth." He flashed me a humorless smile and turned back to his TV set. "But it *is*, by god! And it's almost too good to be true."

My problem—journalistically, at least—has its roots in the fact that I agree with just about everything that laughing, vengeful bastard said that day. We didn't talk much. There was no need for it. Everything Richard Milhous Nixon ever stood for was going up in smoke right in front of our eyes. And anybody who could understand and appreciate *that*, I felt, didn't need many words to communicate. At least not with me.

(The question is: what did he *stand for*, and what next for *that?* Agnew? Reagan? Rockefeller? Even Percy? Nixon was finally "successful" for the same reason he was finally brought low. He kept pushing, pushing, pushing—and inevitably he pushed too far.)

Noon—Tuesday, June 26

The TV set is out on the porch now—a move that involved much cursing and staggering.

Weicker has the mike—*mano a mano* on Dean—and after thirteen minutes of apparently aimless blathering he comes off no better than Talmadge. Weicker seemed oddly cautious —a trifle obtuse, perhaps.

What are the connections? Weicker is a personal friend of Pat Gray's. He is also the only member of the Select Committee with after-hours personal access to John Dean.

"—Live from Senate Caucus Room—"

—flash on CBS screen

Live? Rehearsed? In any case, Dean is livelier than most—not only because of what he has to say, but because he—unlike the other witnesses—refused to say it first in executive session to Committee staffers before going on TV.

Strange—Dean's obvious credibility comes not from his long-awaited impact (or lack of it) on the American public, but from his obvious ability to deal with the seven Senatorial Inquisitors. They seem awed.

Dean got his edge, early on, with a mocking lash at the integrity of Minority Counsel Fred Thompson—and the others fell meekly in line. Dean radiates a certain very narrow kind of authority—nothing *personal*, but the kind of nasal blank-hearted authority you feel in the presence of the taxman or a very polite FBI agent.

Only Baker remains. *His* credibility took a bad beating yesterday. Dean ran straight at him, startling the TV audience with constant references to Baker's personal dealings with "the White House," prior to the hearings. There was no need to mention that Baker is the son-in-law of that late and only half-lamented "Solon" from the Great State of Illinois, Sen. Everett Dirksen.

Dean is clearly a shrewd *executive.* He will have no trouble getting a good job when he gets out of prison.

Now Montoya—the flaccid Mex-Am from New Mexico. No problem here for John Dean. . . . Suddenly Montoya hits Dean head on with Nixon's bogus quote about Dean's *investigation* clearing all members of White House staff. Dean calmly shrugs it off as a lie—"I never made any investigation."

—Montoya continues with entire list of *prior* Nixon statements.

Dean: "In totality, there are less than accurate statements in that . . . ah . . . those statements."

Montoya is *after Nixon's head!* Is this the *first sign?* Over the hump for Tricky Dick?

* * *Recall lingering memory of Miami Beach plainclothes cop, resting in armory behind Convention Center on night of Nixon's renomination—"You tell 'em, Tricky Dick"—watching Nixon's speech on TV . . . with tear gas fumes all around us and demonstrators gagging outside.

4:20 EDT
As usual, the pace picks up at the end. These buggers should be forced to keep at it for fifteen or sixteen straight hours— heavy doses of speed, pots of coffee, Wild Turkey, etc., force them down to the raving hysterical *quick.* Wild accusations, etc. . . .

Dean becomes more confident as time goes on—a bit *flip* now, finding his feet.

Friday morning, June 29. . . . 8:33 A.M.
Jesus, this waterhead Gurney again! You'd think the poor bugger would have the sense not to talk anymore . . . but no, Gur-

ney is still blundering along, still hammering blindly at the receding edges of Dean's "credibility" in his now-obvious role as what Frank Reynolds and Sam Donaldson on ABC-TV both described as "the waterboy for the White House."

Gurney appears to be deaf; he has a brain like a cow's udder. He asks his questions—off the typed list apparently furnished him by Minority (GOP) counsel, Fred J. Thompson—then his mind seems to wander, his eyes roam lazily around the room while Thompson whispers industriously in his ear, his hands shuffle papers distractedly on the table in front of his microphone . . . and meanwhile, Dean meticulously chews up his questions and hands them back to him in shreds; so publicly mangled that their fate might badly embarrass a man with good sense. . . .

But Gurney seems not to notice: His only job on this committee is to *Defend the Presidency*, according to his instructions from the White House—or at least whatever third-string hangers-on might still be working there—and what we tend to forget, here, is that it's totally impossible to understand Gurney's real motives without remembering that he's the Republican Senator from Florida, a state where George Wallace swept the *Democratic primary* in 1972 with 78% of the vote, and which went 72% for Nixon in November.

In a state where even Hubert Humphrey is considered a dangerous radical, Ed Gurney's decision to make an ignorant yahoo of himself on national TV makes excellent sense—at least to his own constituency. They are watching TV down in Florida today, along with the rest of the country, and we want to remember that if Gurney appears in Detroit and Sacramento as a hideous caricature of the imbecilic Senator Cornpone—that's not necessarily the way he appears to the voters around Tallahassee and St. Petersburg.

Florida is not Miami—contrary to the prevailing national image—and one of the enduring mysteries in American politics is how a humane and relatively enlightened politician like Reubin Askew could have been elected Governor of one of the few states in the country where George Wallace would have easily beaten Richard Nixon—in a head-to-head presidential race—in either 1968 or 1972. Or even 1976, for that matter. . . .

And so much for all that. Gurney is off the air now—having got himself tangled up in a legal/constitutional argument with Sam Ervin and Dean's attorney. He finally just hunkered down and passed the mike to Senator Inouye, who immediately re-focused the questioning by prodding Dean's memory on the subject of White House efforts to seek vengeance on their "enemies."

Which Senators—in addition to Teddy Kennedy—were sub-jects of surveillance by Nixon's gumshoes? Which journal-ists—in addition to the man from *Newsday* who wrote unfavorable things about Bebe Rebozo—were put on The List to have their tax returns audited? Which athletes and actors—in addition to Joe Namath and Paul Newman—were put on the list to be "screwed"?

Dean's answers were vague on these things. He's not inter-ested in "interpreting the motives of others," he says—which is an easy thing to forget, after watching him on the tube for three days, repeatedly incriminating at least half the ranking fixers in Nixon's inner circle: Colson, Haldeman, Ehrlichman, Mitchell, Magruder, Strachan, Ziegler, Moore, LaRue, Kalm-bach, Nofziger, Krogh, Liddy, Kleindienst . . . and the evidence is "mind-boggling," in Senator Baker's words, when it comes in the form of verbatim memos and taped phone conversa-tions.

The simple-minded vengefulness of the language seems at least as disturbing as the vengeful plots un-veiled.

5:35 P.M.
Sitting out here on the porch, naked in a rocking chair in the half-shade of a dwarf juniper tree—looking out at snow-cov-ered mountains from this hot lizard's perch in the sun with no clouds at 8,000 feet—a mile and a half high, as it were—it is hard to grasp that this dim blue tube sitting on an old bullet-pocked tree stump is bringing me every un-censored detail—for five or six hours each day from a musty brown

room 2,000 miles east—of a story that is beginning to look like it can have only one incredible ending—the downfall of the President of the United States.

Six months ago, Richard Nixon was the most powerful political leader in the history of the world—more powerful than Augustus Caesar when he had his act rolling full bore—six months ago.

Now, with the passing of each sweaty afternoon, into what history will call "the Summer of '73," Richard Nixon is being dragged closer and closer—with all deliberate speed, as it were—to disgrace and merciless infamy. His place in history is already fixed: He will go down with Grant and Harding as one of democracy's classic mutations.

9:22 P.M.

Billy Graham Crusade on both TV channels. . . . But what? What's happening here? An acid flashback? A time warp? CBS has Graham in Orange County, raving about "redemption through *blood*." Yes, God demands *Blood!* . . . but ABC is running the Graham Crusade in South Africa, a huge all-white Afrikaner pep rally at Johannesburg's Wanderers Stadium. (Did I finally get that right, are these mushrooms deceiving me?)

Strange . . . on this eve of Nixon's demise, his private preacher is raving about *blood* in Los Angeles (invoking the actual bloody images of Robert Kennedy's brain on the cold concrete floor of the Ambassador Hotel kitchen and Jack Kennedy's blood "on his widow's dress that tragic day in Dallas" . . . and the blood of Martin Luther King on that motel balcony in Memphis).

But *wait!* Is that a *black* face I see in the crowd at Wanderers Stadium? Yes, a rapt black face, wearing aviator shades and a green army uniform . . . stoned on Billy's message, along with all the others: "Your *soul* is searching for God! [Pause, body crouched, both fists shaking defiantly in the air. . . .] They tore his flesh! They pulled his *beard* out." Graham is in a wild Charlton Heston fighting stance now: "And while they were doing that, 72 million avenging angels had to be held back . . .

yes . . . by the bloody arm of the Lord . . . from sweeping this planet into *hell.*"

Cazart! Seventy-two million of the fuckers, eh? That threat would never make the nut in L.A. It would have to be 72 *billion* there. But South Africa is the last of the white Nazi bush-leagues, and when you mention 72 million of *anything* ready to sweep across the planet, they *know* what you mean in South Africa.

Niggers. The avenging black horde . . . and suddenly it occurs to me that Graham's act is extremely subtle; he is actually *threatening* this weeping crowd of white-supremist burghers. . . . Indeed. . . . Redemption Thru Fear! It knocked 'em dead in Houston, so why not here?

10:05
The news, and John Dean again—that fiendish little drone. (Did the President seem *surprised* when you gave him this information?) "No sir, he did not."

The junkies are rolling up the tents at Camp David tonight. Mister Nixon has cashed his check. Press reports from "the Western White House" in San Clemente say the President has "no comment" on Dean's almost unbelievably destructive testimony.

No comment. The boss is under sedation. Who is with him out there on that lonely western edge of America tonight? Bebe Rebozo? Robert Abplanalp, W. Clement Stone?

Probably not. They must have seen what Nixon saw today— that the Ervin committee was going to give Dean a *free ride.* His victims will get their shots at him tomorrow—or next week—but it won't make much difference, because the only ones left to question him are the ones he publicly ridiculed yesterday as tools of the White House. Baker's credibility is so crippled—in the wake of Dean's references in his opening statement to Baker's alleged "willingness to cooperate" with the Nixon brain-trust in the days before these hearings—that anything Baker hits Dean with tomorrow will seem like the angry retaliation of a much-insulted man.

And what can poor Gurney say? Dean contemptuously dismissed him—in front of a nationwide TV audience of 70 million cynics—as such a hopele 3 yo-yo that he wouldn't even have to be leaned on. Gurney was the only one of the seven senators on the Ervin committee that Nixon's strategists figured was safely in their pocket, before the hearings started. Weicker, the maverick Republican, was considered a lost cause from the start.

"We knew we were in trouble when we looked at that line-up," Dean testified. There was something almost like a smile on his face when he uttered those words . . . the rueful smile of a good loser, perhaps? Or maybe something else. The crazy, half-controlled flicker of a laugh on the face of a man who is just beginning to think he might *survive* this incredible trip. By 4:45 on Tuesday, Dean had the dazed, still hypertense look of a man who knows he went all the way out to the edge, with no grip at all for a while, and suddenly feels his balance coming back.

Well . . . maybe so. If Dean can survive tomorrow's inevitable counter-attack it's all over. The Harris poll in today's *Rocky Mountain News*—even *before* Dean's testimony—showed Nixon's personal credibility rating on the Watergate "problem" had slipped to a fantastic new low of 15–70% negative. If the Ervin committee lets even half of Dean's testimony stand, Richard Nixon won't be able to give away dollar bills in Times Square on the Fourth of July.

Monday, July 15, 2:10 P.M.
Watergate Hearings
Old Senate Office Building
   *Mystery witness—Alex Butterfield. Impossible to see witness's face from periodical seat directly behind him.
   *Rufus (pipe) Edmisten. Ervin's man, the face behind Baker and Ervin. "Politically ambitious—wants to run for Attorney General of North Carolina"—always sits on camera.
   Butterfield regales room with tales of elaborate taping machine in Oval Office (see clips). Nixon's official *bugger*—"liaison to SS."

BF:—sharp dark blue suit—Yes sir—*it was a great deal more difficult to pick up in the cabinet room.*

Talmadge: Who installed the devices?

BF: SS—Tech. Security Div. . . . To record things for posterity.

T: Why were these devices installed?

BF: Constant taping of all conversations in Oval Office for transcriptions for *Nixon library.* Voice activated mikes all over Nixon's office. . . . With time delay, so as not to cut out during pauses.

Fred Thompson looks like a Tennessee moonshiner who got rich—somebody sent him to a haberdasher when he heard he was going to Washington.

Four 6 × 6 chandeliers—yellow cut glass—hanging from ceiling, but obscured by banks of Colortran TV lites. Stan Tredick and other photogs with cardboard shields taped over lenses to cut out TV lights from above.

2:34—Voting warning signal?
Ah ha! Butterfield will produce Dean-Nixon tape from September 15?

T: No warning signal?

BF: No sir, not to my knowledge.

T: This taping was solely to serve historical purposes?

BF: Yes sir, as far as I know.

??: Key Biscayne and San Clemente?

BF: No recording devices there—at least not by me.

NY Post headline: NIXON BUGS SELF (full page).

*The most obvious difference between being in the hearing room and watching TV is the *scale*—sense of smallness like a football stadium. The players seem human-sized and the grass seems real (in some cases). Room 318 is only about 100 × 100—unlike the vast theater it looks on TV.

*Constant stream of students being run in and out behind us.

Kalmbach sitting right in front of me—waiting to testify. $300 grey linen suit—$75 wing tips—lacquered black hair and tailored shirt—thin blue stripes on off-white. Large, rich. Sitting with silver-haired lawyer.

*Ervin reads letter from Buzhardt. Sends buzz through room—says LBJ did some taping.

Interesting—sitting directly behind witness chair—you can look right at Ervin and catch his facial expressions—as if he was looking at *me*. Nodding—fixed stare—occasional quick notes with yellow pencil.

*Kalmbach/Ulasewicz phone calls—from phone booth to phone booth—like Mafia operations. —Check *Honor Thy Father* for similar.

*Kalmbach ". . . It was about this time that I began to have *a degree of concern about this assignment.*"

4:50: Tedium sets in
Sudden vision of reaching out with Ostrich Lasso and slipping it around Kalmbach's neck then tightening it up and jerking him backwards.

Sudden uproar in gallery

—Cameras clicking feverishly as Kalmbach *struggles* with piano wire noose around his neck

—falling backwards

Unable to control laughter at this image . . . forced to leave hearing room, out of control, people staring at me. . . .

*Ron MacMahon, Baker's press Sec., ex-Tennessee newsman, "How can they *not* give 'em to us? [Nixon office tapes] Down in Tennessee we used to have a courthouse fire now and then. . . ."

Burnhardt J. Leinan, 27, Jerseyville, Illinois 62052. Came to D.C. by train—thirteen cars pulled by steam locomotive, coal tender. With 100 people Chi-Wash. Private train—Southern R.R. Independence Limited ("Watergate Special").

"Most people in Jerseyville only got interested when Dean produced the enemies list."

—Why?

"Because they couldn't understand why certain names were

on it—Newman, Streisand, Channing, Cosby—they couldn't understand why such a list was kept."

*Carol Arms Bar—like a tavern full of football fans—with the game across the street. Hoots of laughter in bar at La Rue's dead-pan account of Liddy's offer to "be on any street corner at any time—and we could have him assassinated."

All *Watergate Groupies* seem to be anti-Nixon—both in the hearing room and bars around Old Senate Building. Like fans cheering the home team—"the seven Blocks of Jelly."

Tuesday July 24
Benton's studio, 8:00 P.M.
PBS in Aspen is off again—even worse than PBS in D.C.

*Ehrlichman takes the oath with Heil Hitler salute/no laughter from spectators.

—Boredom in hearing room, tedium at press tables.

Ehrlichman's face—ARROGANCE. Keep the fucker on TV—ten hours a day—ten straight days.

E: We saw very little chance of getting FBI to move . . . very serious problem.

[Right! The nation's crawling with communists, multiplying like rats.]

Ehrlichman must have seen himself on "Sixty Minutes"—*so he knows how he looks on TV*—keeps glancing sideways at camera. Ehrlichman's "faulty memory" . . . Brookings—didn't remember who authorized fire-bombing—*didn't remember who he called to cancel Brookings bomb plot.*

(Same backgrounds—Civic Club, Country Club, JCC, USC/UCLA—law school, law firms, ad agencies.)

*Attitudes of Thomp-Baker and Gurney are critical—they related to Nixon's survival chances—rats sneaking off a sinking ship.

*E has insane gall to challenge Ervin on constitutional issues—Nixon's *right* to authorize Ellsberg burglary.

Dan Rather says Nixon wants a *confrontation NOW*—and also wants Cox to resign—Nixon, by withholding tapes, makes conviction of Haldeman, Ehrlichman, Dean, etc. impossible . . . thus holding this over their heads—to keep them from talking.

"Hang together or hang separately."

—Ben Franklin

EDITOR'S NOTE:

The following conversation between Ehrlichman and Herb Kalmbach arrived as a third generation Xerox in a package with Dr. Thompson's notebooks. The transcript was released by Ehrlichman himself—he hadn't told Kalmbach he was taping their phone call for possible use in his defense. This was not one of those documents ferreted out by the Select Committee investigators. According to Thompson, the following transcript is "the single most revealing chunk of testimony yet in terms of the morality of these people. It's like suddenly being plunged into the middle of the White House."

**CONVERSATION WITH HERB KALMBACH
—APRIL 19, 1973, 4:50 P.M.**

E: Ehrlichman

K: Kalmbach

E: Hi, how are you?

K: I'm pretty good. I'm scheduled for two tomorrow afternoon.

E: Where—at the jury or the U.S. Attorney?

K: At the jury and I'm scheduled at 5:30 this afternoon with Silver.

E: Oh, are you?

K: Yeah. I just wanted to run through quickly several things, John, in line with our conversation. I got in here last night and there was a call from O'Brien. I returned it, went over there today, and he said the reason for the call is LaRue has told him to ask him to call me to say that he had to identify me in connection with this and he wanted me to know that and so on.

E: Did he tell you about Dean?

K: Nope.

E: Well Dean has totally cooperated with the U.S. Attorney in the hopes of getting immunity. Now what he says or how he says nobody seems to be able to divine but he.

K: The whole enchilada?

E: He's throwing on Bob and me heavily.

K: He is?

E: Yep.

K: He is.

E: And taking the position that he was a mere agent. Now on your episode he told me before he left, so to speak, he, Dan, told me that really my transaction with him involving you was virtually my only area of liability in this thing and I said, well, John, what in the world are you talking about? He said, well I came to you from Mitchell and I said Mitchell needs money could we call Herb Kalmbach and ask him to raise some. And I said, and Dean says to me, and you said yes.

And I said yep, that's right. And he said well that does it. And I said well that's hard for me to believe. I don't understand the law but I don't think Herb entered into this with any guilty intent and I certainly didn't and so I said I just find that hard to imagine. Now since then I've retained counsel.

K: Oh, you have?

E: . . . very good and who agrees with me that it is the remotest kind of nonsense but the point that I think has to be clarified, that I'm going to clarify if I get a chance, is that the reason that Dean had to come to me and to Bob where you were concerned is that we had promised you that you would not be run pillar to post by Maurice Stans.

K: And also that you knew I was your friend and you knew I was the President's attorney.

E: Sure.

K: Never do anything improper, illegal, unethical, or whatever.

E: Right.

K: And . . .

E: But the point is that rather than Mitchell calling you direct Mitchell knew darn well that you were no longer available.

K: Yep.

E: Now this was post April 6, was it not?

K: Yep, April 7.

E: So that Mitchell and Stans both knew that there wasn't any point in calling you direct because we had gotten you out of that on the pretext that you were going to do things for us.

K: That's right.

E: And so it was necessary for Dean to come to me and then in turn to Bob and plead a very urgent case without really getting into any specifics except to say you had to trust me, this is very important, and Mitchell is up his tree, or, you know, I mean is really worked, he didn't use that phrase, but he is really exercised about this. And, John, if you tell me it's that important, why yes.

K: You know, when you and I talked and it was after John had given me that word, and I came in to ask you, John, is this an assignment I have to take on? You said, yes it is period and move forward. Then that was all that I needed to be assured that I wasn't putting my family in jeopardy.

E: Sure.

K: And I would just understand that you and I are absolutely together on that.

E: No question about it, Herb, that I would never knowingly have put you in any kind of a spot.

K: Yeah. Well, and when we talked you knew what I was about to do, you know, to go out and get the dough for this purpose; it was humanitarian.

E: It was a defense fund.

K: . . . to support the family. Now the thing that was disquieting and this thing with O'Brien was that he said that there is a massive campaign evidently under way to indict all the lawyers including you and me, and I was a little shocked and I guess what I need to get from you, John, is assurance that this is not true.

E: Well, I don't know of any attempt to target you at all. My hunch is that they're trying to get at me, they're trying to corroborate. See what they said to Dean is that he gets no consideration from them unless they can corroborate Haldeman and my liability.

K: God, if I can just make it plain that it was humanitarian and nothing else.

E: Yeah, and the point that I undoubtedly never expressed to you is that I continually operated on the basis of Dean's representation to me.

K: Yep. It was not improper.

E: Right.

K: And there was nothing illegal about it.

E: See, he's the house lawyer.

K: Yep, exactly and I just couldn't believe that you and Bob and the President, just too good friends to ever put me in the position I would be putting my family on the line.

K: And it's just unbelievable, unthinkable. Now shall I just— I'll just if I'm asked by Silver I'll just lay it out just exactly that way.

E: Yeah, I wouldn't haul the President into it if you can help it.

K: Oh, no, I will not.

E: But I think the point that I will make in the future if I'm given the chance is that you were not under our control in any sort of a slavery sense but that we had agreed that you would not be at the beck and call of the committee.

K: And, of course, too, that I acted only on orders and, you know, on direction and if this is something that you felt sufficiently important and that you were assured it was altogether proper, then I would take it on because I always do it and always have. And you and Bob and the President know that.

E: Yeah, well, as far as propriety is concerned I think we both were relying entirely on Dean.

K: Yep.

E: I made no independent judgment.

K: Yep. Yep.

E: And I'm sure Bob didn't either.

K: Nope and I'm just, I just have the feeling, John, that I don't know if this is a weak reed, is it?

E: Who, Dean?

K: No, I mean are they still going to say, well Herb you should have known?

E: I don't know how you could have. You didn't make any inquiries.

K: Never. And the only inquiries I made, John, was to you after I talked to John Dean.

E: And you found that I didn't know just a whole helluva lot.

K: You said this is something I have to do and . . .

E: Yeah, and the reason that I said that, as you know, was not from any personal inquiry but was on the basis of what had been represented to me.

K: Yeah, and then on—to provide the defense fund and to take care of the families of these fellas who were then . . .

E: Indigent.

K: Not then been found guilty or not guilty.

E: And the point being here without attempting to induce them to do a damn thing.

K: Absolutely not and that was never, that was exactly right.

K: OK.

K: Now, can I get in to see you tomorrow before I go in there at two?

E: If you want to. They'll ask you.

K: Will they?

E: Yep.

K: Well, maybe I shouldn't.

E: They'll ask you to whom you've spoken about your testimony and I would appreciate it if you would say you talked to me in California because at that time I was investigating this thing for the President.

K: And not now?

E: Well, I wouldn't ask you to lie.

K: No, I know.

E: But the point is . . .

K: But the testimony was in California.

E: The point is. Well, no, your recollection of facts and so forth.

K: Yes, I agree.

E: See, I don't think we were ever seen together out there but at some point I'm going to have to say that I talked to O'Brien and Dean and Magruder and Mitchell and you and a whole lot of people about this case.

K: Yeah.

E: And so it would be consistent.

K: Do you feel, John, that calling it straight shot here, do you feel assured as you did when we were out there that there's no culpability here?

E: Yes.

K: And nothing to worry about?

E: And Herb, from everything I hear they're not after you.

K: Yes, sir.

E: From everything I hear.

K: Barbara, you know.

E: They're out to get me and they're out to get Bob.

K: My God. All right, well, John, it'll be absolutely clear that there was nothing looking towards any cover-up or anything. It was strictly for the humanitarian and I just want . . . when I talked to you I just wanted you to advise me that it was all right on that basis.

E: On that basis.

K: To go forward.

E: That it was necessary.

K: And that'll be precisely the way it is.

E: Yeah, OK. Thanks, Herb. Bye.

5:00 P.M. Monday, July 30
Hearing Room
Old Senate Office Building
*Haldeman opening statement
— Terrible heat from TV lights turned back towards press

and gallery. Barking (sounds of dog kennel) in press room as Haldeman comes on. Not on Nat. TV, but audible in hallway.

"Nor did I ever suggest . . . [The Super Eagle Scout wounded tone of voice—] I had full confidence in Dean as did the President at that time. . . ."

Haldeman's 1951 burr-cut seems as out of place—even weird—in this room as a bearded Senator would have seemed in 1951. Or a nigger in Beta Theta Phi fraternity in the late 1940s.

Haldeman's head on camera looks like he got bashed on the head with a rake.

Total tedium sets in as Haldeman statement drones on . . . his story is totally different than Dean's on crucial points . . . definite perjury here . . . which one lying?

"If the recent speech [August 15] does not produce the results the President wants, he will then do what he has already come to doing. He will use all the awe-inspiring resources of his office to 'come out swinging with both fists.' Divisive will be a mild way of describing the predictable results."
—Joe Alsop, *Washington Post*, 8/17/73

"The clear warning: Mr. Nixon will not do any more to clear himself of the taint of Watergate because he cannot: If the Democrats do not allow him to get back on the job of President, but continue what one high presidential aide called the 'vendetta' against him, his next move will be full retaliation."
—Evans and Novak, *Washington Post*, 8/17/73

" 'When I am attacked,' Richard Nixon once remarked to this writer, 'it is my instinct to strike back.' The President is now clearly in a mood to obey his instinct. . . . So on Wednesday, July 18th, at a White House meeting, it was agreed unanimously that the tapes should not be released. This decision, to use the sports cliches to which the President is addicted, meant an entirely new ball game, requiring a new game plan. The new game plan calls for a strategy of striking back, in

accord with the presidential instincts, rather than a policy of attempted accommodation. . . ."
—Stewart Alsop, *Newsweek,* 8/6/73

Cazart! It is hard to miss the message in those three shots . . . even out here in Woody Creek, at a distance of 2,000 miles from the source, a joint statement, as it were, from Evans and Novak and both Alsop brothers hits the nerves like a blast of summer lightning across the mountains. Especially when you read them all in the same afternoon, while sifting through the mail-heap that piled up in my box, for three weeks, while I was wasting all that time back in Washington, once again, trying to get a grip on the thing.

Crouse had warned me, by phone, about the hazards of coming east. "I know you won't believe this," he said, "so you might as well just get on a plane and find out for yourself—but the weird truth is that Washington is the only place in the country where the Watergate story seems *dull.* I can sit up here in Boston and get totally locked into it, on the tube, but when I go down there to that goddamn Hearing Room I get so bored and depressed I can't think."

Now, after almost a month in that treacherous swamp of a town, I understand what Crouse was trying to tell me. After a day or so in the hearing room, hunkered down at a press table in the sweaty glare of those blinding TV lights, I discovered a TV set in the bar of the Capitol Hill Hotel just across the street from the Old Senate Office Building, about a three-minute sprint from the Hearing Room itself . . . so I could watch the action on TV, sipping a Carlsberg until something looked about to happen, then dash across the street and up the stairs to the Hearing Room to see whatever it was that seemed interesting.

After three or four days of this scam, however, I realized that there was really no point in going to the Hearing Room at all. Every time I came speeding down the hall and across the crowded floor of the high-domed, white-marble rotunda where a cordon of cops kept hundreds of waiting spectators penned up behind velvet ropes, I felt guilty. . . . Here was some ill-dressed geek with a bottle of Carlsberg in his hand, waving a press pass and running right through a whole army of cops, then through the oak doors and into a front row seat just behind the witness chair—while this mob of poor bastards who'd been waiting since early morning, in some cases, for a seat to open up in the SRO gallery.

After a few more days of this madness, I closed up the National Affairs Desk and went back home to brood.

PART III

TO THE MATTRESSES . . . NIXON FACES HISTORY, AND TO HELL WITH THE WASHINGTON POST . . . THE HAZY EMERGENCE OF A NEW AND CHEAPER STRATEGY . . . JOHN WILSON DRAWS 'THE LINE' . . . STRANGE TROIKA AND A BALANCE OF TERROR . . . MCGOVERN WAS RIGHT

"When democracy granted democratic methods to us in times of opposition, this was bound to happen in a democratic system. However, we National Socialists never asserted that we represented a democratic point of view, but we have declared openly that we used the democratic methods only in order to gain power and that, after assuming the power, we would deny to our adversaries without any consideration the means which were granted to us in times of our opposition."

—Josef Goebbels

What will Nixon do now? That is the question that has every Wizard in Washington hanging by his or her fingernails—from the bar of the National Press Club to the redwood sauna in the Senate Gymnasium to the hundreds of high-powered cocktail parties in suburbs like Bethesda, McLean, Arlington, Cabin John, and especially in the leafy white ghetto of the District's Northwest quadrant. You can wander into Nathan's tavern at the corner of M Street and Wisconsin in Georgetown and get an argument about "Nixon's strategy" without even mentioning the subject. All you have to do is stand at the bar, order a Bass Ale, and look interested: The hassle will take care of itself; the very air in Washington is electric with the vast implications of "Watergate."

Thousands of big-money jobs depend on what Nixon does next; on what Archibald Cox has in mind; on whether "Uncle Sam's" TV hearings will resume full-bore after Labor Day, or be either telescoped or terminated like Nixon says they should be.

The smart money says the "Watergate Hearings," as such, are effectively over—not only because Nixon is preparing to mount a popular crusade against them, but because every elected politician in Washington is afraid of what the Ervin committee has already scheduled for the "third phase" of the hearings.

Phase Two, as originally planned, would focus on "dirty tricks"—a colorful, shocking, and essentially minor area of inquiry, but one with plenty of action and a guaranteed audience appeal. A long and serious look at the "dirty tricks" aspect of national campaigning would be a death-blow to the daily soap-opera syndrome that apparently grips most of the nation's housewives. The cast of characters, and the twisted tales they could tell, would shame every soap-opera script-writer in America.

Phase Three/Campaign Financing is the one both the White House and the Senate would prefer to avoid—and, given this mutual distaste for exposing the public to the realities of Campaign Financing, this is the phase of the Watergate Hearings most likely to be cut from the schedule. "Jesus Christ," said one Ervin committee investigator, "we'll have *Fortune*'s 500 in that chair, and every one of those bastards will take at least one Congressman or Senator down with him."

At the end of Phase One—the facts and realities of the Watergate affair itself—the seven Senators on the Ervin committee took an informal vote among themselves, before adjourning to a birthday party for Senator Herman Talmadge, and the tally was 4–3 *against* resuming the hearings in their current format. Talmadge cast the deciding vote, joining the three Republicans—Gurney, Baker, and Weicker—in voting to wrap the hearings up as soon as possible. Their reasons were the same ones Nixon gave in his long-awaited TV speech on August 15, when he said the time had come to end this Daily Bummer and get back to "The business of the people."

Watching Nixon's speech in hazy color on the Owl Farm tube with New York Mayor John Lindsay, Wisconsin Congressman Les Aspin, and former Bobby Kennedy speechwriter Adam Wolinsky, I half expected to hear that fine old Calvin Coolidge quote: "The business of America is business."

And it only occurred to me later that Nixon wouldn't have dared to use that one, because no president since Herbert Hoover has been forced to explain away the kind of root structural damage to the national economy that Nixon is trying to explain today. And Hoover at least had the excuse that he "inherited his problems" from somebody else—which Nixon can't claim, because he is now in his *fifth* year as president, and when he goes on TV to explain himself he is facing an audience of 50 to 60 million who can't afford steaks or even hamburger in the supermarkets, who can't buy gasoline for their cars, who are paying 15 and 20% interest rates for bank loans, and who are being told now that there may not be enough fuel oil to heat their homes through the coming winter.

This is not the ideal audience for a second-term president, fresh from a landslide victory, to confront with twenty-nine minutes of lame gibberish about mean nit-pickers in Congress, the good ole American way, and Let's Get on with Business.

Indeed. That's the first thing Richard Nixon and I have ever agreed on, politically—and what we are dealing with now is no longer hard ideology, but a matter of simple competence. What we are looking at on all our TV sets is a man who finally, after twenty-four years of frenzied effort, became the President of the United States with a personal salary of $200,000 a year and an unlimited expense account including a fleet of private helicopters, jetliners, armored cars, personal mansions and estates on both coasts, and control over a budget beyond the wildest dreams of King Midas . . . and all the dumb bastard can show us, after five years of total freedom to do anything he wants with all this power, is a shattered national economy, disastrous defeat in a war he could have ended four years ago on far better terms than he finally came around to, and a hand-picked personal staff put together through five years of screening, whose collective criminal record will blow the minds of high-school American History students for the next one hundred years. Nixon's hand-picked Vice President is about to be indicted for Extortion and Bribery; his former campaign manager and his former Secretary of Commerce and personal fundraiser have already been indicted for Perjury, two of his ranking campaign managers have already pleaded guilty to Obstruction of Justice, the White House Counsel is headed for prison on more felony counts than I have room to list here, and before the trials are finished. . . .

Sen. Talmadge: "Now, if the President could authorize a covert break-in and you do not know exactly where that power would be limited, you do not think it could include murder, do you?"

John Ehrlichman: "I do not know where the line is, Senator."

With the first phase of the Watergate hearings more or less ended, one of the few things now unmistakably clear, as it were, is that nobody in Nixon's White House was willing to "draw the line" anywhere short of re-electing the President in 1972. Even John Mitchell—whose reputation as a super-shrewd lawyer ran afoul of the Peter Principle just as soon as he became Nixon's first Attorney General—lost his temper in an exchange with Sen. Talmadge at the Watergate hearings and said, with the whole world watching, that he considered the re-election of Richard Nixon in '72 "so important" that it out-weighed all other considerations.

It was a classic affirmation of the "attorney-client relationship"—or at least a warped mixture of that and the relationship between an ad agency executive and a client with a product to sell—but when Mitchell uttered those lines in the hearing room, losing control of himself just long enough to fatally confuse "executive loyalty" with "executive privilege," it's fair to assume that he knew he was already doomed. . . . He had already been indicted for perjury in the Vesco case, he was facing almost certain indictment by Archibald Cox, and previous testimony by John Dean had made it perfectly clear that Nixon was prepared to throw John Mitchell to the wolves, to save his own ass.

This ominous truth was quickly reinforced by the testimony of John Ehrlichman and Harry "Bob" Haldeman, whose back-to-back testimony told most of the other witnesses (and potential defendants) all they needed to know. By the time Haldeman had finished testifying—under the direction of the same criminal lawyer who had earlier represented Ehrlichman—it was clear that somebody in the White House had finally seen fit to "draw the line."

It was not quite the same line Mitchell and Ehrlichman had refused to acknowledge on TV, but in the final analysis it will be far more critical to the fate of Richard Nixon's presidency . . . and, given Mitchell's long personal relationship with Nixon, it is hard to believe he didn't understand his role in the "new strategy" well before he drove down from New York to Washington, by chauffeured limousine, for his gig in the witness chair.

The signs were all there. For one, it had been Haldeman and Ehrlichman—with Nixon's tacit approval—who had eased Mitchell out of his "Number One" role at the White House. John Mitchell, a millionaire Wall Street lawyer until he got into politics, was more responsible than any other single person for the long come-back that landed Nixon in the White House in 1968. It was Mitchell who rescued Nixon from oblivion in the mid-Sixties when Nixon moved east to become a Wall Street lawyer himself—after losing the presidency to John Kennedy in 1960 and then the Governorship of California to Pat Brown in '62, a humiliating defeat that ended with his "You won't have Dick Nixon to kick around anymore" outburst at the traditional loser's press conference.

. . .

The re-election of Mr. Nixon, followed so quickly by the Watergate revelations, has compelled the country to re-examine the reality of our electoral process. . . .

"The unraveling of the whole White House tangle of involvement has come about largely by a series of fortuitous events, many of them unlikely in a different political context. Without these events, the cover-up might have continued indefinitely, even if a Democratic administration vigorously pursued the truth. . . .

"In the wake of Watergate may come more honest and thorough campaign reform than in the aftermath of a successful presidential campaign which stood for such reform. I suspect that after viewing the abuses of the past, voters in the future will insist on full and open debate between the candidates and on frequent, no-holds-barred press conferences for all candidates, and especially the President.

"And I suspect the Congress will respond to the fact that Watergate happened with legislation to assure that Watergate never happens again. Today the prospects for further restrictions on private campaign financing, full disclosure of the personal finances of the candidates, and public finance of all federal campaigns seem to me better than ever—and even better than if a new Democratic administration had urged such steps in early 1973. We did urge them in 1972, but it took the Nixon landslide and the Watergate expose to make the point.

"I believe there were great gains that came from the pain of defeat in 1972. We proved a campaign could be honestly financed. We reaffirmed that a campaign could be open in its conduct and decent in its motivation. We made the Democratic party a place for people as well as politicians. And perhaps in losing we gained the greatest victory of all—that Americans now perceive, far better than a new President could have persuaded them, what is precious about our principles and what we must do to preserve them. The nation now sees itself through the prism of Watergate and the Nixon landslide; at last, perhaps, we see through a glass clearly.

"Because of all this, it is possible that by 1976, the 200th anniversary of America's birth, there will be a true rebirth of patriotism; that we will not only know our ideals but live them; that democracy may once again become a conviction we keep and not just a description we apply to ourselves. And if the McGovern campaign advanced that hope, even in defeat, then, as I said on election night last November, 'Every minute and every hour and every bone-crushing effort . . . was worth the entire sacrifice.' "

—George McGovern in the *Washington Post*,
August 12, 1973

Jesus. . . . Sunday morning in Woody Creek and here's Mc-Govern on the mini-tube beside my typewriter, looking and talking almost exactly like he was in those speedy weeks between the Wisconsin and Ohio primaries, when his star was rising so fast that he could barely hang onto it. The sense of *déjà vu* is almost frightening: Here is McGovern speaking sharply *against the system*, once again, in response to questions from CBS's Connie Chung and Marty Nolan from the Boston Globe, two of the most ever-present reporters on the '72 campaign trail . . . and McGovern, brought back from the dead by a political miracle of sorts, is hitting the first gong of doom for the man who made him a landslide loser nine months ago: "When that [judicial] process is complete and the Supreme Court rules that the President must turn over the tapes—and he refuses to do so—I think the Congress will have no recourse but to seriously consider Impeachment."

Cazart! The fat is approaching the fire—very slowly, and in very cautious hands, but there is no ignoring the general drift of things. Sometime between now and the end of 1973, Richard Nixon may have to bite that bullet he's talked about for so long. Seven is a lucky number for gamblers, but not for fixers, and Nixon's seventh crisis is beginning to put his first six in very deep shade. Even the most conservative betting in Washington, these days, has Nixon either resigning or being impeached by the autumn of '74—if not for reasons directly connected to the "Watergate scandal," then because of his inability to explain how he paid for his beach-mansion at San

Clemente, or why Vice President Agnew—along with most of Nixon's original White House command staff—is under indictment for felonies ranging from Extortion and Perjury to Burglary and Obstruction of Justice.

Another good bet in Washington—running at odds between two and three to one, these days, is that Nixon will crack both physically and mentally under all this pressure, and develop a serious psychosomatic illness of some kind: Maybe another bad case of pneumonia.

This is not so wild a vision as it might sound—not even in the context of my own known taste for fantasy and savage bias in politics. Richard Nixon, a career politician who has rarely failed to crack under genuine pressure, is under more pressure now than most of us will ever understand. His whole life is turning to shit, just as he reached the pinnacle . . . and every once in a while, caving in to a weakness that blooms in the cool, thinking hours around dawn, I have to admit that I feel a touch of irrational sympathy for the bastard. Not as The President: a broken little bully who would sacrifice us all to save himself—if he still had the choice—but the same kind of sympathy I might feel, momentarily, for a vicious cheap-shot linebacker whose long career comes to a sudden end one Sunday afternoon when some rookie flanker shatters both his knees with a savage crackback block.

Cheap-shot artists don't last very long in pro football. To cripple another person intentionally is to violate the same kind of code as the legendary "honor among thieves."

More linebackers than thieves believe this, but when it comes to politics—to a twenty-eight-year career of cheap shots, lies, and thievery—there is no man in America who should understand what is happening to him now better than Richard Milhous Nixon. He is a living monument to the old Army rule that says: "The only *real* crime is getting caught."

This is not the first time Richard Nixon has been caught. After his failed campaign for the Governorship of California in 1962 he was formally convicted—along with H. R. Halde-man, Maurice Stans, Murray Chotiner, Herb Klein, and Herb

Kalmbach—for almost exactly the same kind of crudely illegal campaign tactics that he stands accused of today.

But this time, in the language of the sergeants who keep military tradition alive, "he got caught every which way" . . . and "his ass went into the blades."

Not many people have ever written in the English language better than a Polack with a twisted sense of humor who called himself Joseph Conrad. And if he were with us today I think he'd be getting a fine boot out of this Watergate story. Mr. Kurtz, in Conrad's *Heart of Darkness*, did his thing.

Mr. Nixon also did his thing.

And now, just as surely as Kurtz: "Mistah Nixon, he dead."

JOHN WATERS

WHATEVER HAPPENED TO SHOWMANSHIP?

Perhaps (perhaps?) *best known as a filmmaker* (Pink Flamingos, Polyester, Hairspray), *John Waters has also been a regular contributor to* National Lampoon, Rolling Stone, Playboy, American Film, *and* Vogue. *He is the author of two collections of written work,* Shock Value *and* Crackpot.

Liberace had a word for it. So did *Variety*. The word was "showmanship"—but lately this term seems to have disappeared from movie moguls' vocabulary. After all, with so many bad movies around these days, couldn't the promotional campaigns at least be fun? What's happened to the ludicrous but innovative marketing techniques of yesteryear that used to fool audiences into thinking they were having a good time even if the film stunk? Did the audiences care? Hell, no. They may have hated the picture, but they loved the gimmick, and that's all they ended up remembering anyway.

Who's to follow in the footsteps of the great low-rent Samuel Z. Arkoffs and Joseph E. Levines who used to hype films? Why do today's producers waste untold millions on media junkets, national television spots, and giant print ads when they could come up with something as delightful and effective as handing out vomit bags at horror films? Or how about the high-profile but dirt-cheap antics of the producers of a 1977 red-neck oddity entitled *The Worm Eaters?* Realizing that competition for attention from film buyers at the Cannes Film Festival was fierce that year, these ballyhoo experts blithely ate live worms from a bucket as startled distributors filed into their screening.

We can even go way back in history to *Mom and Dad*, a boring pseudo sex documentary from the forties brilliantly hyped by the great-great-grandfather of exploitation, Kroger Babb. Since the film contained footage of an actual birth of a baby, Mr. Babb realized this was a chance to legally show full-frontal female nudity. Did he figure the voyeuristic audience would just ignore the baby and focus on the anatomy? Four-walling a theater in each city, Babb picked up some added pocket change by having a phony nurse hawk sex-education pamphlets in the aisles before the feature began. He assured further controversy by sexually segregating the audience—women only in the afternoon and men only at night. In what has to be the most outlandish publicity stunt in film history, he would start the film and turn off the ventilation. As the audience grew more and more uncomfortable, he would release noxious gas through the air vents and wait for the first person to pass out. Mr. Babb would immediately call an ambulance and the local media at the same time, then rush outside the theater to smugly watch the heavily photographed "rescue of a shocked patron," knowing it would be front-page news the next day.

Without a doubt, the greatest showman of our time was William Castle. King of the Gimmicks, William Castle was my idol. His films made me want to make films. I'm even jealous of his work. In fact, I wish I *were* William Castle.

What's the matter with film buffs these days? How could they be so slow in elevating this ultimate eccentric director-producer to cult status? Isn't it time for a retrospective? A documentary on his life? Some highfalutin critique in *Cahiers du Cinéma*? Isn't it time to get his marvelous autobiography, *Step Right Up! I'm Gonna Scare the Pants Off America*, back in print? Forget Ed Wood. Forget George Romero. William Castle was the best. William Castle was God.

The picture that first put Mr. Castle on the map was *Ma-*

cabre (1958). Well, not exactly the picture, but the gimmick. *Macabre* was a rip-off of *Diabolique*, and was filmed in just nine days at a cost of $90,000. Realizing that the finished product was nothing special, Castle came up with an idea that would succeed beyond his wildest dreams. He took out a policy with Lloyd's of London insuring every ticket buyer for $1,000 in case they died from fright. Mock insurance policies appeared in all the newspaper ads. Giant replicas of the actual policy hung over the marquees. Hearses were parked outside the theaters and fake nurses in uniform were paid to stand around the lobbies.

Audiences fell hook, line, and sinker. Nobody talked about the movie, but everyone was eager to see if some jerk would drop dead and collect. Of course, no one died. But if they had, it would have been even better. A death of any kind inside the theater would only have cost Lloyd's of London a paltry $1,000, and think of the hype *that* would have generated!

Mr. Castle got so carried away with the promotion that he arrived in a hearse at some of the premieres and made his entrance popping from a coffin. Was this not the ultimate in auteurism? Would Jean-Luc Godard have gone this far? Would he have arrived in a wrecked car to promote *Weekend*? Would Sergei Eisenstein have arrived in a battleship? I think not. I hate that Sergei Eisenstein.

William Castle was no slacker. Not content to rest on his laurels, he set his feverish little mind to work to come up with what the studios wanted—more gimmicks and higher grosses. His next project was *House on Haunted Hill* (1959), a nifty little horror film boasting the director-producer's first real star, Vincent Price. But even Price was upstaged by Castle's new gimmick, "Emergo." Each theater was equipped with a large black box installed next to the screen. At a designated point in the film, the doors to the box would suddenly fly open and a twelve-foot plastic skeleton would light up and zoom over the audience on a wire to the projection booth. Studio executives were initially skeptical when, at the first sneak preview, the equipment failed and the skeleton jumped its wires and sent a *truly* horrified audience running for cover.

After further testing, Emergo was perfected and installed in theaters all over the country. The kids went wild. They screamed. They hugged their girlfriends. They threw popcorn boxes at the skeleton. Most important, they spent their allowance and made the film a huge hit. Was this not the first film to utilize audience participation to an absurd length? It certainly seemed more fun to me than dressing à la Brad and Janet and throwing rice at the screen during *The Rocky Horror Picture Show.*

Next came *The Tingler* (1959), arguably William Castle's masterpiece. Another horror film, once again featuring Vincent Price, in a command performance. But this time the script had a twist. A Tingler was an organism that lived in everyone's spinal column. A cross between a lobster and a crab, it came to life only when a person was frightened. The only way to kill this little bugger was to scream. In the film, the Tingler breaks loose in a movie theater and kills the projectionist. In real theaters where the film was playing, the screen would go white at this point and a voice would announce, "Attention! The Tingler is loose in this theater. Please scream for your life." Naturally, the audience responded by shrieking their lungs out, but this wasn't good enough for the Master of Gimmicks. He came up with "Percepto," "the newest and most startling screen gimmick." Similar to a handshake buzzer, Percepto was nothing more than little motors installed under theater seats and activated by the projectionist at the exact moment the audience was in a frenzy. As the patrons got their asses buzzed, the theater would erupt in pandemonium. Castle estimated in his autobiography that he buzzed more than twenty million American asses.

Naturally, there were problems. In Philadelphia one beefy truck driver was so incensed that he ripped his entire seat from the floor and had to be subdued by five ushers. In another city, the management dutifully installed the Percepto equipment the night before the film was scheduled to open. That night the smart-alecky projectionist decided to test the fanny buzzers on a group of older women who were watching *The Nun's Story* on the last night of its run. I'm sure Audrey Hepburn never got such a vocal reaction before or after this "electrifying" screening.

Looking back, *The Tingler* is the fondest moviegoing memory of my youth. I went to see it every day. Since, by the time it came to my neighborhood, only about ten random seats were wired, I would run through the theater searching for the magical buzzers. As I sat there experiencing the miracle of Percepto, I realized that there could be such a thing as Art in the cinema.

I didn't have to wait long for a follow-up. *13 Ghosts* (1960), his next picture, offered "Illusion-O." Each spectator was given a "ghost-viewer," an obscure twist on 3-D glasses. If you looked through the red plastic part, you could see the ghosts; if you looked through the blue, you couldn't. Audiences seemed bewildered by this imperfect technical breakthrough, but still bought the gimmick.

(Recently, the Thalia Theater in New York was brave enough to revive the film—on a double bill with Arthur Knight's *The Wild, Wild World of Jayne Mansfield* yet. Imagine my surprise when I entered the theater and was handed a piece of red plastic—the Thalia's own makeshift version of the long-unavailable Illusion-O glasses. Wild with excitement, I took my seat and trembled at the thought of how creative theater management could be. I noticed a few grumpy film purists refusing the ghost-viewer, but they nonetheless legitimized the film, because without any kind of glasses, *13 Ghosts* is still unique—beautifully surreal, almost arty.)

Trying to better Alfred Hitchcock's smash 1960 hit, *Psycho*, William Castle unleashed his own transvestite-themed shocker, *Homicidal* (1961). Although some critics howled about cinematic plagiarism, they conveniently overlooked the fact that it was Hitchcock who ripped off Castle first, not vice versa. Forget the shower scene in *Psycho*. What initially attracted the throngs to this "classic" was the stunt of strictly enforcing the "No one will be admitted to the theater after the feature has begun" gimmick. Castle must have reacted to this competition in panic, because he retaliated with a campaign for *Homicidal* so ridiculous and bizarre that many in the industry felt he had gone off the deep end.

Homicidal has the dubious distinction of being the first film in cinematic history to utilize the "Fright Break." Two minutes before the picture ended, the screen would once again go blank and the voice of Castle himself would announce, "This is a Fright Break. You hear that sound? The sound of a heartbeat? It will beat for another sixty-five seconds to allow anyone who is too frightened to see the end of the picture to leave the theater. *You will get your full admission refunded!*" Naturally exhibitors were wary of this campaign because it violated the golden rule of exploitation: *Never* offer a money-back guarantee.

The first time the Fright Break was tested, the entire audience stampeded to the box office and Mr. Castle nearly collapsed. He soon figured out the problem—the audience loved the picture, but the gimmick created such a word of mouth that they figured out how to get the last laugh. They simply stayed and saw the film a second time and then tried to cash in. Mr. Castle was no dummy. He began issuing different-colored tickets for each show. It worked. Now about one percent asked for a refund. This one percent seemed to be Castle's ultimate challenge: He went to unheard-of lengths to humiliate the adventurous ticket buyer who had the nerve to ask for his money back.

William Castle simply went nuts. He came up with "Coward's Corner," a yellow cardboard booth, manned by a bewildered theater employee in the lobby. When the Fright Break was announced, and you found that you couldn't take it anymore, you had to leave your seat and, in front of the entire audience, follow yellow footsteps up the aisle, bathed in a yellow light. Before you reached Coward's Corner, you crossed yellow lines with the stenciled message: "Cowards Keep Walking." You passed a nurse (in a yellow uniform? . . . I wonder), who would offer a blood-pressure test. All the while a recording was blaring, *"Watch the chicken! Watch him shiver in Coward's Corner!"* As the audience howled, you had to go through one final indignity—at Coward's Corner you were forced to sign a yellow card stating, "I am a bona fide coward." Very, very few were masochistic enough to endure this. The one percent refund dribbled away to a zero percent, and I'm sure that in many cities a plant had to be paid to go through this torture. No wonder theater owners balked at booking a William Castle film. It was all just too damn complicated.

Mr. Castle's career as gimmick monger may have reached its zenith at this point, but he kept on going. He used the "Punishment Poll," perhaps his weakest gimmick, to promote his next opus, *Mr. Sardonicus* (1961). On entering the theater, you were given a day-glow card featuring a thumbs-up, thumbs-down design similar to a playing card. Like spectators at the Roman Coliseum, the audience was allowed to decide the fate of the villain. As a (presumably) humiliated usher conducted the Punishment Poll, spectators held up their Mercy/No Mercy verdict to be counted. Not realizing how bloodthirsty audiences really could be, Castle needlessly supplied every print with two endings, just in case. Unfortunately, not *once* did an audience grant mercy, so this one particular part of the film has *never* been seen. Why all this current fuss about the "lost" half hour of *A Star Is Born*? How about the lost footage from *Mr. Sardonicus*? Can't the vaults be searched? Isn't Radio City Music Hall available? Can't something be done to preserve this important footnote to film history?

After *Mr. Sardonicus*, Castle seemed to be suffering from the too-much-of-a-good-thing syndrome. Critics panned his efforts, claiming he was incapable of producing a hit without a gimmick. He tried it again with *13 Frightened Girls* (1963), but all he could come up with was a worldwide talent hunt for the prettiest girl in each of thirteen countries who, when cast, would receive $300, hotel accommodations, and a "first-class" new wardrobe.

Audiences, too, were getting weary of his "Gyro Gearloose" approach to filmmaking. And the moneymen were getting stingy. They gave him their final ultimatum: *No more gimmicks!* But Castle fooled his detractors by apparently acquiescing to their demands with his new film, *Straight Jacket* (1964), while at the same time employing the biggest gimmick of them all—Joan Crawford. Wisely realizing that all movie stars are merely high-priced gimmicks in themselves, he sent Miss Crawford to the theaters for promotion. Joan got so carried away by being a live, in-person gimmick that she once invited the entire audience to join her for hamburgers in the restaurant next door to the theater, ensuring a riot and front-page coverage. But Mr. Castle was showing his insecurities. At the last minute he panicked and ordered thousands of bloody cardboard axes to be distributed free to his fans.

A great career was limping to a close. The day of the gimmick seemed to be over. His final attempt at horror gimmickry was *I Saw What You Did* (1965), again starring Joan Crawford. (Castle did go on to produce films like *Rosemary's Baby* and *Bug*, but they are not relevant to this discussion.) The plot concerns teenage pranksters who call random strangers and pant, "I saw what you did." Accidentally, they reach a real murderer, who tries to track them down. At first, the phone company cooperated with Castle's promotion by allowing him to hang huge plastic phones over the marquee. But when teenagers began imitating the script in real life and the phone company was swamped with complaints, Ma Bell showed her usual humor-impaired company policy by refusing to let Castle even mention phones in the ads. Undaunted, he came up with a hastily hatched gimmick, his last and, touchingly, most pathetic. The back three rows of each theater were turned into a special "Shock Section." Longtime fans were disappointed to find that it was nothing more than seat belts on each chair to prevent you from being jolted out from fear. RIP William Castle. You certainly deserve it.

This magnificent career raises some pertinent questions for today. What has happened to showmanship? Is it completely dead? How can we lure people away from the dreaded VCRs, whose sole reason for popularity is that most of us don't have the nerve to masturbate in movie theaters? Sure, some exhibitors have caused a little excitement, but usually by accident.

Think of the drive-ins that routinely cause car crashes by unveiling hard-core porno in full view of speeding, merging traffic. Or grind houses (where waiting in line is always scarier than the film itself), which have given new meaning to the term "horror film" by allowing huge rats to stroll about.

The big studios have certainly been no help. Think of that irritating Dolby Sound, which mistakenly assumes that all moviegoers want to become sound mixers. Or the annoying 3-D, brilliantly revived and exploited by Andy Warhol and Paul Morrissey for their *Frankenstein*, and then bludgeoned into the ground by more serious attempts to "perfect" this tired gimmick. Porno, finally, is the only genre to demand the third dimension. Remember *The Stewardesses?* Huge breasts spilling out from the screen. Or *Heavy Equipment?* Gay male porno with, well, life itself gushing into the audience's lap.

The industry as a whole should put on its collective thinking cap and realize that even with today's computer-printout method of filmmaking, there's still room for outlandish showmanship. Stop fooling around and go for broke. The possibilities are endless. Every time an expensive Hollywood bomb opens, theaters could profit by letting the audience in for free and making them pay to get *out*. Show *Inchon* over and over and make a fortune. If your highly self-touted international epic turns out to be boring, why not give out copies of the deal memo that got the thing financed. Think of the yawns that could be stifled when the audience figures out how all this cash was wasted in the first place.

Try variations of the movie-star lookalike contests, but instead of intimidating audiences by forcing them to imitate such impossible classics as Marilyn Monroe or James Dean, pick someone as unremarkable as Jill Clayburgh and let everybody win. Go for community support! Let Mothers Against Drunk Drivers sponsor a car-crash festival—*Death Race 2000, Eat My Dust!* and so on.

All kinds of films could benefit. The producers of *Porky's* et al., pretend their films aren't made for dirty, filthy twelve-year-old lechers, but why not be honest and sponsor a circle-jerk for Cub Scout troops with the winner receiving a call girl for the night? If you want to be civic minded and publicize your newly installed handicap ramps, show *The Crippled Masters*, an honest-to-God karate film with two heroes—one has no arms, the other no legs. Everybody beats them up until one jumps on the other's shoulders, and together they become a killing machine.

If the Edie Sedgwick biopic, *Ciao! Manhattan*, opens weakly, have the top fag hag in each community pretend to OD in the theater and afterward local hamburger shops could sponsor rap sessions on the tragedy of the whole situation.

Even highbrow, critically acclaimed Oscar winners could up their grosses. Drag enthusiastic members of the *Reds* audience before mock Senate hearings in the lobby. Close the concession stand for *Gandhi* and let the patrons get into the spirit of the thing by starving to death.

What's the matter, Hollywood? Are you going to just sit there with your head in the sand? People are getting bored with the theatergoing experience! Can't you come up with something? Will everyone just sit at home with their video machines? William Castle, where are you when we really need you?

RUSSELL BAKER

I REMEMBER PAPA

A Pulitzer Prize winner (for his memoir about growing up during the Depression), Russell Baker has been possibly the most popular columnist The New York Times *has had in this century. His wit and smooth delivery mask a keen eye, and though he might sometimes wear white gloves, you'll find that he's gone for your throat and is choking you to death—with laughter, of course. The many volumes of his work include* So This Is Depravity *and* The Rescue of Miss Yaskell and Other Pipe Dreams.

Yet another collection of anecdotes about the literary giants: One afternoon in Paris, Ernest Hemingway and Morley Callaghan challenged Scott Fitzgerald and me to a bout of team wrestling. Hemingway, who was vain about his half nelson, became enraged halfway to the first fall when Edna St. Vincent Millay jumped into the ring and broke her umbrella over his skull, crying, "You monosyllabic brute! Get that half nelson off the finest American writers of our generation!"

Ernest was so stunned—possibly by the umbrella blow, possibly by hearing Scott and me described as his literary superiors—that he grabbed his partner, Morley Callaghan, and was about to pin him with a body slam when Morley flattened him with a right hook to the jaw. Ernest never forgave Scott and me.

John O'Hara and I were drinking late one evening in Tim Costello's when Ernest Hemingway came in to do some betting. "See that blackthorn walking stick hanging over the bar? I'll bet $5 I can break it over your skull," he told John.

"You're pretty good at breaking sticks," O'Hara said, "but not worth a damn at knitting."

"Oh, yeah?" said Ernest. "I'll bet $10 I can knit a pair of baby bootees faster than you can."

O'Hara accepted the challenge and they went at it. Hemingway was furious when O'Hara completed two masterfully crafted baby bootees before Ernest had even learned to hold the knitting needles. In his rage, Hemingway seized the blackthorn walking stick and broke it over my head, so I sued him for the hospital bill and the courts made him pay. Ernest never forgave me.

One day I was having tea with T. S. Eliot at the Plaza when Ernest Hemingway dropped in with Dorothy Parker. "Meet the wittiest woman in the world," Ernest said to Eliot.

"Delighted," T. S. said to Dottie, rising, hooking his umbrella over the back of the chair and shaking her hand. "Say something witty."

"Tell me Calvin Coolidge is dead," said Dottie.

"Gladly," said Eliot. "Calvin Coolidge is dead."

"How can they tell?" said Dorothy.

"Can you top that?" Hemingway roared with appreciation, until I pointed out that Coolidge had been dead for twenty-five years and that General Eisenhower was now President.

"So what?" scowled Ernest.

"So ask me what they call the White House since Eisenhower moved in," I said.

"What do they call the White House since Eisenhower moved in?" asked T. S.

"The tomb of the well-known soldier," I said.

I got to Eliot's umbrella one step ahead of Ernest and broke it over the teapot. Ernest never forgave me.

Once, at lunch around the Algonquin Round Table, Noel Coward challenged Ernest Hemingway to drink a double martini out of Gertrude Stein's slipper. I was dismayed when Ernest accepted the challenge because Gertrude had phoned me the previous night to ask if I could recommend an effective ointment for athlete's foot.

"Ernie," I whispered, as he lifted the gin-filled slipper with an olive toward his lips.

"Don't interrupt, or I'll never forgive you," he growled, draining the slipper and smashing the olive over Noel Coward's head.

After that, Hemingway started growing his beard to conceal a skin problem. Ernest never forgave me.

Herman Melville and Petroleum V. Nasby called on me one afternoon while I was lying under a beach umbrella at Key West. They wanted a favor.

"Neither Herman nor I have ever met Ernest Hemingway," said Petroleum.

"Better keep quiet about it," I cautioned. "If Ernest finds out you haven't met him, he'll never forgive you."

"The problem," said Melville, "is, if we never meet him, we will never have the chance to be involved in a Hemingway literary anecdote, and our names will disappear from the history of American literature."

Naturally, I wanted to give the poor devils a shot at fame so I hailed Hemingway, who happened to be in his boat just offshore hunting for Nazi submarines.

He was in an uncharacteristically genial mood and could not have been more charming. He said he thought Herman was one of the finest writers in the language and he told Petroleum that any man who could make Abraham Lincoln laugh was all right with Papa.

"That's all very well, Ernie," I said, "but these fellows need a little anecdotal action. Why don't you break the beach umbrella over their skulls?"

Ernest absolutely refused. "That wouldn't be very polite to fellows who came all the way to Key West to shake my hand," he said, and walked away with a cheerful wave. Herman and Petroleum never forgave him.

VACATION '58

These days John Hughes is known for his deft, effective, and remarkably thoughtful teenage movies such as Sixteen Candles, The Breakfast Club, *and* Pretty in Pink, *but he had another life before moviemaking. For a period he was a copious contributor to the* National Lampoon, *writing material for the magazine's "News" section as well as some features. Those who have seen the movie* Summer Vacation *with Chevy Chase will recognize and celebrate the following wonderful* Lampoon *piece, which formed the germ of that film.*

If Dad hadn't shot Walt Disney in the leg, it would have been our best vacation ever. We were going to Disneyland. It was a dream come true. The rides! The thrills! The Mouseketeers! I was so excited that I spent the whole month of May feeling like I had to go to the bathroom. When school finally let out on a Tuesday, I sprinted home as fast as I could, even though we weren't leaving until Friday.

Dad picked up our brand-new 1958 Plymouth Sport Suburban Six station wagon on Thursday morning. The speedometer had only six and three-tenths miles on it. Dad said that it would be a pleasure to travel for six days in a car that smelled as good as our Plymouth. It was nice to see Dad excited about our trip. For months Mom had to act moody and beg to get him to drive out to California. "What good will it do the kids to see their country from an airplane seat?" she wanted to know. Finally, Dad gave in and said we would get a station wagon and drive the 2,448 miles from 74 Rivard

Boulevard, Grosse Pointe, Michigan, to 1313 Harbor Boulevard, Anaheim, California.

It took almost all day Friday to pack the car. Dad loaded and unloaded it again and again to save a square foot here, a square inch there. Then he simonized the car and hung litter bags in the front and back seats, attached a compass to the dashboard, and put a first aid kit in the glove compartment. Then he called everyone outside to take one item apiece out of the car so he could close the back.

After dinner, Dad ran the Plymouth up to Richie's Marathon Service to gas up and have Richie check under the hood to see if everything was A-O.K. When Dad backed out of the driveway the car scraped bottom. Not a little scrape but a *sccccccrrrrrraaaaaape!*

Dad got back at 8:00. We heard the *scccrrrraaaaape!* and knew it was him. Richie had said that everything was beautiful under the hood. The car was gassed up, there was plenty of oil, the tire pressure was perfect, the AAA maps were organized in the glove compartment, and the speedometer read exactly 20.00 miles.

"Okay, all you Indians! Time for bed!" Mom said.

"But it's only 8:30!" I protested.

"We have to get up at 4:00 in the morning! I want to make Chicago by lunch!" Dad said, shooing us upstairs.

The telephone rang at 9:45 the next morning. It was Grandpa Pete calling to see why we hadn't gone yet. We had all overslept—even the baby. Dad was furious. I could hear him screaming and pounding his fists on the bathroom sink.

"We're five hours behind schedule!" he yelled. "And we haven't even left the goddamn house!"

"*I* wasn't the one who sat up all night rearranging the suitcases!" Mom yelled back.

Everyone hurried downstairs, dressed and ready to go.

"We don't need breakfast, Mom," I said.

"I'm still full from last night," Patty said, grinning in a way that she hoped would calm Dad. He was even angrier after he had tried to shave real fast.

Mom insisted that we all sit down and have a good breakfast, and Dad argued that no one ever died from skipping *one* breakfast. We gobbled down our pancakes and bacon, and chugged our juice. Dad sat outside in the car revving the engine. By the time we were ready to leave, the car had stopped, and Dad couldn't get it going again.

"Goddamn Plymouth Motors! I should have gone with a Ford—they know how to make an ignition! These damn Plymouths!"

"Just calm down, Clark!" Mom snarled. "You're making the whole neighborhood smell of gasoline!"

After we sat for five minutes quietly listening to Dad breathe in and out of his nose, the car started and we backed out of the driveway. Mr. McMillan came running up to the car.

"Hey! You folks left your sprinkler on!"

Not only did we leave the sprinkler on, but when we got to the Edsel Ford Expressway, Mom said she thought she left the oven on, and we had to turn around and go all the way back home only to find that she hadn't left it on. While Mom was inside the house checking the oven, the phone rang. It was my Aunt Catherine calling to say that Great Aunt Edythe needed a ride to her son's house in Tucson, Arizona, and would we mind taking her since we were going in that general direction anyway.

It looked like we were finally on our way when Mom said that it was almost lunchtime and we could save some money by having lunch at home.

She had thrown out all the milk so that it wouldn't sour and smell up the refrigerator, so Dad had to go up to Kroger's and get a fresh quart. That took almost an hour because Dad locked the keys in the car by accident and had to wreck the vent window to get in.

Dad was so exhausted from being mad all morning that when he got home he said we would leave the next day.

"But I told Catherine that we would be there on Sunday, and if we lose today and tonight we won't make it," Mom said.

"Call her back and tell her we'll see her on Monday instead."

"Well," Mom said cautiously, "Auntie Edythe wants to be in Tucson by Wednesday."

"What?"

"I told Catherine that we would drive Auntie Edythe to Normie's in Tucson. It's on our way, and she's such a sweet thing."

Dad didn't say a word until we reached Battle Creek and then all he said was, "Shut up back there!" He made up a rule about no eating in the car, and he wouldn't let us listen to the radio or roll down the windows. All through Michigan he went over the speed limit, except when we went under bridges and past clumps of trees where a State Police car might be hiding. I wanted desperately to belt Patty for not sharing the jujubes she was sneaking. She had brought along a whole bunch of stuff she'd bought with baby-sitting money, and she wouldn't share any of it with me. There was absolutely nothing to do but stare out the window at the moonlit fields of corn.

Mom pleaded with Dad to stop at a motel when we got to Springfield, Illinois. Several times he crossed completely over the median lines and drove in the opposite lane. Once, while going through a little town, Dad drove up on the sidewalk and ran over a bike and some toys. Mom accused him of being asleep at the wheel, but he said he was just unfamiliar with Illinois traffic signs.

He took off his shoes, rolled down the window, turned the radio way up, and made us all sing the Michigan State fight song. But after a few minutes we were all sound asleep, our new station wagon racing down U.S. 55 like a bedroom on wheels. I don't know how far we traveled like that. Fortunately, there wasn't much traffic at that hour so we didn't hit anything. We finally woke up when Missy asked Dad to get her a drink of water and Dad said, "Go ask Mommy, Daddy's sleeping." I heard that and so did Mom, and she screamed and Dad slammed on the brakes, and the luggage tumbled forward onto the back seat and Dad's golf clubs scattered all over the highway.

We slept beside the road for the rest of the night. When we woke we all felt miserable. Our teeth were coated with night slime, our necks were stiff, and we all had to go to the bathroom. We hadn't eaten dinner, so we were all hungry. Dad was even crabbier because he hadn't had any coffee yet.

After we washed our faces and brushed our teeth at a gas station and ate breakfast, we felt a little better. Even Dad managed a smile, and when we pulled back out on the highway, he suggested a game of Auto Bingo.

We rolled into Aunt Catherine's driveway about 10:00 P.M. She lived in Wichita, Kansas, in a farmhouse that was not on a farm but in town. She and Uncle Stan had two kids: Dale, who was my age, and Vicki, who was a year younger than Patty. I hated the two of them like I hated the flu. I was glad we were only staying the night.

I had to sleep in Dale's room on a bed that was lumpy and smelled funny. Patty and Vicki slept together and got along fine, but I think it was just because Patty was trying to act big in front of Vicki, who was a hick. The baby and Missy slept with Mom and Dad in Aunt Catherine's room. Uncle Stan was a baby about having to sleep on the couch in the family room. "I work tomorrow, you know," he said.

I didn't remember Aunt Edythe because the last time I had seen her I was practically a baby. I tried to be polite and not register my horror when I saw her. She looked like the Mummy with a wig on. She smelled like a combination of mothballs and vitamin pills. I couldn't believe that I had to ride next to her.

"Put her by the window," Dad whispered to Mom as Uncle Stan helped Aunt Edythe into the car. "I don't want to upchuck on the seats."

"She can't sit by the window!" Mom snapped. "She might fall out."

We were ready to go when Dale came around the side of the house with a beagle on a leash.

"Here he is, Uncle Clark," he said. "All walked and everything!"

"Who is he?" Dad asked.

"Auntie Edythe's dog. His name is Dinkie," Dale said. "He's neato. He watches 'Ed Sullivan.' "

We had to rearrange the seating so that the dog would be way in the back. Mom didn't want him near the baby. She was afraid the dog might bite his face or lick his breath away. So we ended up with the baby in the front, the dog in the back, Patty next to the window, Missy beside her, then Aunt Edythe, and then me by the other window. Aunt Edythe was pressed right up against me so tight I could feel her nose breath on my arm.

At Mullinville we jogged northwest about twenty miles across the Arkansas River, which wasn't as much a river as a gash filled with water the color of beef broth. I tried to spit in it as we crossed, but succeeded only in "frogging" my cheek.

"You don't want to take Highway 50," Aunt Edythe said to Dad. "You want to stay on U.S. 54."

"We're going to Dodge City," Dad shouted so that Aunt Edythe could hear.

"Why in heavens would you want to go to that filthy, dirty tourist trap?"

Unfortunately, Aunt Edythe was right about Dodge City. It wasn't the authentic frontier town I had dreamed it would be. It was sort of like St. Claire Shores, Michigan, only dustier and minus a lake. There were used car lots named after Wyatt Earp and Doc Holliday and trailer homes right in town. The Long Branch Saloon smelled like popcorn and toilet ice. Dad refused to pay seventy-five cents for a beer so we left.

"If you really want to see something," Aunt Edythe said in an "I-told-you-so" voice, "you get back on U.S. 54 like I told you before and go down to Liberal and see the House of Mud. It's entirely made out of mud and it's really something to see!"

There was no House of Mud. At one time, a gas station attendant told us, there was a House of Mud, but just after World War I it caved in, killing the curator and his family.

"If you want to see something special," he said, "go back to Mullinville and take Highway 50 up to Dodge City."

At first glance, Oklahoma looked the same as Kansas. At second and third glance, it also looked like Kansas. Even after

Dad pointed out that the portion of Oklahoma that we were traveling through was one of the nation's top producers of fossils and dinosaur bones, it still looked like Kansas. As a matter of fact, it looked like Kansas deep into Texas, where we stopped for the night.

The Ranger Inn was like my friend Earl Denkinger's attic bedroom in his stepfather's house. It had a rug made out of rags, cowboy beds, a horseshoe on the door, a bathtub with feet, a chipped mirror, and only half a roll of toilet paper. The rooms were so small that Dad had to get three. Aunt Edythe and her dog had one room; Mom, Dad, and Mark had another; and Missy, Patty, and I had the other. Although it was sort of scary being alone in a strange room, it gave me an opportunity to bash Patty for being so stingy with her Milk Duds.

Everyone except Aunt Edythe was real cheerful when we got in the car the next day. Her arthritis was flaring up and she claimed that it would kill her before we got to Tucson.

"Beans, baloney, and horseflies!" Dad said under his breath to Mom. "No one ever died from stiff fingers."

"Don't be so sure, Mr. Know-It-All," Aunt Edythe barked. She swatted Dad with her *Reader's Digest*.

Dad's face turned as red as the flashing Highway Patrol lights behind us. That's the way it is with old people: claiming they are hard of hearing, they make you shout, but as soon as you say something about them, they can hear 100 percent. Later on Dad told me that Aunt Edythe could hear an ant fart, but set an H-Bomb off in her drawers and she wouldn't hear a thing.

That flashing red light got closer and closer. Dad edged over to the let the patrolman pass, but he didn't want to pass. He wanted Dad to pull over.

"I haven't gone over seventy miles per hour," Dad said.

"Well, he's not stopping you to chat," Mom said in her voice that sounds pleasant to children, but nasty to adults.

Dad pulled over and reached for his wallet. The cop came to the window. "What's the problem, officer?" Dad asked, offering his driver's license.

"You better step out of the car for a moment, sir."

Dad got out of the car and walked around behind it. His mouth dropped open and his eyes showed white. I jumped into the back and looked out the rear window. It was the most sickening thing I'd ever seen in my life. Aunt Edythe's dog was laying on the ground behind the car. He was flat on his belly with his legs out to the sides and his neck stretched out, so that he looked a beagle version of a bear rug. There was a wide red trail leading up to his body.

"We have anti-cruelty laws in this state," the cop told Dad.

"My God, you can't think I'd do a thing like that on purpose!" Dad protested, looking away from the carcass. "I tied the dog to the bumper while I put my wife's aunt in the car. It takes so long to get her in and out, I guess I forgot about him."

The cop bought Dad's explanation. He kneeled down and tenderly examined the dog.

"I had one of these when I was a boy," he said with a sad smile. "From the looks of his foot pads I'd say this little guy kept up with you for half a mile or so."

After the cop pulled away, Dad untied the leash from the bumper and got back in the car. He just drove away telling everyone that we had a loose license plate and the cop was helping fix it. He must have figured Aunt Edythe wouldn't miss the dog now if she hadn't missed him all day.

On Wednesday we got off to a good, early start. Dad had consented to a side trip to Carlsbad Caverns. Carlsbad, Mom explained, was the largest cave in the world and New Mexico's only national park.

Mom took out all the maps and spread them across the front seat. Mark got ahold of one corner of the map and sucked it soft from Kermit, Texas, to Artesia, New Mexico, including Carlsbad. His tongue was spotted black with trip planner's ink, which Mom was afraid might be poisonous. Dad pointed out that thousands of kids suck on maps and that the government wouldn't let the auto club use poison ink. It didn't make much difference whether or not the map was wrecked because no map showed the road we were on. We had gotten on it by mistake after missing a couple of detour-this-way signs. After a few miles, we drove off a cliff.

It wasn't a big cliff. It was only about four feet high. But it was enough to blow out the front tire, knock off the back bumper, break Dad's glasses, make Aunt Edythe spit out her false teeth, spill a jug of Kool-Aid, bump Missy's head, spread the Auto Bingo pieces all over, and make Mark do number two.

We sat there stunned, rubbing our banged-up arms and shins. Aunt Edythe howled about her internal organs getting the shock of their lives. Mom was in a panic because she thought a flying orange had hit Mark's soft spot. Dad just sat gripping the steering wheel and clicking his tongue. Personally, I enjoyed the accident and was particularly impressed with the distance Dad had gotten out of a heavy, loaded-up station wagon.

Dad cut all the adhesive strips of the Band-Aids and taped his glasses together. He stood on the roof of the car and studied the landscape to determine the best route back to civilization.

"Where's my little dog?" Aunt Edythe suddenly screamed. "Has he gotten loose in the desert? Where is he? I have to find him!" She tried to get out of the car.

"Stay in the car," Mom said sternly. "It's hot and dangerous out there."

"Don't you tell me what to do!" Aunt Edythe shot back. "I'll do what I want. I should never have come on this trip! I should have taken the airplane!"

She pointed a finger at Dad. "He can't even drive," she shouted.

Dad drew back his fist to deck her, but Mom got to her first, grabbing her arm and firmly pressing her back into her seat. "You move and I'll split your lip!" Mom yelled.

A glorious desert sunset bathed the tow truck in orange light as it hauled our car back to the dirt detour road.

"I never seen nothin' so mother bless'ed dumb," the toothless tow driver said to Dad. "You musta got shit fer yer brains!"

Dad would have punched the guy in the mouth, but he knew

there probably wasn't another tow truck in Loco Hills, New Mexico. He didn't even complain when all the men at the gas station laughed when he asked how much the tow and tire repair was.

"Well, how much? Five bucks? Ten bucks? What?" Dad inquired. The men laughed. Dad sort of laughed along with them.

"How much you got?" the avocado-shaped station owner asked.

"I'm asking how much the charge is," Dad said. "Why on earth do you need to know how much money I have to tell me how much it costs to tow my car?"

" 'Cause I'm a-gonna charge you all the money you got."

It cost us $588 dollars. They even took the money out of Aunt Edythe's shoe. The owner of the station made it a point to explain to Dad that what he was doing wasn't robbery. "I should know," he laughed. "I'm the sheriff."

We spent the night in Alamagordo, New Mexico. Since the only money we had was Patty's twenty-nine dollars from baby-sitting, Dad had to rob the motel in the morning when he went to check out. He didn't actually rob it; he just reached into the cash register and took a handful of money. The manager came out of the back room, where he had been checking on our breakfast charges, and saw Dad. He was pretty old and he didn't move too fast, so we got away clean.

About five miles outside of Lordsburg, Patty and I were singing "One Hundred Bottles of Beer on the Wall." All of a sudden Dad shouted, "Hold your hats!" He gunned the engine and we lunged forward. I could hear sirens wailing. I looked out the back. A highway patrol car was chasing us.

"Pull over, Clark!" Mom shouted. "Pull over!"

"Not on your life!" Dad growled. He pounded his fist on the steering wheel. "Come on, you gas-eating bastard, *go!*"

The cop was gaining on us. His Ford was light and tuned-up. Our Plymouth was heavy and loaded-down, and it shimmied and vibrated from driving off the cliff. The cop jerked his car into the passing lane. A truck coming in the opposite direction forced him back. He came up almost to our bumper.

"Throw out the ice chest!" Dad shouted to me. "Throw it out the back window!"

I crawled back and lowered the window, and the rush of air and the change in pressure sucked a baby sheet and a Wichita newspaper out of our car and onto the windshield of the cop car. The cop swerved and ripped into the dirt shoulder, sending up a rooster tail of dirt and gravel. Dad laughed.

"What are you doing?" Mom screamed. She didn't know about the robbery. I knew, but Dad made me promise not to tell Mom.

"I'm running from the law!"

"What? Are you crazy?"

"I robbed the Roadrunner Motel!" he shouted. "To get money!"

The cop was back on our tail. A second car was coming from behind him.

"This is so cool!" I yelled out the back window.

"I have to go tinkle!" Missy cried.

Suddenly Dad slammed on the brakes. The Plymouth fish-tailed to a screeching, rubber-stink stop. The cops locked up their brakes and dove to the sides of the road. Dad put the hammer down and we took off. One of the cops was stuck in the ditch. The other was in pursuit after a moment. That's when I threw out the ice chest. It hit the front of the cop car on the first bounce. The cop lost momentary control of his car and sideswiped a convertible in the other lane.

"It pays to watch 'Dragnet'!" Dad laughed.

Mom was in a trance, shaking her head. Tears were collecting in her eyes. Missy had wet her dress and was crying. Patty was saying her prayers, Mark was sleeping, and Aunt Edythe was looking sort of sick. I was having a great time planning what I would throw out the back trap next if some cop got brave enough to try and run in my Dad.

"Uh-oh!" Dad said.

I looked out the front and saw a flickering mass of lights.

"Roadblock," Dad said. He leaned forward and tried to coax a little more speed out of the Plymouth. "We'll run it!"

We split a row of sawhorses as if they weren't even there,

and then plowed into two cop cars joined at the front bumpers, opening them up like supermarket doors. We smacked them so hard, they spun around until they met at the rear bumpers.

Dad kept it to the floorboards until we came to San Simon Creek, Arizona. He slowed down and cut off the main highway onto a dirt service road. That road ran into a larger road and then we were back on pavement. Dad calmed down and breathed a sigh of relief. He even let us stop at a place called the Horrors of Mexico, which was a barn that had a dead person in a bottle and some wads of hair mounted in cases. There was also a chicken with five legs.

An hour later we arrived in Bisbee. Dad wanted to show us the largest openpit copper mine in the country. "It says in the guidebook that this mine would hold nearly one billion pillows!"

As we examined the mine, Dad switched license plates with a car belonging to an elderly couple from Michigan. Then Dad called us back into the car and we got onto Highway 80 and headed north to Tucson to drop off Aunt Edythe, who, by now, didn't look very good at all.

"Leave her alone," Dad said to Mom. "She's sleeping. If you wake her, we'll just have to listen to her guff."

"I wonder if she's hungry," Mom replied. "We didn't wake her for lunch."

"Old people sleep a lot. She's fine."

Only she wasn't fine.

"Mom!" Patty said about an hour later. "Mom!"

"What is it!" Mom said angrily. She had just gotten Mark to stop screaming.

"Aunt Edythe is leaning on me and she won't get off. And I can't wake her up."

"Pull over, Clark," Mom said.

"We'll be in Tucson in another twenty minutes. She'll be fine."

"Pull over! She's not fine!"

Dad pulled over to the side of the road. Mom hurried out and opened the back door. Patty jumped out and Aunt Edythe slowly fell over, sort of like a tree being cut down. She stayed in a sitting position, even though she was on her side.

"She's dead!"

Patty shrieked and rubbed the spot on her arm where Aunt Edythe's head had rested. Dad pounded the steering wheel.

"Well, goddamn it anyway!" he yelled.

We figured that she must have died back around Deming, New Mexico. That's the last time anyone could remember her saying anything. She told us to roll the windows up because she was freezing cold. She was dead about ten hours and missed out on the cop chase.

"What are we going to do, Clark?" Mom asked, choking back tears.

"We could leave her here and call Normie and you could tell him to come and . . ."

"We can't do that!"

"Well, hell, then let's take her to Tucson. I just don't want to get caught up in questioning and funerals and all that baloney."

"How can you be so cold and insensitive?" Mom asked.

"I'm not being insensitive, I'm being practical. We have only three days at Disneyland at the tops—three days. It was your idea to take a car vacation to Disneyland, not mine. I didn't rob a motel, ruin my car, and kill a dog to spend my vacation at a funeral for a crusty old bag."

Mom could hardly argue with that so we continued on to Tucson with Aunt Edythe on the roof covered with Dad's raincoat. She was real light and Dad was able to get her up there by himself, which was good because no one else would touch her.

"Come on, let's play I Spy," Dad said, trying to cheer us up and make us forget that there was an eighty-four-old dead woman on our roof. "I spy something . . . green!"

When we got to Tucson, we had to stop at a gas station and get a fill-up. Mom looked up Normie's address in the phone book. He lived over near the University of Arizona. The gas station attendant helped us with directions, and we found the house with no trouble at all. The only problem was, Normie wasn't home. His neighbor said he went up to Flagstaff for the week.

"I hope he don't get this rain," the man said as he hurried inside his house. He shouted from the porch, "First rain in eleven weeks!"

"It's a damn good thing it's night," Dad said as he carried Aunt Edythe into Normie's backyard and sat her down in a patio chair.

"You can't leave her here," Mom said. "It's raining."

"Is she going to catch a cold and die?"

"No, but have some respect!"

"Up your ass with a red hot poker!" Dad finally lost his temper. He stormed back to the car and lit up a cigarette.

Mom found her umbrella in the back and opened it up. She fixed it so it rested in Aunt Edythe's hand and protected her from the rain. Then she wrote a note and stuck it between Aunt Edythe's knees. The note said, "Sorry, Normie. Will talk later. Love, Ruth and Clark and the kids."

The vacation sort of went downhill after that. Mom continued to feel badly about how we just dumped Aunt Edythe on the porch and how upset Normie would be to find his Mom all wet and dead. Dad tried to be cheerful from time to time, but it wasn't sincere. He couldn't cheer anyone up, not the way he felt.

We ran into a little excitement the next day at the Yuma Proving Grounds, near the Arizona/California border. Dad thought that we might enjoy a brief trip to the Imperial Dam. At Roll, Arizona, we took a little dirt road that both Mom and Dad thought would go through to the reservoir and dam. Instead, it went through the proving grounds, and on that particular day they were proving missiles.

We were just driving along trying to ignore the bumps and chuckholes, when all of a sudden a missile cleared the top of the car by a foot and exploded about a half mile away. The force of the explosion rocked the car and woke up the baby.

Another missile zinged past and blew up.

"Holy Christ! Someone's shooting at us!"

Dad hit the gas and we all dove on the floor and covered our heads. "Gimme your walkie-talkie!" Dad shouted to me. I fumbled around on the floor and found my Kaptain Kismet walkie-talkie set.

"Come on, you idiot! Hand it over!"

I gave it to Dad and he pressed the button. *"Weeeeeeeee-ooooooooowop!"* Dad screamed into the little plastic walkie-talkie.

I looked up and saw a missile explode in front of us.

"See, son? Missiles are radio controlled. I just interfered with its signal and changed its course!"

"But Dad . . ."

"Here comes another! *Weeeeeeeeeooooooooowop!*"

"But Dad!"

"Look out!"

That was it! *Blam!* The force of the exploding shell knocked the car over on its side. We all fell against the passenger doors. Dad's glasses broke again. Patty chipped her two-thousand-dollar front teeth. Mom just started to whimper and coo and tap her foot on the floor.

"Dad," I finally said, "there isn't any batteries in it."

"Aren't any batteries," Mom said softly.

Dad and I were able to get the car back on its wheels. No missiles came by until we were on our way again. At first, Dad didn't do anything but drive. It was as though we were going down Woodward Avenue in Detroit and the exploding missiles were pigeon poops. Then one came pretty close and Dad jumped on the accelerator and we took off again. Dad dodged and swerved, stopped, sped up, spun around. He got so good at avoiding missiles that I felt a little disappointed when we reached the north entrance to the range.

A pair of startled guards approached the car. Dad rolled down the window and grinned. "You better hope to God that the Russians aren't flying Plymouth station wagons, 'cause they're invincible!"

We drove off and had a good laugh. As a matter of fact, we laughed nonstop until the Indian attack.

We crossed the Colorado River, stopping to admire its

muddy brown majesty. Then we continued driving through the Yuma Indian reservation. Highway 80 cut through the southwest corner of the reservation, which was littered with beat-up trailers, tin sheds, garbage, pickup trucks, and semi-naked kids. It smelled of sewage.

As we passed a driveway, a truck pulled out and followed us. Every driveway had a pickup truck and every pickup truck pulled out and followed us. The lead truck pulled out and passed us. He slowed to a crawl as the other trucks came alongside.

"Lock your doors!" Mom ordered.

Dad honked the horn and waved for the Indians to let us pass. They responded with a shower of beer cans and liquor bottles.

"Indian attack!" I shouted.

"But they're Yuma Indians. The guidebook says that they are primarily agrarian people with no tradition of warfare!" Mom said.

"Look out!" Dad shouted. "A rifle!"

Five rifles poked out from the truck windows. Dad coasted to a stop, steering with his knees so he could keep his hands up in the air. One of the Indians got out of his truck. He knocked on the window with his rifle. Dad rolled it down a crack.

"Yes! May I help you?" Dad said with a smile.

"Give me your money," the Indian mumbled. He was drunk.

Dad counted out the last of the stolen money. He slipped a twenty, a five, and three ones out the window.

"Open the hood of your car."

"Why?"

The Indian trained his rifle on Dad. He reached down and pulled the hood latch. A couple of the other Indians began robbing the engine of parts. The rest of the Yumas surrounded the car and made lewd remarks and gestures at Patty and Mom.

"Hey, look here!" Dad said. "If you take too much of my engine, we won't be able to drive away."

We let the Indians fleece us. They took everything, even

Dad's Pall Malls. They took our hubcaps, headlights, chrome strips, radio, antenna, and air filter. Then one of the Indians asked for our tires. He said he would trade his tires for ours. Three Indians helped jack-up the front and got the front tires off, while two other Indians jacked-up the back and took off those tires. Another truck came by loaded with screaming Indians waving bottles in paper bags.

"Let's fergit this," the leader said, and they left us with one tire on and three off. The three that were off were snow tires and slightly larger than the original tire that remained.

At about sun-up we passed through Joshua Tree National Monument. Dad slammed on the brakes and made us all get out of the car. "See," he said. "That's a Joshua tree." Then he made us get back in and we sped off. It was sort of scary.

We hit Riverside, California, around breakfast, but no one dared suggest we stop. At Ontario it began to rain. Dad turned on the wipers. They started up and then stopped. Dad had to slow down because the rain formed an opaque film on the glass and he couldn't see. When he slowed down, the wipers went on. As he accelerated, they slowed and stopped. That's when he started to cry. We all started to cry. There we were crawling down U.S. 10, bawling like babies.

We idled into Pomona. The rain cleared and Dad punched it, and we roared south to Anaheim.

"We're getting close," I shouted as I spotted a Disneyland sign. "We're going to make it!"

Our odyssey was nearing an end, and even though we had less than a day to spend in the fabled fun capital of America, it didn't matter. Our tears were now for joy. I patted Dad on the back and said in a choked voice, "Thanks, Dad. I love you." Mom gave him a kiss and so did Patty, and Missy grabbed him around his neck and squeezed.

"*There it is! I see it!*" I screamed when I saw the turrets of Cinderella's castle.

"Oh, my God! It's Disneyland!" Mom cried. She thanked God and made us give thanks, which we gladly did.

We pulled into the massive parking lot. It was empty.

"We have the place to ourselves!" Dad announced with a smile that quickly turned to a drooling idiot's frown as he read a sign that said CLOSED FOR REPAIRS AND CLEANING.

"There is no god!" Mom shouted. "No god would treat us like this!"

"Don't say that, Mom," Patty pleaded.

"We are in the hands of the devil! We have sinned, we bathed in sin, and the devil stole our souls!" Mom grabbed out at us. We started to cry.

"Closed for repairs and cleaning," Dad fumed. "You son-of-a-bitch prick! I watched your son-of-a-bitch-program every Sunday! I bought a son-of-a-bitch color TV just to watch your son-of-a-bitch program! You owe me! You owe Clark W. Griswold, Jr.! *You owe him!*"

Dad threw the car in reverse and floored it. The thrust jerked us all forward in our seats. Then he slammed on the brakes and threw it into forward. We screeched off toward the freeway. When we got to L.A., Dad got off the freeway and stopped at a sporting goods store. He took the checkbook off the dashboard and went inside.

A few minutes later, Dad came out of the store with a bag under his arm. He got into the car and kissed Mark. He started the engine and we drove back to the freeway. We got off at Santa Monica Boulevard and headed toward Beverly Hills and Bel Air.

"Clark?" Mom said. "Where are we going?"

Dad didn't answer. He just continued driving, being very careful now to observe speed limits and all the rules of the road.

"Clark? Clark? Clark?" said Mom, over and over again.

When we got to Beverly Hills, Dad pulled over. There was an old sedan parked ahead of us. A man wearing a straw hat came up to our car. He held up a map of the stars' homes.

"Hello, folks," he said. "Welcome to Hollywood!"

"Give me the map," Dad demanded as he drew a revolver out of the bag and pressed it against the man's nose. The man handed Dad the map. "Thank you."

We drove away, leaving the man standing in the middle of the road, shaking his head and stroking his white hair.

We stopped in front of a rambling mansion surrounded by a high fence. Dad turned off the motor. He loaded his revolver and stuck it in his belt. Without saying a word, he got out of the car and made for the fence. I followed him. Mom was too nuts to prevent me.

I never knew Dad was in such good shape, but he just climbed up the fence like it was a four-foot backyard stockade fence. I could see where he was going. There was a group of men sitting around a swimming pool having some kind of meeting. Dad crawled on his belly through the flower beds up to the house; then he stood still. A dog on a chain leaped from the patio toward the flower bed where Dad was standing. He fired and drilled the dog in midair.

"I've got your number, Disney! I'm Clark W. Griswold, and you owe me!"

The men who were reviewing drawings and papers on a large table turned in Dad's direction. A woman screamed and dropped a tray of drinks.

"I'll give you to the count of three, Walt Disney!"

"Can't we talk?" Disney said in the familiar voice that I recognized from the weekly introductions to his TV program.

"You closed your fantasy park, and that was a mistake!" Dad shouted as he waved his revolver at Mr. Disney. "I'm giving you to the count of three to run. I'm giving you a chance! You can run or I can blast your ass right here!"

Mr. Disney looked at the other three men. He looked at the woman who had dropped the drinks and was now frozen with her hands over her mouth. A security guard came running around the corner of the house. He saw Dad and stopped, dropping his pistol on the lawn and raising his hands over his head.

"One!" Dad shouted.

Walt waited a moment, then dashed down the long stretch of grass. Dad dropped to one knee, followed Mr. Disney, and fired. Mr. Disney tumbled to the ground clutching his upper thigh. His momentum carried him into the flower beds. Two Beverly Hills policemen leaped on Dad and wrestled the weapon from his hand.

Mom, Patty, Missy, Mark, and I were cleared of conspiracy charges. They held Dad for attempted murder, assault with a deadly weapon, illegal use of a firearm, and two violations of the Beverly Hills noise code. He had to stay behind. We went home.

Mom called Grandpa Pete from the police station, and he arranged for tickets to be waiting for us at the airport. The police let us say good-bye to Dad. I felt really sorry for him, especially when he kissed me and said that he hoped I'd had at least a few minutes of fun on our vacation. I assured him I did. I also told him that I hoped he would beat the rap and be home real soon and that I didn't begrudge him for shooting such a neat guy as Mr. Disney.

We sort of forgot about Dad as soon as the engines on the airplane trembled and sputtered and moved us around in a graceful arc, then nosed up into the sky. Our hearts pounded with excitement as we watched L.A. shrink below us. We drank Coca-Cola and sailed over the desert valleys that we had fought our way across just the day before. We enjoyed sandwiches as we flew into the pollen-free Arizona air.

"Isn't this marvelous?" Mom sighed. She exhaled and shook her head. "It seems foolish now to drive when you can fly. Maybe this is the way to see the country. Look, down there below us, children!"

"Ladies and gentlemen, this is Captain Fred Freeman. Off to the right side of the aircraft you will see the Grand Canyon. Formed millions of years ago, it is . . ."

Al Sarrantonio, writer, editor, House Dad, is the editor of the Fireside Treasury of Great Humor, *the author of the science fiction novel* Moonbane, *the mystery novel* Cold Night, *and the horror novels* House Haunted, The Boy with Penny Eyes, Totentanz, Campbell Wood, *and* The Worms. *His forty short stories have appeared in such magazines as* Heavy Metal, Isaac Asimov's Science Fiction Magazine, *and* Twilight Zone, *as well as in such anthologies as* Laughing Space, Great Ghost Stories, Westeryear, *and* The Year's Best Horror Stories. *He is horror book reviewer for* Mystery Scene *magazine; writes a humorous column on astronomy; and is also the author of a column for the* Horror Writers of America Newsletter. *A new horror novel,* October, *and a new detective mystery,* Summer Cool, *will be published in 1990. He lives in New York's Hudson Valley with his wife and two sons.*